THE WINNING RUN—"HOW IS IT, UMPIRE?"

GUIDE TO
BASEBALL LITERATURE

Guide To Baseball Literature

Edited by Anton Grobani

With an Introduction by Ken Smith,
Director, The National Baseball
Hall of Fame and Museum

Gale Research Company * Book Tower * Detroit, Michigan 48226

**Library of Congress
Cataloging in Publication Data**

Grobani, Anton.
  Guide to baseball literature.

  Includes bibliographical references.
  1. Baseball--Bibliography. I. Title.
Z7514.B3G76   016.796357   74-17223
ISBN 0-8103-0962-9

Contents

Contents

Foreword

by Ken Smith, Director,
The National Baseball Hall of Fame and Museum

The scope of baseball is vast and to all corners of its world the written word finds its way, like sunshine through a crack in the wall.

Boys played with wagon tongue, twine and tape ball, and stone base without anything in the paper about it at first, though a woodcut would appear in the early nineteenth century of a boy with a ball and club. Now, it is to be mused if the country were stripped of printing, suddenly baseball would be reduced to the idle pastime of its infancy. And that would still be fun. As it is, its foundation is what is printed about it.

Whether it is Roger Maris and Hank Aaron chipping at Babe Ruth's 60th and 714th home runs; voting for the annual All-Star team; signing a players' contract; or scouting a juvenile, it all depends on the record book. As Casey Stengel said, you could look it up. Maris could have hit 75 home runs in 1961 and Aaron could have piled up 775 in 1974, the numerals wouldn't have meant anything without Ruth. The structure of the sport is Baseball Guide, as certain as Dow Jones and Standard and Poor.

Every time a player stepped to the plate in the major leagues since 1871 is recorded. If we hadn't seen this statistical phenomenom we would have scoffed that the phases, facets, and tangents of baseball diamond literature could be assembled into a bibliographical publication readable by any other than a librarian with a doctor's degree from M.I.T. and twenty-five years attendance in the bleachers.

You muse if there is so much variety of literary form in the arts and sciences as bat and ball, where there is biography, comparative studies of teams and players, evolution, history, World Series, graphs, instruction, computation, elocution, art, broadcasting, writing, acting, controversy, music, humor, poetry, photography, sophisticated fiction, yarns, analysis, law. And always the averages, sheets, bound copies, separated in categories and circulated to the ends of the earth.

From 8 Men Out, reviewing the Black Sox scandal, to the musical comedy hit Damn Yankees; from Earnshaw Cooke's Percentage Baseball, a slide rule furnished with purchase, to Fred Russell's Bury Me in an Old Press Box. One day, Bob McGarigle's Baseball's Great Tragedy, the inside of Ray Chapman's death, the only fatality on the diamond. Next day you are engrossed in Harold Rosenthal's Baseball Is Their Business or Leonard Koppett's A Thinking Man's Baseball or Donald Davidson's Caught Short. The gamut extends to Japan and to the Sphinx in Egypt where the Giants and White Sox played an informal game. In the bullpen, clubhouse, on the plane, in the hotel, spring training, winter occupation, dinners, smokers, tours, ground keeping, trainers, costumes, diets, public announcers, practice swing, bat weights, equipment managers, bat boys, concessions. There is no end to what somebody has written a book about.

You trust that art, literature, science, theology, and economy expertise is in sounder minds, considering modern writers who essay the Babe Ruth story from exaggerated myths. Alas, Shakespeare and Washington suffer like the Babe, so do DeMille, Capra, and Hitchcock. Publishers do not always demand literary or subject matter authority, when wheedled for an assignment, but in the main the batting order is as formidable as the lineup they write about.

Douglas Wallop turned out two first class baseball books with no telltale signs he didn't hold a baseball writers' card. A professor wrote a penetrating and entertaining essay. The subject: second base.

The writing genius who put baseball in the drawing room, the ladies' afternoon literary society agenda, and the authors' association reading list was Ring W. Lardner, who traveled with the White Sox for a Chicago newspaper and enchanted Saturday Evening Post readers who didn't know anything about ball games, but asked for more "You Know Me Al," "Alibi Ike," and "Elmer the Great." The contents of this five-cent but distinguished and enormously circulated weekly were devoured nationwide. Keeping up on their Lardner, first thing you knew people began following Walter Johnson and Ray Schalk: they didn't want to be considered ignorant. Roger Kahn's more recent Boys of Summer had a similar influence on non-fans.

Charles E. Van Loan brought people with him when he put baseball in his curriculum. Irvin S. Cobb, another of the Post team, a pal of New York Evening World daily ball writer Bozeman Bulger, associated some of his writing with the game. Baseball boasted having H. Allen Smith on its side. Zane Gray mixed shortstops and base hits with his Riders of the Purple Sage style. Bernard Malamud's The Natural was called a classic. A recent production: Mark Harris' Bang the Drum Slowly.

Professional baseball writers counter by putting away their press box cards and turning out first class books far from the diamond - Robert Ruark, Bob Considine, Quentin Reynolds, John Kieran, Damon Runyon, Drew Middleton, Paul Gallico, Francis Wallace, Jim Breslin, Jack Kofoed, Arthur Mann. The latter two in younger times ground out pulp by the bale. I don't know a writer of any kind in America more prolific than Kofoed, always currently sharp. Ethel Barrymore, an occasional patron of the Polo Grounds first base section, and later a play-by-play listen-in-er between acts, nevertheless once objected to a drama criticism by Heywood Broun because he was a baseball writer, who produced The Sun Field amid his political pieces. At the slightest hint of absence of erudition in the press box, any ball writer instantly claimed Kieran, celebrated nature authority and radio interrogation wizard, as a fellow worker.

The term is still used, "Who does he think he is, Grantland Rice!" Patron saint of the press box. Will Wedge, of the New York Sun, scoured bookstores on road trips, so did Dan Daniel, New York World Telegram, and Howell Stevens of Boston, a sample of many who seized advantage of their nomadic assignment. At Leary's five floors of books, in Philadelphia in 1929, they found less than ten books on the subject that had brought them miles from home. Not counting fiction, record books, and stories for boys. People were raised on A.G. Spalding's America's National Game. William B. Hanna from Harvard wrote meticulously for the New York Herald Tribune. Hearst's George E. Phair, educated by Jesuits, began his day's ball game report in verse. But they weren't writing books in their day. Now, among a computed healthy percentage of baseball readers in the book field, the public is kept supplied steadily, with not one but a handful of approaches to a current subject like the Mets or Hank Aaron, whose exploits in 1974 brought Babe Ruth back to the shelves. New York Journal correspondent Ford C. Frick wrote Babe Ruth's Own Book of Baseball in 1928, the first biography on the classic ball player who is still the subject of books, an outburst of forty-six years later. Great, authentic Ruth books followed - by his roommate, Waite C. Hoyt, who writes as delightfully as he (a) pitched, (b) spoke, (c) sang, and (d) painted; by Dan Daniel who traveled the twenty years with him; by Tom Meany, companion of the trains; by Bob Considine, as literarily articulate as anybody; and by Jimmy Cannon, another associate who wrote with Claire Ruth over his shoulder. Christy Walsh, business manager of the great man and a stable of other athletes, employed the biggest fleet of ghost writers ever, so the shelves at Leary's were jammed from then on. Baseball can boast that its commissioner from 1951 to 1965 was a man whose knowledge of the sport was wider than anyone else's, extending to the talent to write a book on the subject himself. His Games, Asterisks and People in 1973 measured the printed facts many miles, many years, and many thousands of ball games since A.G. Spalding's and Thomas Richter's histories and will escort researchers behind the scenes through the generations.

It could be that there are more newspaper baseball writers who have written books on the subject than not, which is one of the best reasons for this bibliography, the only place where the list of them is to be found, every single one of them.

Boys books, millions of them, counting total circulation. A pioneer author was Noah Brooks. American Boy, Boys' Life, and Youth's Companion wouldn't think of coming out without a baseball subject. The names of Ralph Henry Barbour, William Heyliger, Lester Chadwick, Edward Strohmyer, and Harold M. Sherman were found on book covers under the Christmas tree in most of the houses across the USA. And of course Burt L. Standish, who signed up Frank and Dick Merriwell for the most famous juvenile series. It was really Mr. Gilbert Patten but the army of the generation wasn't concerned with that. Frank Merriwell is today a known name. His books are not in circulation, they are scarce in the collectors' field, but his name lives on as a symbol of unfailing triumph. Bozeman Bulger wrote Christy Mathewson's Pitching in a Pinch. The celebrated pitcher was called author of Pitcher Pollock, Catcher Craig, and First Base Faulkner. Later, players themselves wrote books, Hoyt, the pioneer. A computer would be a candidate for Matteawan, attempting to file brass doublers where they belong. Some men make deals with publishers to grind out books and make it their business. Some books are best sellers, like

Glory of Their Times and Boys of Summer, displayed with dignity and reviewed in the big newspaper book sections. Nearby may be seen one without substantial background. It is this kaleidoscope of merit as well as subject that can place a consultant of baseball bibliography in a dither, attempting to work out any common denominator. Thumb through it and you'll know what I mean.

The game is over, the crowd gone home, but it is still being played as the man reads The Glory of Their Times presented by Professor Lawrence Ritter, compiled by tape recorder under the midnight light. The season is ended, the snow piled high outside, but the ball game is going on through the wintry night, as the boy thrusts deep in the fourth chapter of Baseball Joe in the Central League. In the manner of the baseball legendary beside the bootblack at the ball game, a college professor upstairs exercises his brain on strategical technique while the boy on the third floor figures the batting averages and sorts his gum card collection.

Acknowledgments

A.P. DeWeese, The New York Public Library

H.D. Fortner, The Sporting News.

Goodwin Goldfaden, Adco Sports Book Exchange.

Dave Grote, The National League.

Robert Holbrook, The American League.

Clifford Kachline, The National Baseball Hall of Fame and Museum.

Joseph McKenney, The American League.

Ron Menchine, Washington, D.C.

Roy Nelson, All-American Sports Books.

John F. Redding, The National Baseball Hall of Fame and Museum.

Ken Smith, Director, The National Baseball Hall of Fame and Museum.

James Tobin, The New York Public Library.

Karl Wingler, The Baseball Blue Book.

Explanatory Notes

In cases where a title differs on the cover and title page, the title by which the work is best known is given in the heading. The variant title is listed in the descriptive paragraph, and both are included in the index.

Works listing A.G. Spalding & Brothers as publisher include those published by the American Sports Publishing Company.

Works listing The Sporting News as publisher include those published by Charles C. Spink & Son.

In the bibliographic references, "to date" means through 1972.

Reference Sources

Allegheny College Library

Cleveland Public Library

Detroit Public Library

Harvard College Library

Library of Congress

National Baseball Hall of Fame and Museum

National Union Catalogue

New York Public Library

Ohio State University Library

Material gathered from the Editor's private collection.

1. Early Club Constitutions

1-1   Constitution of Olympic Ball Club of Philadelphia. John Clark.
       1838. Booklet.

       Town ball was one of the forerunners of baseball and
       contained many of its features. The Olympic Club
       of Philadelphia was organized in 1833. The constitu-
       tion was codified in December 1837.

1-2   Constitution and By-laws of the Olympic Ball Club. Ashmead
       Printer. 1866. Booklet.

       The original town ball team changed over to baseball
       in the 1860's. A history of the club, yearly rosters,
       rules.

1-3   By-laws and Rules of the Eagle Ball Club. Douglass & Colt. 1852.
       Booklet.

       First baseball publication. The club, membership,
       meeting, officers, dues, penalties, rules. Organized
       in New York City in 1840.

1-3A   Revised Constitution, By-laws and Rules of the Eagle Ball Club.
       Oliver & Brother. 1854. Booklet.

1-4   Constitution and By-laws of the Pioneer Baseball Club of Jersey
       City. W. & C.T. Barton. 1855. Booklet.

       Organized June 1855.

1-5   Constitution and By-laws of the Excelsior Baseball Club. 1856-65.
       George Scott Roe. 1856. Wilbur & Hastings. 1860. L.H.
       Bigelow & Co. 1865. Booklet.

       Constitution, by-laws, roster. National Association
       rules and regulations. Organized in Brooklyn, New
       York, in December 1854.

1-6   By-laws, Rules and Regulations of the Mazeppa Baseball Club.
       E. Hoyt. 1858. Booklet.

       Organized in October 1858 in Stamford, Connecticut.

1-7   By-laws and Rules and Regulations of the Newburgh Baseball Club. Gray and Lawson. 1858. Albert Saifer. 1969, reissue. Booklet.

Organized in September 1858, in Newburg, New York.

1-8   Constitution and By-laws, with Rules and Regulations of the Louisville Baseball Club. Hanna & Co. 1858. Booklet.

Organized in June 1858.

1-9   By-laws of the Independent Baseball Club. Bowne & Co. 1858. Booklet.

With the rules and regulations of the National Association of Baseball Players. Organized in Brooklyn, New York.

1-10   By-laws and Rules of Order of the Takewambait Baseball Club of Natick. G.W. Ryder & Co. 1858. Booklet.

With the rules and regulations of the game of baseball as adopted by the Massachusetts Association of Baseball Players. Officers, membership roster. Organized in Natick, Massachusetts.

1-11   Constitution and By-laws of the Olympic Baseball Club of South Brooklyn. William D. Roe. 1858-59. Booklet.

With the rules and regulations of the National Association of Baseball Players. Officers, club members, member clubs of the National Association. Organized in August 1858.

1-12   By-laws, Regulations and Rules of the Knickerbocker Baseball Club. Wilbur & Hastings. 1858-60. Biglow & Bleecker. 1861-65. F.F. Taylor. 1866. Booklet.

The team started on an informal basis in New York City in 1842, and was expanded into a regular organization by Alexander Cartwright in September 1845. Adopted the first set of baseball rules on September 23, 1845.

1-13   By-laws of the Harlem Baseball Club. William Manwaring. 1859. Booklet.

Organized in Harlem, New York, in 1859.

1-14   Constitution and By-laws of the Mercantile Baseball Club. Grattan & Co. 1859. Booklet.

Organized in Philadelphia in December 1859.

1-15   Revised Constitution, By-laws and Rules. Quinnipiack Baseball

Club. 1860. Booklet.

Organized in New Haven, Connecticut.

1-16 By-laws, Regulations and Rules of the New York Baseball Club. J.A.H. Hasbrouck & Company. 1861.

Organized in New York City in October 1860.

1-17 Constitution By-laws and Rules of the "M.M. Van Dyke" Baseball Club. H.C. Stoothoff. 1865. Booklet.

Organized in New York City in August 1865.

1-18 Constitution and By-laws with Rules and Regulations of the Detroit Baseball Club. Jno. B. Firmin. 1868. Booklet.

Rules, regulations, list of members.

1-19 Constitution of the National Baseball Club of Washington, D.C. Gibson Brothers. 1867. Booklet.

Organized in November 1859.

1-20 Haymaker Baseball Club. 1878. Booklet.

Rules governing players. Organized in Troy, New York, in 1860.

1-21 Rules and By-laws of Baseball. Putnam Baseball Club. No date. Booklet.

Organized in Brooklyn, New York, in 1856.

Stealing the bases.

2. General Works

2-1   Manual of Cricket and Baseball. Mayhew & Baker. 1858. Pa-
        perbound.

> First baseball publication issued for public sale. Club
> rules, how to play the Massachusetts game, diagram
> of the field.

2-1A   Baseball Players' Pocket Companion. 1859-69. Mayhew & Baker.
        1859, 1860. A. Hudge & Son. 1861. Booklet.

> Continuation of 2-1. Background, history, rules and
> regulations of the Massachusetts and New York games.
> Constitution, by-laws, rules, regulations, and officers
> of seven clubs of the Massachusetts Association and the
> National Association of Baseball Players. The 1861
> edition contained rules of the fly game.

2-2   The Baseball Players' Book of Reference. Henry Chadwick. J.C.
        Haney. 1866-68. Peck & Snyder. 1869-72. Paperbound.

> Rules, explanatory appendix, umpiring and scoring
> instructions, playing pointers. Averages appeared in
> the 1866 edition only.

2-3   The Game of Baseball. Henry Chadwick. George Munro & Co.
        1868. Cover title: Chadwick's American Game of Baseball.
        Clothbound.

> First clothbound baseball book. How to learn, play,
> and teach the game. Sketches of noted players. Box
> scores of notable games of the previous ten years.

2-4   Ball and Bat. Champion Publishing Co. 1882. Booklet.

> Instructions, rules and regulations, scores of outstand-
> ing games.

2-5   Baseball. Henry Chadwick. J.B. Lippincott, Inc. 1888. Pa-
        perbound.

> A reprint from Chambers' Encyclopedia. Rules, his-
> tory, playing instructions.

2-6   Chadwick's Baseball Manual. Henry Chadwick. Theodore Holland. 1888, 1889. Title Page: The American Game of Baseball. Paperbound.

            Playing instructions, rule interpretations, history.

2-7   Chadwick's Baseball Manual. Henry Chadwick. G. Routledge & Sons. 188?. Title Page: Chadwick's Baseball Manual. Clothbound.

            Compiled by Chadwick in 1874, but not issued until the 1880's. Published in London for British players. New rules as revised at the 1874 convention. Excerpts on rules, regulations and play of each position from Chadwick's Convention Baseball Manual and Chadwick's Baseball Manual 3-6, 3-6A. Cricketeers as baseball players, U.S. tour by English players in 1868. Noteworthy contests of 1873.

2-8   Baseball. Newton Crane. George Bell & Sons, London. 1891. Clothbound.

            British publication. History, English background. Explanations, playing instructions, rules.

2-9   Baseball. Richard G. Knowles and Richard Morton. G. Routledge & Sons. 1896. Paperbound.

            British publication. A review of the present position of the game in the United States and an account of its recent rise in popularity in England. Duties of each position, rules, scoring. Illustrations of British players and games. Review of American and British 1895 seasons.

2-10   Baseball and Football. John Ward and Ralph D. Paine. Macmillan Co. 1905. Paperbound.

            British publication.

2-11   Baseball. Henry J. Wehman. DeWitt's Standard Handbook Series. R.M. DeWitt. 1895. Booklet.

            Rise and progress of the game, rules, how to play, how to score.

2-12   Ad-Vantage. Bachmeyer-Lutmer Press. June 1929. Baseball Edition. Booklet.

            Articles on a variety of baseball topics.

2-13   The Big Baseball Book for Boys. Mary G. Bonner and Alan Gould. McLoughlin Brothers, Inc. 1931. Clothbound.

            History, stars of past and present, duties of each

position. World Series history, records, terms, rules.

2-14   Play Ball - The Cubs. Chicago National League Ball Club. 1934.
        Booklet.

        Instructions by Chicago Cub players. Chicago Cub
        historical data and player sketches.

2-15   Baseball, The Fans' Game. Gordon (Mickey) Cochrane. Funk &
        Wagnalls. 1939. Clothbound.

        General instructions with personal reminiscences and
        anecdotes. Chronicle of a major leaguer in the
        making. Qualifications, handling the pitcher, strat-
        egy and psychology. Tips for fans, glossary.

2-16   Major First Events in a Century of Baseball. Edwina Guilford.
        C.E. Line. 1939. Paperbound.

        Historical firsts, sketches of Hall of Fame members,
        questions and answers. Color stamps.

2-17   Diamond Facts, Figures and Fun. Al Schacht. The Sporting News.
        1944. Booklet.

        Stories, glossary, chronology. Records of Hall of
        Famers, World Series results.

2-18   Walt Tulley's Baseball Recorder. Walt Tulley. Sports Books.
        1946. Paperbound. Armed Forces Edition. 1946, reissue. Book-
        let.

        Origin of baseball, ready reference history of the
        major leagues, yearly team and player champions.

2-19   A Handy Illustrated Guide to Baseball. Samuel Nisenson. Perma-
        books. 1950. Clothbound.

        Rules, records, Hall of Fame, World Series. Instruc-
        tions, strategy, digest of outstanding achievements.

2-20   Big-Time Baseball. Hart Publishing Co. 1950. Clothbound and
        Paperbound. 1956-65. Paperbound. Harold H. Hart and Ralph
        Tolleris. 1950, 1956, 1957. Ben Olan. 1958-61, 1963-65.
        M.W. Hart. 1962.

        Biographies of all-time stars, anecdotes, outstanding
        feats, humor. Records, statistics.

2-21   Big League Baseball. Clark Kinnaird, Walter L. Johns and Ralph
        Hollenbeck. Avon Books. 1951. Paperbound.

        History, oddities, memorable events. All-time major
        league all-star teams, records.

2-22   <u>The Ins and Outs of Baseball</u>. Otto Vogel. C.V. Mosby & Co. 1952. Clothbound.

Instructions, development of baseball, records, photos.

2-23   <u>Inside the Majors</u>. Joe Reichler. Hart Publishing Co. 1952. Paperbound.

Sketches of leading players, records, facts.

2-24   <u>Baseball Fans' Roundup</u>. Hector Stevens. Hart Publishing Co. 1952. Paperbound.

Biographical sketches, records, anecdotes, statistics, outstanding feats.

2-25   <u>Radio and TV Baseball</u>. Hy Turkin. A.S. Barnes & Co. 1953. Paperbound.

Records, rosters, rules, schedules, glossary. Broadcasting information, photos.

2-26   <u>Baseball</u>. Mort Cornin. S. Gabriel Sons. 1955. Clothbound.

Instructions and facts for boys from 9-14. Great players, outstanding rookies, Hall of Fame, superstitions, World Series, anecdotes.

2-27   <u>Frankie Frisch's Baseball Roundup</u>. Zander Hollander. 1956. Booklet.

Player sketches, facts.

2-28   <u>Mutual Baseball Annual</u>. Van Patrick. Doubleday & Co. 1960. Paperbound.

Records, statistics, rosters, schedules. Previews, player sketches, photos.

2-29   <u>Major League Baseball Annual</u>. Tom Meany. Grosset & Dunlap. 1960. Paperbound.

Previews, reviews, records, World Series.

2-30   <u>Major League Baseball Facts</u>. McCagie Brooks Rogers, Sr. 1960. Paperbound.

Rosters, reviews, records, World Series.

2-30A   <u>Major League Baseball Digest</u>. McCagie Brooks Rogers, Sr. and Cecil L. Freeman. 1962. Paperbound.

Continuation of 2-30.

2-30B   <u>Major League Rosters with Hall of Fame Immortals</u>. McCagie Brooks Rogers, Sr. 1964. Booklet.

Player lists.

2-31   Famous Baseball Plays and Players. Ted Werth. Harvey House. 1962. Paperbound.

Glossary, player sketches, oddities, World Series highlights, records, quiz.

2-32   Inside Big League Baseball. Roger Kahn. Macmillan Co. 1962. Clothbound.

An inside view of the major league and major leaguers. Players, spring training, the season, the pennant race, the World Series.

2-33   Baseball's Baedeker. Pete Whisenant. Whisenant, Glenn. 1962-64. Paperbound.

A guide to major league cities. Hotels, restaurants, points of interest. Rosters, statistics, major and minor league schedules.

2-33A   Baseball's Guide Book. Pete Whisenant. Whisenant, Glenn. 1965-68. Paperbound.

Continuation of 2-33.

2-34   Major League Baseball Funbook. Thomas Moran. Doubleday & Co. 1963. Paperbound.

For boys. Jokes, games, quizzes, poems, stories, records, facts.

2-35   Arrow Book of Baseball Fun. Ellen Stern Ryp. Scholastic Book Services. 1967, 1971. Paperbound.

Similar to 2-34.

2-36   The Thinking Man's Guide to Baseball. Leonard Koppett. E.P. Dutton & Co. 1967. Clothbound.

Views on a variety of topics. The game on the field, behind the scenes, personalities, and propositions. Analysis of baseball's financial structure, anecdotes.

2-37   NBC Sports Baseball. William Mehlman, ed. National Broadcasting Co. Grosset & Dunlap. 1967. Paperbound.

Team reviews and previews, playing instructions, statistics, records, features.

2-38   Baseball Is an Exciting Game. Robert Thum. Carlton Press. 1969. Clothbound.

2-39   Batters-up. Sportsline Publishers, Inc. 1970. Magazine.

Records, articles, playing instructions.

2-40   Heroes on the Base Paths. Greyhound Corp. 1970. Booklet.

Historical sketch of base stealing. Career records of current stolen base leaders, all-time statistics, pointers.

2-41   This Great Game. Major League Baseball Promotion Co. Rutledge Books, Prentice-Hall. 1971. Clothbound.

A pictorial review. History, an analysis of the game, articles on general topics.

2-42   Pitchers and Pitching. George Sullivan. Dodd, Mead & Co. 1972. Clothbound.

An analysis of pitching. Instructions, strategy, training. Great pitchers and pitching performances, all-time records.

3. Guides

3-1   <u>Constitution and By-laws of the National Association of Baseball Players.</u> 1858-70. Wilber & Hastings. 1858, 1859. Various printers. 1860-70. Paperbound.

> First guide. Issued by the first baseball organization. Proceedings of the annual convention, game scores, averages, rules and regulations.

3-1A   <u>Baseball Rules and Regulations of the National Association of Baseball Players.</u> J.C. Haynie. 1871. Paperbound.

> Continuation of 3-1. Rules and regulations as revised at the 14th annual convention. Proceedings of the first conventions of the Amateur Association and the Professional Association, held in 1870. Scores of professional games played in 1870. The Professional Association evolved in 1871 into the first major league, The National Association of Professional Baseball Players.

3-2   <u>Convention of the National Association of Professional Baseball Players.</u> National Association of Professional Baseball Players. 1871. Booklet.

> Proceedings, constitution and by-laws, rules, memberships. Covered the same convention as that reviewed in 3-1A.

3-3   <u>Beadle's Dime Baseball Player.</u> Henry Chadwick. Beadle & Co. 1860-81. Paperbound.

> First guide produced for public sale. Averages first appeared in the 1861 edition. Club records, best yearly averages since 1858, noteworthy games. Box scores of Fashion Course Matches. The 1860 edition covered history, first codified rules, the National Convention, playing instructions, current rules and regulations, the Massachusetts Game, and delegates to and member clubs of the National Association.

3-4   <u>Dewitt's Baseball Guide.</u> R.M. DeWitt. 1868-85. Michael J.

Kelly. 1868. Henry Chadwick. 1869-85. Paperbound.

Official publication of the Amateur and Professional Association, 1872-76. Averages first appeared in the 1872 edition. Playing instructions, rules.

3-5   Birth of a Nation's Pastime. Gene Kessler. James Mulligan Printing Co. 1933. Paperbound.

Historical highlights, interview with old-time player Jim White. Reproduction of the 1872 edition of 3-4.

3-6   Chadwick's Convention Baseball Manual. Henry Chadwick. National Chronicle. 1870. Paperbound.

National Association history, noteworthy events of the past decade, monthly review of previous season. Playing instructions and rules, averages and statistics.

3-6A   Chadwick's Baseball Manual. Henry Chadwick. American News Co. 1871. Paperbound.

Continuation of 3-6.

3-7   George Wright's Book for 1875. George Wright. Norfolk County Gazette. 1875. Booklet.

Record for 1874, with special coverage of the Boston team. Averages, scores, review of the English trip, playing instructions.

3-8   Constitution and Playing Rules of the National League of Professional Baseball Clubs. 1876-to date. Reach & Johnston. 1876. A.G. Spalding & Brothers. 1877-1941. The National League. 1942-to date. Paperbound booklet.

The 1876 edition was the first National League publication. Compiled by A.G. Spalding, it was the first of the Reach Sports publications. The 1877 edition was the first National League book to contain statistics and averages, and also the first in the long line of Spalding Sports publications. Contained minutes of the annual meeting, convention coverage, and rosters. Became known as the "League Book."

3-9   Spalding's Official Baseball Guide. A.G. Spalding & Brothers. 1878-1939. A.G. Spalding and Lewis Meacham. 1878. A.G. Spalding. 1879-80. Henry Chadwick (not listed as editor until 1890). 1881-1908. John Foster. 1909-39. Paperbound.

Best-known and most widely-distributed guide of its day. History, season review, records, averages, statistics. Scores of each team's home games, rules. Minor league statistics omitted, 1908-24. Official

National League Guide from 1878 on. East and
West regional editions furnished different minor league
schedules.

3-10 Spalding's Official Baseball Guide, Foreign Editions. A.G. Spalding & Brothers. British. 1889-1907. Australian. 1889-90.
Spanish-American. 1906-14. Cuban. 1916. Paperbound.

3-11 Spalding's Official Baseball Record. John Foster. A.G. Spalding & Brothers. 1908-24. Paperbound.

Chronology of the previous season, all-time records,
major and minor league statistics and averages.

3-12 Reach Baseball Guide. 1883-1939. A.J. Reach & Co. 1883-
1927. A.J. Reach, Wright & Ditson, Inc. 1928-34. American
Sports Publishing Co. 1935-39. Paperbound.

3-12A Reach's Official American Association Baseball Guide. 1883-91.

3-12B Reach's Official Baseball Guide. 1892-1901.

3-12C Reach's Official American League Baseball Guide. 1902-05.
Cover title: The Reach Official American League Baseball Guide.

3-12D The Reach Official American League Baseball Guide. 1906-39.
Francis Richter. 1902-26. Thomas Richter. 1927. James Isaminger. 1928-39.

The 1900 and 1901 editions gave full coverage to the
new American League. The guide's overall coverage
through the years was generally more comprehensive
than that of the rival Spalding Guide.

3-13 Spalding-Reach Official Baseball Guide. John Foster and A.C.
Isaminger. American Sports Publishing Co. 1940, 1941. Paperbound.

During their last two years of publication the two
guides were combined into a single edition.

3-14 Our Boys' Baseball Rules. Henry Chadwick, ed. N.L. Munro.
1877, 1878. Booklet.

"Our Boys" was a boys' weekly sporting paper which
sponsored amateur teams in various cities. Playing
rules, National League scores and statistics, coverage
of amateur games.

3-15 Constitution and Playing Rules of The American Association of
Baseball Clubs. American Association. Louis H. Mahn. 1882.
Booklet.

The American Association was a major league from

1882-91. Constitution, rules, convention proceedings.

3-16   Wright & Ditson's Baseball Guide. Wright & Ditson. 1884
86, 1910-12. T.H. Murnane. 1910-12. Paperbound booklet.

> Official Union Association guide, 1884. Major league
> statistics and records.

3-17   Universal Baseball Guide. J.C. Eckel. Rand, McNally. 1890.
Paperbound.

> History of Baseball and the Brotherhood. Major and
> minor league coverage.

3-18   Players' National League Official Guide. F.H. Brunnell. 1890.
Paperbound.

> Background and history of the Brotherhood, by John
> Montgomery Ward. History of the Players' League,
> by Tim Keefe. Chronology, major and minor league
> coverage, World Series.

3-19   Sporting Life Guide. Francis Richter. Sporting Life Publishing
Co. 1891. Paperbound.

> Major and minor league statistics, records. Extensive
> Players' League coverage: history, averages, detailed
> account of its war with the National League and Amer-
> ican Association, and its demise.

3-20   Victor Baseball Guide. Overman Wheel Co. 1896, 1897. Paperbound.

> How to play, by J.M. Ward. Development of base-
> ball, rule explanations, playing instructions. Major
> and minor league averages. The 1896 edition con-
> tained an editorial opposing the National League
> Monopoly and control of the minor leagues.

3-21   Victor Federal League Guide. Overman Wheel Co. 1914. Paperbound.

> Coverage of the outlaw Federal League. Major and
> minor league records.

3-22   American League Rules and Records. Fred Ratsch. Chicago Sporting Goods Manufacturing Co. 1903-05. Paperbound.

> Similar in design to 3-12. The 1903 edition contained
> the peace treaty signed by the American and National
> Leagues.

3-23   McGraw Baseball Guide. John J. McGraw. R.K. Fox. Paperbound.

3-23A   The Science of Baseball.   1904.

         Playing instructions, rules, major league schedules.
         No statistics.

3-23B   McGraw's Official Baseball Guide.   1905.

         Playing instructions, rules, major and minor league
         statistics.

3-23C   Scientific Baseball.   1906-13.

         Similar to 2-23B in coverage.

3-24   Lajoie's Official Baseball Guide.   Napolean Lajoie and M.A. Bo-
brick.   American League Publishing Co.   1906-08.   Paperbound.

         Major and minor league review and statistics, season's
         chronology.

3-25   Bull Durham Baseball Guide.   Baseball Publishing Co.   1910,
1911.   Paperbound.

         Major and minor league coverage.   Averages, statis-
         tics, review of season.

3-26   Official National Baseball Guide.   George Moreland.   National
Baseball Guide Co.   1911.   Paperbound.

         Major and minor league coverage.   Averages, statis-
         tics, unusual records.   Pictures and sketches of stars.

3-27   Baseball.   Leslie O'Connor.   Baseball Commissioner's Office.
1943.   Paperbound.

         Official guide, known as the "Commissioner's Guide."
         Extensive major and minor league coverage.   Season
         review, team histories.

3-28   Official Baseball.   Leslie O'Connor.   A.S. Barnes & Co.   1945,
1946.   Paperbound.

         Became known as the "Barnes Baseball Guide."   Of-
         ficial guide.   Continuation of 3-27, but not as exten-
         sive.   The 1945 edition contained averages and sta-
         tistics for the 1944 and 1943 seasons.

3-29   Sportings News Baseball Guide.   The Sporting News.   1942-to
date.   Paperbound.

3-29A   Official Baseball Record Book.   1942.

3-29B   Baseball Guide and Record Book.   1943-46.

3-29C   Official Baseball Guide.   1947-to date.   J.G. Taylor Spink,

Ernest Lanigan and Paul Rickart. 1942-46. Spink, Lanigan, Rickart and Clifford Kachline. 1947-59. Spink, Rickart and Kachline. 1960-62. C.C. Johnson Spink, Rickart and Kachline. 1963-65. Kachline and Chris Roewe. 1966, 1967. Roewe and Oscar Kahane. 1968. Roewe and Paul McFarlane. 1969. Roewe, McFarlane and Larry Wigge. 1970. Roewe, McFarlane, Wigge and Larry Vickry. 1971-to date.

> Complete, extensive major and minor league records, statistics, averages, review, etc. Official guide from 1947 on.

3-30   Illustrated Digest of Baseball. Art Poretz and Edward Smith. Stadia Sports Publishing. 1971-to date. Paperbound.

> Team reviews and previews. Rosters, statistics, records, player sketches, photos.

3-31   Official Major League Baseball Record Book. Nicholas Acocella, ed. Major League Baseball Promotion Corp. Fawcett World Library. 1971-to date. Paperbound.

> Official publication of the major leagues. Rosters, 1970 results, all-time player and team records and statistics, World Series, All-Star games, Hall of Fame.

4. Record Books

General

4-1   <u>Baseball Ready Reference Book</u>. W.C. Elliott. 1880. Booklet.

Rosters, averages, schedules, umpires.

4-2   <u>Boston Pocket Directory and Baseball Guide</u>. Boston Publishing Co. 1888. Paperbound.

Major league records and averages. City directory.

4-3   <u>Morse's Annual Baseball Book</u>. Jacob C. Morse. 1889. Booklet.

Organizational data, records, rosters, rules, schedules, collegiate coverage.

4-4   <u>Little Encyclopedia of the National League of Professional Baseball Clubs</u>. Morgan and Bingham. 1895. Paperbound.

4-5   <u>Sporting News Record Book</u>. The Sporting News. 1908-41. J.G. Taylor Spink. 1908-24. Paul Rickart. 1925-28. Ernest Lanigan. 1929-41. Booklet.

Extensive compilations of records, statistics. Season review, facts.

4-6   <u>Sporting News Dope Book</u>. The Sporting News. 1942, 1948-66. Leonard Gettleson. 1942. J.G. Taylor Spink, Ernest Lanigan, Paul Rickart and Clifford Kachline. 1948. Spink, Rickart, and Kachline. 1949-62. C.C. Johnson Spink, Rickart, and Kachline. 1963-65. Kachline and Chris Roewe. 1966. Cover titles: <u>Sporting News Dope Book</u>. 1942, 1948-63. <u>The Dope Book</u>. 1964, 1965. <u>Baseball Dope Book</u>. 1966. Paperbound.

The 1942 edition contained all-time individual and team records in various categories. Subsequent editions consist of rules, averages, miscellaneous records and statistics, facts.

4-6A   <u>Baseball Dope Book</u>. The Sporting News. 1967-to date. Clifford Kachline and Chris Roewe. 1967. Roewe and Dick Kaegel. 1968. Roewe and John Duxbury. 1969. Roewe and Joe Marcin. 1970-to date. Paperbound.

Continuation of 4-6.

4-7 Sporting News Baseball Guide and Record Book. Radio Editions. The Sporting News. 1942, 1943, 1948, 1950, 1952, 1954. Various titles: Baseball Record Book, Radio Edition. 1942. Baseball Guide and Record Book, Red Barber Radio Edition. 1943. Baseball Guide, The Red Barber Radio Edition. 1948. Title page: Baseball Guide and Record Book, Radio Edition. Harry Caray and Gus Mancuso. Harry Caray and Gabby Street Baseball Guide. 1950. Baseball Guide, The Sporting News Special Radio Edition. 1952. Budweiser Baseball Guide, Special Radio and TV Edition. 1954. Title page: Budweiser Baseball Guide. Paperbound.

Collaboration by various broadcasters on each edition.
Extracts from 3-29 and 4-6, plus other information.

4-8 Bert Wilson's Official 1942 Baseball Book. The Sporting News. 1942. Booklet.

Similar to 4-7.

4-9 Official Baseball Book. Lifebuoy. The Sporting News. 1942. Booklet.

Extracts from 3-29 and 4-6.

4-10 Bike Web Baseball Record Book. Len Gettleson. The Sporting News. 1949. Booklet.

Extracts from 3-29 and 4-6.

4-11 Sporting News Baseball Record Book. The Sporting News. 1950, 1963. Booklet. J.G. Taylor Spink and Paul Rickart. 1950.

Rules, records, definitions, facts.

4-12 Sporting News Baseball Rule and Record Book. J.G. Taylor Spink and Paul Rickart. The Sporting News. 1951. Booklet.

Similar to 4-11.

4-13 Knot Hole Gang Baseball Guide. The Sporting News. 1954. Booklet.

Extracts from 3-29 and 4-6.

4-14 Budweiser Baseball Guide and Record Book. The Sporting News. 1955, 1956. Booklet.

Extracts from 3-29 and 4-6. Similar to 4-7.

4-14A Busch Bavarian Baseball Guide. The Sporting News. 1957-60. Booklet.

Continuation of 4-14.

4-15   Schaeffer and Lucky Strike Baseball Guide and Record Book. The
Sporting News. 1956, 1957. Booklet.

> Extracts from 3-29 and 4-6. Similar to 4-7. Facts
> on Brooklyn Dodger baseball.

4-16   Roi-Tan Baseball Guide and Record Book. The Sporting News.
1958, 1959. Booklet.

> Extracts from 3-29 and 4-6. Similar to 4-7.

4-17   Dual Filter Tareyton and Roi-Tan Cigar Baseball Guide and Record
Book. The Sporting News. 1960-63. Booklet.

> Extracts from 3-29 and 4-6. Similar to 4-7.

4-18   Moreland's Baseball Records and Percentage Book. George Moreland. International Baseball Bureau. 1907-09, 1909 revised.
Booklet.

> The 1909 editions are numbered vol. 3 and vol. 4.
> League, team and player statistics and records. His-
> tory, playing pointers, facts. Percentage tables.

4-18A   Chicago Daily News Baseball Records and Percentage Book. George
Moreland. Chicago Daily News. 1909. Booklet.

> Same as 4-18.

4-19   Burton's Pocket Baseball Guide. I.R. Burton. 1908. Booklet.

> Major and minor league statistics and records. Rules.

4-20   Baseball Dope. Walter M. Berry. 1909. Booklet.

> Chronology, averages, statistics, facts.

4-21   Just Baseball. Newark Evening News. 1909-16. Booklet.

> Rules, schedules, statistics, records, facts.

4-22   Pittsburgh Gazette Times Record Book. Pittsburgh Gazette-Times.
1909, 1910. Booklet.

> Statistics, records, facts.

4-23   The Fan, His Book. W. McKay. Guardian Savings Trust Co.
1910. Booklet.

4-24   The Fan's Book. Detroit Journal. 1911. Booklet.

> Statistics, records, facts.

4-25   The Sunday American Baseball Guide. American Journal-Examiner.
1911. Booklet.

> Statistics, records, facts.

4-26   <u>Gillette Baseball Annual</u>. Frank Riley. Gillette Safety Razor Co. 1911, 1912. Booklet.

         Statistics, game recapitulations.

4-27   <u>Gillette Baseball Blue Book.</u> Gillette Safety Razor Co. 1916, 1917. Booklet.

         Records, statistics.

4-28   <u>Heilbroner Baseball Yearbook.</u> 1912-18, 1920-to date. Heilbroner Baseball Bureau. 1912-51. Baseball Blue Book, Inc. 1952-to date. Paperbound.

4-28A   <u>Heilbroner's Records.</u> 1912-18, 1920.

4-28B   <u>Baseball Yearbook.</u> 1921-45.

4-28C   <u>Baseball Year and Notebook.</u> 1946-to date.

         The bureau serves as the clearing house for all organized baseball records. Averages, records, statistics, rosters. Directories, reserve lists, other data. Supplements issued during season. Much of the player data is not to be found elsewhere. Early editions were known as "Heilbroner's Red Book." Later editions erroneously listed 1918 as the year of missed publication.

4-29   <u>Richter's History and Records of Baseball.</u> Francis C. Richter. The Dando Co. 1914. Clothbound.

         History, team and player records, development of the playing code. Great players and writers. An enlarged edition of 6-7.

4-30   <u>Offerman's Pocket Baseball Guide and Calendar.</u> Frank J. Offerman. 1914. Booklet.

         Coverage of American, National, and International Leagues. Records, averages, history, World Series, chronology.

4-31   <u>Facts for Fans.</u> William Phelon. Felix Mendelsohn. 1911-16. Booklet.

         Rules, statistics, records, schedules, miscellaneous data.

4-32   <u>Balldom.</u> George Moreland. Balldom Publishing Co. 1914. Clothbound. 1926, 1927. Paperbound.

         History, chronology, records, all-time roster of each major league team.

4-32A   <u>Supplement to Balldom.</u> George Moreland. Balldom Publishing

Co. Booklet.

Records, statistics, facts for the 1914-19 seasons.

4-33 What Authorities Say of Balldom. George Moreland. 1932.
Booklet.

Testimonials from baseball figures promoting the forth-
coming 1933 edition of 4-32 which was not published.

4-34 Born's Blue Book of Baseball. M. Born Co. 1917. Booklet.

Miscellaneous facts, data.

4-35 Stove League Baseball Record. J.L. MacDaniel Printing Co.
1917. Booklet.

Line scores of the 1917 major and high minor league
games. Records, statistics, World Series coverage.

4-36 James J. Corbett's Baseball Guide and Sporting Encyclopedia.
New York American. King Features. 1917. Booklet.

Statistics, records, schedules.

4-37 Baseball Guide and Rule Book. Thomas E. Wilson & Co. 1918-
26. Booklet. Irwin Howe. 1918-24.

Records, statistics, schedules, rules.

4-37A Wilson Baseball Record Book. Thomas E. Wilson & Co. 1920-
26. Booklet.

Continuation of 4-37.

4-38 The Famous Slugger Yearbook. Hillerich & Bradsby. Booklet.

4-38A Famous Sluggers. 1921, 1932-34.

4-38B Famous Sluggers of (date of previous season). 1927-31, 1936-38.

4-38C How to Raise Your Batting Average and Famous Sluggers of the
1934 Season. 1935.

4-38D The Famous Slugger Yearbook. 1939-to date. Variant title pages:
Famous Sluggers and Their Records of (date of previous season).
1932-34. All You Need to Know About Bats and Batting. 1936-
38.

Records of leading hitters, unusual batting feats, batting tips, other data.

4-39 Rheingold Facts for Baseball Fans. Rheingold Brewery. 1921.
Paperbound.

4-40   <u>Baseball Cyclopedia.</u> Ernest Lanigan. Baseball Magazine. 1922. Paperbound.

> Yearly supplemental inserts, 1923-33. History, team and player records, box scores.

4-41   <u>Baseball Dope.</u> Vincent Treanor. Martin Ray. 1922. Booklet.

> Records, statistics, schedules, facts.

4-42   <u>Rawlings Baseball Record Book.</u> Ernest Lanigan; Paul Rickart. Rawlings Manufacturing Co. 1922-40. Booklet.

> Records, statistics, rosters, rules, schedules.

4-43   <u>Black's Annual.</u> Joe Black. 1923-41, 1946-48. Paperbound.

> Records, rosters, statistics, schedules, daily chronology. Some coverage of other sports.

4-44   <u>Walter H. Teodecki Baseball Record and Rule Book.</u> Walter Teodecki. Bradley Knitting Co. 1924. Title page: <u>Baseball Record and Rule Book.</u> Booklet.

> Records, review. Similar to 4-5.

4-45   <u>Evening World Baseball Record and Rule Book.</u> New York Evening World. 1926. Booklet.

4-46   <u>Los Angeles Times Baseball Record and Rule Book.</u> Los Angeles Times. 1926. Booklet.

4-47   <u>Batter Up! Illustrated Royal Rooter Annual and Baseball Almanac.</u> J.F. Murphy. Baseball Almanac and Royal Rooter Publishing Co. 1927-39. Variant titles. Booklet.

> Photos, player sketches, rosters, articles. Emphasis on Boston Red Sox and Braves. Some editions were issued in newspaper format. Later editions contained records, averages, World Series results.

4-48   <u>Data on American League Recruits.</u> Henry P. Edwards. The American League. 1929, 1931-36. Paperbound.

> Revised editions issued during the season, 1930-32. Rosters and sketches of new players. Records were first included in the 1936 edition.

4-48A   <u>Revised Data on American League Clubs.</u> Henry P. Edwards. The American League. 1930. Paperbound.

> Same as 4-48.

4-48B   <u>American League Rookie and Record Book.</u> The American League. 1937-42. Henry P. Edwards. 1937-41. Earl J. Hilligan. 1942.

Continuation of 4-48. Cover title: Rookie and Record Book. Paperbound.

League history, rosters, records, statistics. Sketches of new players. 1937 and subsequent issues bear incorrect edition numbers. Edition imprinted number 8 is actually number 9, etc.

4-48C   American League Red Book. The American League. 1943-to date. Paperbound. Earl J. Hilligan. 1943-59.

Continuation of 4-48. Edition numbers are incorrect: edition imprinted number 14 is actually number 15, etc.

4-49   New Players for Season with All Clubs of the National League. The National League. 1930-33. Booklet.

Player sketches, rosters.

4-49A   Records of New Players Acquired During Past Year and Complete Rosters of National League Clubs. The National League. 1934. Booklet.

Continuation of 4-49.

4-49B   National League Green Book. The National League. 1934-to date. Bill Brandt. 1941-45. Charley Segar. 1946-51. Dave Grote. 1952-to date. Paperbound.

Continuation of 4-49A. Rosters, rookies, all-time player and team records, records, statistics.

4-50   Chicago Daily News Record Book. Irwin Howe. Chicago Daily News, Howe News Bureau. 1934. Booklet.

Statistics, records, facts.

4-51   Cities Service Baseball Guide. Grantland Rice. Cities Service Oil Co. 1953. Booklet.

Records, World Series results, baseball immortals.

4-52   Official Baseball Facts. Carl Hubbell. Heffelfinger Publications. 1937. Cover title: Carl Hubbell's 1937 Baseball Book. Booklet.

Records, photos, schedules, World Series.

4-53   Major League Baseball. Harry Heilmann, H.G. Salsinger, and Don Black. 1937-39, 1941-53. Whitman Publishing Co. 1937-45. Dell Publishing Co. 1946-53. Paperbound.

Facts, statistics, records, rules.

4-54   Esso Baseball Handbook. Christy Walsh. Standard Oil Co. of New Jersey. 1939. Booklet.

Issued in commemoration of baseball's centennial.
Records, rules, history, instructions.

4-55   Baseball Fact Finder. Calling All Boys Magazine. Calling All Boys, Inc. 1946. Booklet.

Listing of statistical leaders in various categories.

4-56   Indianapolis Baseball Book. Incar Printing Corp. 1946. Paperbound.

American League, National League, and American Association averages, records, and reviews.

4-57   Official Baseball Rules. Leslie O'Connor. A.S. Barnes & Co. 1947, 1948. Booklet.

Statistics, records, rules.

4-57A   Baseball Almanac. Don Schiffer. A.S. Barnes & Co. 1949. Booklet.

Continuation of 4-57.

4-58   Book of Baseball Facts. Dan Daniel, Stan Lomax, and Joe DiMaggio. C.H. Pearson. 1949. Booklet.

Anecdotes, records, statistics, World Series records.

4-59   Baseball Reference Book. Trunz Co. 1949. Booklet.

Records and statistics, with emphasis on the Brooklyn Dodgers.

4-60   Zenith TV and Radio Baseball Score Book. Merchant Sales Corp. 1950. Paperbound.

Records, history, Hall of Fame, other data.

4-61   Royal Book of Baseball Facts. Stan Musial. C.H. Pearson. 1951. Booklet.

Records, statistics.

4-62   Blatz Baseball Guide. National Sports Almanac. Albert M. Anderson. 1951, 1952. Booklet.

Records, statistics, review.

4-63   Official Encyclopedia of Baseball. Hy Turkin and S.C. Thompson. A.S. Barnes & Co. 1951, 1956, 1959, 1963, 1968. Clothbound. 1955. Paperbound. 1964. Clothbound and Paperbound.

History, yearly standings, minor leagues, administration. World Series, Hall of Fame, all-time records.

Playing hints, unusual facts, umpire roster. Lifetime playing records for every major league player since 1871. The 1955 edition was a pocket-sized condensation.

4-63A   The Official Encyclopedia of Baseball 1952 Supplement. Hy Turkin and S.C. Thompson. A.S. Barnes & Co. 1952. Paperbound.

Review, records, statistics of the 1951 season. Career statistics of active players.

4-64   Peek Size Baseball Guide. E.W. Peek & Co. 1953. Booklet.

Separate edition for each American Association team. Records, schedules of the American and National Leagues and American Association.

4-65   Mutual Baseball Almanac. Doubleday & Co. 1954, 1955. Roger Kahn and Al Helfer. 1954. Roger Kahn and Harry Wismer. 1955. Clothbound.

Statistics, records, rules, rosters, facts.

4-65A   Illustrated Mutual Baseball Yearbook. Roger Kahn, Harry Wismer and Paul Lapolla. Doubleday & Co. 1956. Clothbound.

Continuation of 4-65.

4-66   Baseball Almanac. Hy Turkin. A.S. Barnes & Co. 1955. Clothbound. Pocket Books. 1955, reissue. 1956. Paperbound.

Averages, records, rules, schedules. Playing tips, World Series highlights, biographical sketches. Coverage of amateur ball, radio and TV information.

4-67   Dizzy Dean Baseball Guide. Masthead Corp. 1957. Booklet.

Rosters, records.

4-68   1959 Baseball Story. Phillies Cigars. 1959. Booklet.

Rosters, schedules, statistics, records, team reviews.

4-68A   1960 Baseball Story. Phillies Cigars. 1960. Booklet.

Continuation of 4-68.

4-69   Baseball Player Guide. Norman Paulson. 1959-64. Paperbound.

Detailed statistics and records of all players in organized baseball.

4-70   Big League Player Guide. Norman Paulson. 1961-64. Paperbound.

Rosters, schedules, averages, data.

4-71   Major League Baseball Handbook. 1961-64. Pocket Books. 1961-
        63. Paperbound. Thomas Nelson & Sons. 1961, reissue. Cloth-
        bound. J. Lowell Pratt. 1964. Paperbound. Don Schiffer.
        1961-63. Dave Anderson. 1964.

        Records, statistics, rosters, schedules, previews, re-
        views, player sketches.

4-72   Don Schiffer's Major League Baseball Handbook. Don Schiffer.
        Pocket Books. 1964. Paperbound.

        Previews, reviews, player sketches, rosters. Sched-
        ules, records, statistics.

4-72A   Major League Baseball. Pocket Books. 1965-to date. Jack
        Zanger. 1965-70. Brenda Zanger and Dick Kaplan. 1971.
        Brenda Zanger. 1972. Paperbound.

        Continuation of 4-72.

4-73   Era Baseball Record Book. Everett Roundy. Era Enterprises. 1962.
        Booklet.

        Batting, fielding, pitching statistics.

4-74   Ronald Encyclopedia of Baseball. Joe Reichler. Ronald Press.
        1962, 1965. Clothbound.

        General history, team histories and records, player
        records. All-Star game and World Series records.
        Year-by-year records of all major league players since
        1876, including home runs, runs-batted-in and shut-
        outs.

4-75   Nelson's 20th Century Encyclopedia of Baseball. Murray Older-
        man. Thomas Nelson & Sons. 1963. Clothbound.

        Records, history, review since 1900.

4-76   Official Baseball Almanac. William Wise. Fawcett Publishing
        Co. 1963-65. Paperbound.

        Records, statistics, schedules, team analyses.

4-77   Baseball Guide. Snibbe Sports Publications. 1965-to date. Nor-
        man Miller. 1965. Jack Clary. 1966-to date. Booklet.

        Previews, schedules, rosters, records, statistics.

4-78   All-Time Rosters of Major League Baseball Clubs. S.C. Thompson.
        A.S. Barnes & Co. 1967. Clothbound.

        Yearly team rosters and player records.

4-79   Official American League Averages. Howe News Bureau. 1968-
        to date. Booklet.

Official batting, pitching, fielding and championship series statistics and records.

4-80   Official National League Averages. Elias Sports Bureau. 1968-to date. Booklet.

Official batting, pitching, fielding and championship series statistics and records.

4-81   The Baseball Encyclopedia. Information Concepts, Inc. Macmillan Co. 1969. Clothbound.

A statistical reference work in which computer programming was employed in order to reconstruct player statistics and records which were previously unavailable. Player, pitcher and manager registers, World Series, All-Star games, all-time team and player records.

4-82   Complete Handbook of Baseball. Zander Hollander. Lancer Books. 1971-to date. Paperbound.

Previews, reviews, player sketches, rosters, records, statistics.

Player Statistics

4-83   Statistics on Baseball Players. B.A. Younker. G.A. Miller. 1891. Booklet.

Player records and statistics.

4-84   Who's Who in Baseball. 1912, 1916-to date. Booklet. Baseball Magazine. 1912-57. Who's Who in Baseball Magazine Co. 1958-to date. Clifford Bloodgood. 1940-51. Joseph Lilly. 1952. Sid Feder. 1953. Allan Roth. 1954-to date.

Year-by-year minor and major league batting and pitching statistics for each major league player. The 1912 edition did not contain pitching records. Career major league totals were carried from 1925 on. World Series records were included from 1924 on. A special edition honoring Babe Ruth was issued in 1921, including his life story and records.

4-85   Baseball Bat Bag. Al M. Elias. Baseball Magazine. 1922-25. Booklet.

Team and player statistics, all-time records, rosters.

4-86   Who's Who in Major League Baseball. Harold (Speed) Johnson. Buxton Publishing Co. 1933. Clothbound.

Full page photo, sketch and record of each major
league player. A paperbound prospectus containing
excerpts was issued prior to publication.

4-86A   Who's Who in the Major Leagues. Harold (Speed) Johnson. B.E.
Callahan. 1935-37. Clothbound and Paperbound.

Continuation of 4-86. Player sketches, photos,
statistics, records. The 1935 edition was also published in two separate books.

4-86B   Who's Who in the American League.

4-86C   Who's Who in the National League.

4-86D   Who's Who in the Major Leagues Baseball. John P. Carmichael.
B.E. Callahan. 1938-55. Title page: Who's Who in the Major
Leagues. Clothbound and Paperbound.

Continuation of 4-86A.

4-87   Daguerreotypes of Great Stars of Baseball. The Sporting News.
1934, 1951, 1958, 1961, 1968, 1971. J.G. Taylor Spink. 1934.
Spink and Paul Rickart. 1951, 1958. Spink, Rickart, and Ray
Nemec. 1961. Paul McFarlane and Leonard Gettleson. 1968,
1971. Paperbound.

Year-by-year batting, fielding and pitching records
of former stars. Biographical data.

4-88   Baseball Register. The Sporting News. 1940-to date. J.G. Tay-
lor Spink. 1940-42. Spink and Paul Rickart. 1943-50. Spink,
Rickart, and Joe Abramovich. 1951-62. C.C. Johnson Spink,
Rickart, and Abramovich. 1963. Abramovich and Rickart. 1964.
Charles Pickard, Clifford Kachline, and Rickart. 1965. John
Duxbury and Kachline. 1966, 1967. Duxbury. 1968, 1969.
Joe Marcin. 1970-to date. Paperbound.

Year-by-year minor and major league batting, fielding and pitching statistics for each major league player. Photos, biographical data. Editions through 1963
contained an introductory article on a player or specific phase of the game.

Abridged editions:

All-Star Edition. 1941.
Coverage of Chicago National and American League
players.

Servicemen's Edition. 1944, 1945.

4-89   Baseball Register Index. The Sporting News. 1967-to date.
Booklet.

Alphabetical listing of players, with years played.

4-90　　　Good Hitting Pitchers. Baseball-For-Fans Publications. 1968.
　　　　　Paperbound.

Lifetime batting statistics of all major league pitchers.

4-91　　　The Book. Baseball-For-Fans Publications. 1968. Paperbound.

Player performance analyses covering the 1967 season
thru the use of pitch-by-pitch statistics. Six volumes:

4-91A　　New York Mets Batter Performance.

4-91B　　New York Mets Pitcher Performance.

4-91C　　California Angels Batter Performance.

4-91D　　California Angels Pitcher Performance.

4-91E　　Don Drysdale.

4-91F　　Juan Marichal.

4-92　　　Player Profile Ratings. Baseball-For-Fans Publications. 1968-to
　　　　　date. Paperbound.

Ratings based on various offensive elements. Comparison charts.

4-93　　　Player Performance Handbook. Baseball-For-Fans Publications.
　　　　　1968-to date. Paperbound.

Performance analyses of major league batters and pitchers. Lifetime statistics.

4-94　　　Player Win Averages. Eldon G. Mills and Harlan D. Mills. A.S.
　　　　　Barnes & Co. 1970. Clothbound and Paperbound.

A computerized statistical measurement of a player's
contribution to a win or loss. 1969 figures.

Pitching

4-95　　　Smallwood's Pitchers's Record Book. W.J. Smallwood. Lone
　　　　　Star Publishing Co. 1932. Booklet.

Records of 160 pitchers against each team as starters
and relievers.

4-96　　　Pitcher's Record Guide. Samuel Georgeson. 1935-51. Booklet.

Records of each pitcher against opposing clubs. Schedules, rosters.

4-97   Major League Pitchers Record Book. William Bartleson. 1940,
        1941. Booklet.

        Detailed record of each game pitched by each pitcher.
        Season records.

4-98   Pitching Record Book. Gorham Press. 1943-45. Booklet. Ath-
        letic Publications. 1946-48. Booklet.

        Game-by-game records. Schedules.

4-98A   Baseball Pitching Record Book. Athletic Publications. 1949.
        Booklet.

        Continuation of 4-98.

4-99   Pitching Record Form. Gorham Press. 1943-46. Booklet.

        Weekly. Game-by-game records. Schedules.

4-100   Kings of the Mound. Ted Oliver. 1944, 1947. Paperbound.

        Yearly records and ratings of all major league pitchers
        since 1894. The 1947 edition contained high minor
        league records.

4-101   Pitcher Performance Handbook. R.H. and L.E. Lewis. Baseball-
        For-Fans Publications. 1966, 1967, 1972. Paperbound.

        Pitch-by-pitch game analyses. Performance analyses
        and detailed statistics.

4-102   The Book of Pitcher Performance Profiles. Research Analysis As-
        sociates. Baseball-For-Fans Publications. 1968. Paperbound.

        Monthly statistical analyses, May thru October per-
        formance, effectiveness and capabilities.

All-Time Records

4-103   Here's Something New: Highspots in Baseball. Charles Mears.
        Lezius Printing Co. 1919. Paperbound.

        Best and worst major league fielding records by posi-
        tion, 1871-1918.

4-104   Little Red Book of Baseball. 1926-32, 1934-71. A.G. Spalding
        & Brothers. 1926-32. Paperbound. C.D. White. 1934-37.
        Paperbound. Elias Baseball Bureau. 1938-71. Charlie White and
        John Foster. 1926-32. Charlie White. 1934-37. Frank C.
        Lane. 1938-48. Lester Goodman and Richard Bennett. 1949.

Lester Goodman. 1950-52. Seymour Siwoff. 1953-71. Cloth-bound and Paperbound.

All-time team and player records in various categories. Unusual records and statistics.

4-104A   The Book of Baseball Records. Seymour Siwoff. Elias Baseball Bureau. 1972. Clothbound and Paperbound.

Continuation of 4-104.

4-105   Newsom's Pocket Baseball History. Theodore Newsom. 1937. Booklet.

All-time records, facts.

4-106   One Hundred Years of Baseball. Duquesne Brewing Co. 1939. Booklet.

All-time records.

4-106A   One Hundred Years of Baseball. Enterprise Brewing Co. 1939. Booklet.

Same as 4-106.

4-107   Baseball Dope Book. Russell Hicks. 1940, 1941. Booklet.

4-108   Baseball Record Book. Leonard Gettleson. Bauer and Black. 1949. Booklet.

All-time records.

4-109   One for the Book. The Sporting News. 1949-71. Paperbound.

All-time player and team records in various categories.

4-109A   Baseball Record Book. The Sporting News. 1972. Paperbound.

Continuation of 4-109.

4-110   Major League Baseball Record Book. Jack Brickhouse. WGN Continental Broadcasting Co. 1950-58. Cover titles: Complete Baseball Record Book. 1950. Jack Brickhouse's Major League Baseball Records. 1951. Paperbound.

All-time player and team records in various categories.

4-110A   Major League Baseball Records Book. Jack Brickhouse. WGN Broadcasting Co. 1959-65. Cover title: Jack Brickhouse's Latest Major League Baseball Records. 1959-62. Paperbound.

Continuation of 4-110.

4-110B   Baseball Major League Records. Jack Brickhouse. WGN Broad-casting Co. 1966-69. Paperbound.

Continuation of 4-110A.

4-110C   <u>Baseball Records</u>. Jack Brickhouse. WGN Broadcasting Co. 1970-to date. Paperbound.

Continuation of 4-110B.

4-111   <u>Baseball Records</u>. Joe Reichler. Dell Publishing Co. 1957, 1958. Paperbound.

The walking delegate:
"Say, pard, shake hands; we both make our livin' callin' strikes."

5. Annuals

5-1 Who's Who and What's What in Baseball. C.M. Klump. 1910.
Magazine.

Records, terminology, cartoons, verse. Illustrations.

5-1A America's National Game. W.W. Aulick. Publisher's Printing
Co. 1912. Paperbound.

Reprint of 5-1.

5-2 The Wind-Up Baseball Annual. Stan Carlson. 1939, 1940. Magazine.

Major and minor league coverage. Statistics, records,
reviews, photos.

5-3 Street and Smith Baseball Yearbook. 1941-to date. Street and
Smith. 1941-61. Conde Nast. 1962-to date. Magazine.

5-3A Street and Smith's Baseball Pictorial Yearbook. 1941-48, 1951-
58.

5-3B Pic Quarterly Baseball Pictorial. 1949.

5-3C All-Star Sports Baseball. 1950.

5-3D Street and Smith's Baseball Yearbook. 1959-to date.

Team previews, rosters, statistics. Feature articles,
minor league review, photos.

5-4 Negro Baseball. Sepia Sports Publications. 1944-46. Magazine.

Photos, articles, records, statistics.

5-5 Baseball Illustrated. Elbak Publishing Co. 1946-49. Magazine.

Statistics, articles, photos.

5-5A Sports Review Baseball. Elbak Publishing Co. 1950-53, 1955-62.
Magazine.

Continuation of 5-5.

5-6   Baseball Stars. Dell Publishing Co. 1949-57. Magazine.

5-6A   Dell Sports Baseball Stars. Dell Publishing Co. 1958, 1959. Magazine.

     Continuation of 5-6.

5-6B   Dell Sports Magazine Baseball Stars. Dell Publishing Co. 1960-63.

     Continuation of 5-6A.

5-6C   Dell Sports. Dell Publishing Co. 1964-68. Magazine.

     Continuation of 5-6B. Material appeared in May issue.

5-7   Sports Album. Dell Publishing Co. 1951, 1952. Magazine.

     Baseball issues: Spring and Summer. Player sketches, team previews.

5-8   Baseball Life Stories. Dell Publishing Co. 1952-56. Magazine.

     Sketches, photos of past and present stars.

5-9   Official Baseball Annual. Dell Publishing Co. 1952. Magazine.

     Player and team records. Detailed statistics. Team and player chronologies, reviews.

5-9A   Dell Baseball Annual. Dell Publishing Co. 1953-57. Magazine.

     Continuation of 5-9.

5-9B   Dell Sports Baseball. Dell Publishing Co. 1958, 1959, 1970-to date. Magazine.

     Continuation of 5-9A.

5-9C   Dell Sports Magazine Baseball. Dell Publishing Co. 1960-63. Magazine.

     Continuation of 5-9B.

5-9D   Dell Sports. Dell Publishing Co. 1964-68. Magazine.

     Continuation of 5-9C. Material appeared in March issues.

5-10   Baseball. Dell Publishing Co. 1953. Magazine.

     Team reviews, records, statistics.

5-11   Who's Who in the Big Leagues. Dell Publishing Co. 1953, 1955-57. Magazine.

     Sketches, records, photos.

5-11A   <u>Dell Sports Who's Who in the Big Leagues.</u> Dell Publishing Co. 1958, 1959. Magazine.

                 Continuation of 5-11.

5-11B   <u>Dell Sports Magazine Who's Who in the Big Leagues.</u> Del Publishing Co. 1960–63. Magazine.

                 Continuation of 5-11A.

5-11C   <u>Dell Sports.</u> Dell Publishing Co. 1964–68. Magazine.

                 Continuation of 5-11B.

5-12   <u>True Baseball Yearbook.</u> True Magazine. Fawcett Publishing Co. 1950–54, 1956–to date. Magazine.

5-12A   <u>Baseball Yearbook.</u> 1950–54, 1956–61.

5-12B   <u>True's Baseball Yearbook.</u> 1962–to date.

                 Reviews, previews, feature articles, photos.

5-13   <u>Baseball's Best Hitters.</u> Sport Magazine. Bartholomew House. 1952, 1957. Magazine.

                 Records and sketches of current long-ball hitters.

5-14   <u>Baseball's Best.</u> Sport Magazine. Bartholomew House. 1952, 1953, 1957–60. Magazine.

                 Sketches of current stars.

5-15   <u>Baseball's All-Stars.</u> Sport Magazine. Bartholomew House. 1953, 1958. Magazine.

                 Greatest games of 34 current stars.

5-16   <u>Baseball Review.</u> Sport Magazine. Bartholomew House. 1959. Magazine.

                 Reviews and previews of teams and stars.

5-17   <u>Inside Baseball.</u> Sport Magazine. Bartholomew House. 1961–65. Magazine.

                 Team and player reviews, previews.

5-18   <u>Baseball All-Stars.</u> Maco Magazine Corp. 1953-57. Magazine.

                 Records, photos, reviews.

5-19   <u>Sports All-Stars Baseball.</u> Maco Magazine Corp. 1957–to date. Magazine.

                 Records, photos, review.

5-20   <u>NBC Complete Baseball.</u> Maco Magazine Corp. 1961, 1962.

Magazine.

Team analyses and rosters.

5-20A   Baseball Guidebook. Maco Magazine Corp. 1964-to date. Magazine.

Continuation of 5-20.

5-21   Baseball Heroes. Whitestone Publishing Co. 1958-60. Magazine.

Sketches, records of major league stars.

5-22   Baseball. Whitestone Publishing Co. 1960-to date. Magazine.

Team reviews and previews.

5-23   Official Baseball Annual. Fawcett-Whitestone Publishing Co. 1962-to date. Magazine.

Articles, photos.

5-24   Sports Forecast Baseball. E.J. O'Malley Publishing Co. 1959, 1960, 1961. Magazine.

Statistics, rosters, sketches, previews.

5-25   The Box Scores of the Major League Season of 1959. Sports World Publishers. 1959. Magazine.

5-26   Sportscope Baseball. Sport Scope Publishing Co. 1960. Magazine.

Reviews, previews, rosters, statistics, photos.

5-27   Baseball Thrills. 1961. Magazine.

Outstanding events.

5-28   Sports Action Magazine Baseball. Cape Magazine Corp. 1961. Magazine.

Reviews, previews, photos.

5-29   Major League Baseball. 1961-to date. Cavalier Magazine. 1961, 1962. Fawcett-Whitestone Publishing Co. 1963-to date. Magazine.

Sketches, reviews, previews, photos.

5-30   Complete Baseball. Natlus, Inc. 1961. Magazine.

Articles, photos.

5-30A   Baseball. Complete Sports Publications. 1962-67. Magazine. Three issues in 1962.

Continuation of 5-30. Articles, records, reviews, previews, photos.

5-30B   Complete Sports. Complete Sports Publications. 1968-to date. Magazine.

Continuation of 5-30A. Material appears in spring issue.

5-31   Baseball Review. Complete Sports Publications. 1961-67. Magazine.

Articles, records, reviews, previews, photos. Material incorporated into 5-30B, 1968-to date.

5-32   Power Baseball. Complete Sports Publications. 1962. Magazine.

Mathematical analyses of past and present home run hitters.

5-33   Willie Mays Baseball. Complete Sports Publications. 1963. Magazine.

Articles, reviews, previews, photos.

5-34   Sport Heroes. Complete Sports Publications. 1964-to date. Magazine.

Baseball issue. Photos, sketches of major league stars.

5-35   Baseball Illustrated. Complete Sports Publications. 1965-to date. Magazine.

Color photos, player-sketches, previews, reviews, statistics.

5-36   Home Run Hitters. Ideal Publications. 1962, 1963. Magazine.

Sketches of all-time sluggers.

5-37   Phil Rizzuto's Baseball. Popular Library. 1962. Magazine.

Player sketches, records, previews.

5-37A   Baseball Yearbook. Popular Library. 1963-71. Magazine.

Continuation of 5-37. Team analyses, player sketches.

5-37B   Popular Sports Baseball. Popular Library. 1972. Magazine.

Continuation of 5-37A.

5-38   Home Run. Popular Library. 1969. Magazine.

Player sketches, articles, photos.

5-39   Grand Slam. Popular Library. 1970-to date. Magazine.
Articles, photos.

5-40   Press Box Baseball. P.S.L. Publishing Co. 1964. Magazine.
Sketches, articles, reviews, photos.

5-41   Baseball in Action. P.S.L. Publishing Co. 1965. Magazine.
Sketches, articles, photos.

5-42   Sports Special: Baseball. Tempest Publishing Co. 1964-to date.
Magazine.
Statistics, articles.

5-43   Sports Extra: Baseball. Tempest Publishing Co. 1968-to date.
Magazine.

5-44   United States Baseball. Official Sports Magazine. 1964. Numbered vol. 1, no. 4. Magazine.

5-45   Big-Time Baseball. Official Sports Magazine. 1964. Magazine.
Articles, player ratings.

5-46   Baseball Official Forecast. Official Sports Magazine. 1964.
Numbered vol. 1, no. 6. Magazine.
Sizeups of the pennant races by the managers in each
major league.

5-47   Official Sports Magazine Baseball. Royal Publications. 1965.
Magazine.
Reviews and previews.

5-48   All-Star Baseball. Herald House. 1965. Magazine.
Sketches of most valuable players in both major leagues
from 1931-to date. Photos.

5-49   All-Star Baseball. Topical Magazines. 1965. Magazine.
Player sketches, articles, statistics, photos.

5-50   Big League Baseball. A.D. Publishing Corp. 1965. Magazine.
Sketches, forecasts, photos.

5-51   Sports Quarterly Presents Baseball. Counterpoint Publishing Co.
1965-to date. Magazine.
Articles, records, team reviews and previews, photos.

5-52   Sports Quarterly Presents Baseball Extra. Counterpoint Publishing

Co. 1971–to date. Magazine.

Articles, records.

5-53   Sports World. Reese Publishing Co. 1965–to date. Magazine.

Baseball issue. Articles, photos.

5-54   All-Star Sports Special. Reese Publishing Co. 1972. Magazine.

Baseball Preview issue. Articles, photos.

5-55   Sports Review's Baseball. Splendid Publications. 1966–to date.
Magazine.

Articles, photos.

5-56   Baseball Stars. Major League Baseball Players Association. 1968,
1969. American League and National League editions. Magazine.

Records, sketches, color stamps.

5-57   Today's All Stars. Major League Baseball Players Association.
Sports Collectors, Inc. 1968, 1971. Magazine.

Statistics, color stamps of players.

5-58   Sports Stars Photostamp Album. Major League Baseball Players
Association. Glendale Publishing Co. 1970. Magazine.

Player sketches and color stamps. Records, articles.

5-59   Baseball Sports Stars. Hewfred Publishing Co. 1968–to date.

Team previews, player sketches.

5-60   Baseball Report. Cord Communications. 1969–to date. Magazine.

Team previews, statistics.

5-61   Baseball News. Cord Communications. 1969–to date. Magazine.

Articles, previews, sketches, photos.

5-62   Chris Schenkel's Sportscene: Baseball. America Equity Press.
1970–to date. Magazine.

Articles, schedules, statistics.

5-63   Action Sports Baseball Guidebook. Rostam Publishing Co. 1971.
Magazine.

Player sketches.

5-63A   Action Sports Baseball Yearbook. Rostam Publishing Co. 1972.
Magazine.

Continuation of 5-61.

5-64   <u>All-Time Baseball Greats.</u> Three El Publishing Co. 1972. Magazine.

Articles, records.

The Catcher's signals are
not always considered in good form.

6. General Histories

6-1   The Book of American Pastimes. Charles A. Peverelly. 1866.
Cover title: American Pastimes. Clothbound.

         Sketches of all National Association Clubs. Rosters,
scores. The definitive history of early baseball.

6-2   Sphere and Ash. Jacob Morse. J.F. Spofford & Co. 1888.
Booklet.

         Reviews of all championship series, early tours, extra-
inning games.

6-3   Baseball, 1845-1871. Seymour Church. 1902. Clothbound.

         Numbered vol. 1, but no others were published. His-
torical background, rules, explanation of the game,
box scores of outstanding games. Baseball on the Pacific Coast, unusual facts. Color photos.

6-4   Baseball History. Pocket Manual. Buck Printing Co. 1907.
Booklet.

         History, records, statistics.

6-5   Sol White's Baseball Guide. Sol White. H. Walter Schlichter.
1907. Cover title: History of Colored Baseball. Paperbound.

         A review of Negro baseball. History, championship
games, pitching feats, sketches of current stars and
oldtime players. Discussion of managerial problems,
the color line, and Cap Anson's opposition to Negroes
in the major leagues. By a star Negro player and
manager.

6-6   Only the Ball Was White. Robert Peterson. Prentice-Hall. 1970.
Clothbound.

         The story of Negro baseball. An account of the Ne-
gro leagues and players. Records.

6-7   A Brief History of Baseball. Francis Richter. Sporting Life Publishing Co. 1909. Paperbound.

> Origin and design of the game. Yearly summary and standings of major leagues. World championship series, minor league coverage.

6-8 The National Game. Alfred Spink. National Game Publishing Co. 1910, 1911, reissue. Clothbound.

> The 1911 edition bears a 1910 copyright date. The notation of its being the second edition appears on p. LXII. History, rosters, detailed records. Player sketches, photos.

6-9 America's National Game. Albert G. Spalding. American Sports Publishing Co. 1911. Cover title: Baseball. Clothbound.

> History of the game by one of the pioneer giants. Anecdotes, recollections, illustrations, photos.

6-10 The Book of Baseball. William Patten and J.W. McSpadden. P. F. Collier & Son. 1911. Clothbound.

> Historical background, the National League, the American League. Review of the 1910 season. Pitching instructions, star players, the minor leagues.

6-11 Casey Reminiscences. Col. William H. Rowe, Jr. Volunteer Press. 1911. Booklet.

> An anecdotal sketch in rhyme of baseball from 1871–77.

6-12 Baseball and Baseball Players. Elwood A. Roff. 1912. Clothbound.

> History of the game and its important events. Box scores of outstanding games, records, unusual occurences. Subject index, statistical appendix.

6-12A What Baseball Experts Say of Roff's Great History. Elwood A. Roff. 1912. Booklet.

> Testimonials from various baseball personalities.

6-13 The First One Hundred Years of Baseball. George Moreland. 1929. Paperbound.

6-14 Inaugural Baseball Game. N.Y. State Joint Legislative Committee. 1938. Paperbound.

> An account of the first baseball game and the growth of the sport. A study prepared in connection with the 1939 Baseball Centennial observance.

6-15   The True Story of the Origin of Baseball. Ralph Birdsall. Freeman's Journal Co. 1938. Title page: The Origin of Baseball.
Booklet.

                Reprinted from a chapter in "The Story of Coopers-
town," 1917. An embellishment of the Doubleday
legend.

6-16   A Century of Baseball. Freeman's Journal Co. 1940. Clothbound.

                Published in cooperation with the National Association
of Professional Baseball Leagues as part of the centennial observance. Development of baseball, sketch of
Abner Doubleday, description of the centennial cele-
bration and dedication ceremonies.

6-17   Baseball, The National Sport. Henry P. Isham. Ditto, Inc.
1941. Paperbound.

                A history of the game. Published as a doctoral thesis.

6-18   Baseball's First Regular Game. General Foods. 1946. Baseball.

                Commemoration of the 100th anniversary of the game
between the New York Nine and the Knickerbockers
on June 19, 1846. Background of the game, rules
in effect, reprints of early illustrations.

6-19   Ball, Bat and Bishop. Robert W. Henderson. Rockport Press.
1947. Clothbound.

                Origin and development of ball games, with emphasis
on baseball. Written to refute the legend of Doubleday and Cooperstown. A list of fifteen references to
baseball in literature prior to 1840. Preliminary research published in Bulletin of the New York Public
Library, XLIII, 1939, entitled "Baseball and Rounders".

6-20   The Story of Baseball. John Durant. Hastings House. 1947,
1949, 1959. Clothbound.

                An illustrated history. Records, Hall of Fame.

6-21   Baseball. Robert Smith. Simon & Schuster. 1947, 1970. Clothbound.

                Narrative, in-depth history.

6-22   Hits, Runs, and Errors. Robert Smith. Dell Publishing Co. 1949.
Paperbound.

                Excerpts from 6-21.

6-23   Baseball in America. Robert Smith. 1961. Clothbound.

An illustrated narrative history.

6-24   The Baseball Story. Frederick Lieb. G.P. Putnam's Sons. 1950.
        Clothbound.

        Narrative history and chronology.

6-25   One Hundred Years of Baseball. Lee Allen. Bartholomew House.
        1950. Clothbound.

        Narrative history. Records of great players.

6-26   Times at Bat. Arthur Daley. Random House. 1950. Clothbound.

        A half-century of baseball. History, anecdotes, play-
        er sketches, records, photos.

6-26A   Inside Baseball. Arthur Daley. Grosset & Dunlap. 1950. Cloth-
        bound.

        Abridged edition of 6-26.

6-27   American League Golden Anniversary. Earl J. Hilligan. The
        American League. 1951. Booklet.

        Issued by the American League Office. Pictorial his-
        tory of the league.

6-28   The Official History of the National League. Charles Segar.
        The National League and Jay Publishing Co. 1951. Clothbound.

        An illustrated history of the league and each of its
        teams. Issued by the league in celebration of its
        seventy-fifth anniversary.

6-29   The Six Perfect Games of Baseball History. Bill Shelton. 1955.
        Booklet.

        And almost the seventh. Box score and detailed ac-
        count of each game.

6-30   Baseball, An Action History. O. Goerger. Columbia Records.
        1958. Booklet.

        Booklet accompanying a record album. History, facts,
        records, photos.

6-31   The History of Baseball. Allison Danzig and Joe Reichler. Pren-
        tice-Hall. 1959. Clothbound.

        Narrative history. All-time teams, best by position,
        great hitters and pitchers, outstanding managers. Re-
        cords, photos.

6-32   Baseball's Unforgettable Games. Joe Reichler and Ben Olan.
        Ronald Press. 1960. Clothbound.

Accounts and box scores of one hundred games, with emphasis on the New York teams.

6-33   The Rise of Major League Baseball to 1891. Harold Seymour. Cornell University. University Microfilms. 1956. Paperbound.

College thesis.

6-34   Baseball, the Early Years. Harold Seymour. Oxford. 1960. Clothbound.

A detailed history. Economic aspects, social implications. Index.

6-35   Baseball, the Golden Age. Harold Seymour. Oxford University Press. 1971. Clothbound.

A definitive history covering the 1903-30 period.

6-36   Baseball, 1845-81. Preston Orem. 1961. Clothbound.

A yearly history derived from newspaper accounts. Pictures, box scores, standings, all-star games.

6-36A   Baseball from the Newspaper Accounts. Preston Orem. 1966-67. Paperbound.

Continuations of 6-36. Ten separate editions covering the years 1882 through 1891.

6-37   Twelve Perfect Innings. Weldon Myers. Commercial Press. 1961. Booklet.

A play-by-play in verse of the game pitched by Harvey Haddix on May 26, 1959, in which he pitched 12 perfect innings, then lost the game in the 13th.

6-38   The National League Story. Lee Allen. Hill & Wang. 1961, 1965. Clothbound.

Official history. Narrative account. Photos, index.

6-39   The American League Story. Lee Allen. Hill & Wang. 1962, 1965. Clothbound.

Official history. Narrative account. Photos, index.

6-40   The Story of Baseball. John Rosenburg. Random House. 1962. Clothbound.

Informal history. Photos.

6-41   Play Ball! Dan Daniel. Bowne & Co. 1964. Booklet.

A sketch of baseball in 1858 with Homer Davenport illustrations. Includes a reprint of 1-8.

6-42   The American Diamond. Branch Rickey and Robert Riger. Simon
        & Schuster. 1965. Clothbound.

        An illustrated documentary history. Great players,
        playing instructions.

6-43   Heritage of a National Game: Social Baseball, 1845-75. John
        D. Cleaver. State University of New York. 1965. Clothbound.

        A Master of Arts thesis in which the development of
        baseball is tied in with the development of American
        mores and customs.

6-44   The Game of Baseball. Samuel and Beryl Epstein. Garrard Pub-
        lishing Co. 1965. Clothbound.

        Historical sketch, photos.

6-45   The Home Run Story. Zander Hollander and Larry Fox. W.W.
        Norton & Co. 1966. Clothbound.

        A discussion of the home run and home run hitters.
        Sketches of outstanding sluggers. Records, photos,
        index.

6-46   American Baseball: From Gentleman's Sport to the Commissioner's
        System. David Q. Voigt, University of Oklahoma Press. 1966.
        Clothbound.

        A history from post-Civil War days to 1920, with
        emphasis on the 1870-99 period.

6-47   American Baseball: From the Commissioners to Continental Expan-
        sion. David Q. Voigt. University of Oklahoma Press. 1970.
        Clothbound.

        The development and evolution of baseball in the
        twentieth century.

6-48   Baseball. Earl S. Miers. Grosset & Dunlap. 1967, 1970, re-
        issue. Clothbound.

        An informal narrative history for boys. Photos.

6-49   Great Pennant Races of the Major Leagues. Frank Graham. Ran-
        dom House Little League Library. 1967. Clothbound. Reissued
        as Major League Library.

        Descriptions of seven close races. Photos, index.

6-50   Major League Baseball Chronology. William Puckner. K. Puk-
        ner. 1967, 1969. Paperbound. L.E. Hamlett. 1971. Paper-
        bound.

        All-time major league rosters.

6-51   The Day They Made the Record Book. Milton J. Shapiro. Julian
        Messner, Inc. 1968. Clothbound.

        Accounts of seven outstanding feats. Records, index.

6-52   Great No-Hit Games of the Major Leagues.- Frank Graham, Jr.
        Random House Little League Library. 1968. Clothbound. Reis-
        sued as Major League Library.

        Descriptions of ten games.

6-53   No-Hitter. Phil Pepe. Four Winds Press. 1968. Clothbound.
        Scholastic Book Services. 1969, reissue. Paperbound.

        Accounts of no-hit games, with a listing of all those
        pitched since 1875.

6-54   Baseball's Memorable Boxscores. Robert Schmierer. 1968. Paper-
        bound.

        Boxscores of memorable games from 1876-1968. Pri-
        vately printed.

6-55   Professional Baseball, the First 100 Years. Major League Baseball
        Promotion Corp. Poretz-Ross. 1969. Paperbound.

        Historical background, great players, memorable mo-
        ments. 1969 team previews, player sketches, records.

6-56   Baseball, an Informal History. Douglass Wallop. W.W. Norton
        & Co. 1969. Clothbound. Bantam. 1970, reissue. Paper-
        bound.

        A narrative history of the game.

6-57   Nite Time Baseball. James Weygand. Press of the Indiana Kid.
        1970. Clothbound.

        Reprints of newspaper accounts of the first night base-
        ball game, which was played between two amateur
        teams in Fort Wayne, Indiana, on June 3, 1883.

6-58   Famous Firsts in Baseball. Joseph Cook. G.P. Putnam's Sons.
        1971. Clothbound.

        Descriptions of notable firsts such as the first profes-
        sional game, World Series, double no-hit game, night
        game, etc.

6-59   I Hate the Yankees. John Bizzelle. Vantage Press. 1971. Cloth-
        bound.

        A narrative history of baseball, with emphasis on the
        New York Yankees.

6-60   The Glory Years of Baseball. Don Smith. Stadia Sports Publishing Co. 1972. Booklet.

> A narrative sketch of the game covering great players and teams through 1941. Photos.

6-61   Baseball: Diamond in the Rough. Irving Leitner. Criterion Books. 1972. Clothbound.

> A narrative account of the early days of baseball. Reproductions of period illustrations.

6-62   Baseball. Wendell Rydell. Abelard-Schuman. 1972. Clothbound.

> History, terminology.

6-63   Baseball Highlights. Baseball Associates. No date. Booklet.

> Historical data.

7. Team Histories

7-1   Record of the Boston Baseball Club, 1871-74. George Wright.
       Rockwell and Churchill. 1874. Baseball.

       Divided into sections, each covering one season.
       Player sketches, newspaper account of season's first
       game. Scores, averages, box scores of unusual games,
       standings. Reprints of newspaper reviews.

7-2   A History of the Boston Baseball Club. George V. Tuohey. M.
       F. Quinn. 1897. Cover title: Boston Baseball Club, 1871-97.
       Clothbound.

       History, player sketches, photos.

7-3   The Braves, the Pick and the Shovel. Al Hirshberg. Waverly
       House. 1948. Clothbound.

       Informal history of the Boston Braves since 1914.

7-4   The Boston Braves. Harold Kaese. G.P. Putnam's Sons. 1948.
       Clothbound.

       History since 1871. Photos.

7-5   The Milwaukee Braves. Harold Kaese and R.G. Lynch. G.P.
       Putnam's Sons. 1954. Clothbound.

       Revised edition of 7-4 to include the franchise trans-
       fer to Milwaukee.

7-6   Milwaukee's Miracle Braves. Tom Meany. A.S. Barnes & Co.
       1954. Clothbound. Grosset & Dunlap. 1956, reissue. Cloth-
       bound.

       An account of the franchise transfer and recent history.

7-7   The Fabulous Milwaukee Braves. Robert Allen. 1959, 1960.
       Magazine.

       A seven-year history. Composite roster, team and
       individual leaders, batting and pitching statistics,
       yearly averages. Won and lost records versus each

team, trades, attendance, chronology.

7-8   Miracle in Atlanta. Furman Bisher. World Publishing Co. 1966.
       Clothbound.

           The story of Milwaukee Braves franchise transfer to
           Atlanta. Discussion of federal antitrust legislation,
           secret meetings between Milwaukee Braves and Atlan-
           ta officials. Historical sketch of the Braves since
           1871.

7-9   Baseball in Cincinnati. Harry Ellard. Press of Johnson and Har-
       din. 1907, 1908, reissue. Clothbound.

           1907 edition limited to 500 copies. Development of
           baseball and history in Cincinnati from 1860-1906.

7-10   The Cincinnati Reds. Lee Allen. G.P. Putnam's Sons. 1948.
       Clothbound.

           Narrative history since 1868. Photos.

7-11   Fanfax of Cubs and Sox. George Moreland. 1916. Booklet.

           All-time rosters, records, statistics, facts for the Chi-
           cago White Sox and Cubs.

7-12   Baseball in Old Chicago. Federal Writers' Project. A.C. Mc-
       Clurg & Co. 1939. Paperbound.

           Narrative account covering the nineteenth century.
           Photos, records.

7-13   The Chicago Cubs. Warren Brown. G.P. Putnam's Sons. 1946.
       Clothbound.

           Narrative history since 1876. Photos.

7-14   Fanfax. George Moreland. Fanfax Publishing Co. 1930. Book-
       let.

           A statistical history of baseball in Detroit.

7-15   Iffy's Book of Tiger Tales. Detroit Free Press. 1935. Magazine.

           Selected stories of the Detroit Tigers reprinted from
           the Detroit Free Press.

7-16   Detroit in Baseball. Detroit Baseball Co. 1939. Magazine.

           Centennial souvenir presented to opening day patrons
           at Briggs Stadium, Detroit, in 1939. History of the
           game, all-time record of the Detroit team.

7-17   The Detroit Tigers. Frederick Lieb. G.P. Putnam's Sons. 1946.
       Clothbound. Armed Forces edition. 1946, reissue. Paperbound.

History since 1887. Photos.

7-18   Tiger Feats. W.G. (Billy) Evans. 1948. Booklet.

A record of Detroit in the American League. Anecdotes, all-time records.

7-19   Tiger Records. Fred T. Smith. 1949, 1950. Booklet.

All-time Detroit Tiger player and team records since 1907.

7-20   Detroit Tigers' Hall of Fame. Phillies Cigars. 1959. Booklet.

Sketches, photos of present and past stars. Records, statistics.

7-21   The New York Yankees. Frank Graham. G.P. Putnam's Sons. 1943, 1943, reissue, 1945, 1946, 1948, 1951, 1958. Clothbound.

Narrative history since 1903. Photos.

7-22   The Yankee Doodles. Milton Gross. House of Kent. 1948. Clothbound.

Stories of contemporary New York Yankee players.

7-23   The Yankees. John Durant. Hastings House. 1949, 1950. Clothbound.

A pictorial history of the New York Yankees.

7-24   The New York Yankees. Dan Daniel. Packard Motor Car Co. 1952. Booklet.

Great players and teams of the past and present. Records, statistics.

7-25   The Thrilling True Story of the Baseball Yankees. Harvey Jones. Fawcett Publishing Co. 1952. Booklet.

A history in comic book form of the New York Yankee team. Player profiles.

7-26   The Magnificent Yankees. Tom Meany. A.S. Barnes & Co. 1952. Clothbound. Grosset & Dunlap. 1953, reissue. Clothbound.

The story of the current New York Yankee team. Player profiles.

7-27   The Yankee Story. Tom Meany. E.P. Dutton & Co. 1960. Clothbound.

A narrative history of the New York Yankees.

7-28   The Miracle New York Yankees. Phil Rizzuto and Al Silverman. Coward-McCann. 1962. Clothbound.

An account of the 1961 team, with a comparison to past great Yankee teams. Records, statistics, game photos.

7-29   The Decline and Fall of the New York Yankees. Jack Mann.
Simon & Schuster. 1967. Clothbound.

> An analysis of the factors contributing to the decline
> of the Yankees, who finished in last place in 1966,
> after winning 29 pennants since 1920. Photos, re-
> cords, index.

7-30   The St. Louis Cardinals. Frederick Lieb. G.P. Putnam's Sons.
1944, 1945, 1947. Clothbound.

> A narrative history since 1876. Photos.

7-31   The Gashouse Gang and a Couple of Other Guys. J. Roy Stockton. A.S. Barnes & Co. 1945. Clothbound. Bantam Books.
1948, reissue. Paperbound.

> The story of the St. Louis Cardinals of the late 1920's
> and early 30's. Additional chapters on other baseball
> topics.

7-32   Connie Mack. Frederick Lieb. G.P. Putnam's Sons. 1945.
Clothbound.

> A biography of Mack and narrative history of the
> Philadelphia Athletics since the 1880's. Photos.

7-33   The Kansas City Athletics. Ernest Mehl. Henry Holt & Co. 1956.
Clothbound.

> The story of the transfer of the Philadelphia Athletics
> franchise to Kansas City.

7-34   The Brooklyn Dodgers. Frank Graham. G.P. Putnam's Sons.
1945, 1948. Clothbound. Armed Forces Edition. 1945, reissue.
Paperbound.

> A narrative history since 1890. Photos.

7-35   The Dodgers. John Durant. Hastings House. 1948. Clothbound.

> A pictorial history of the Brooklyn Dodgers.

7-36   The Story of the Brooklyn Dodgers. Ed Fitzgerald, ed. Bantam
Books. 1949. Paperbound.

> A collection of magazine articles on the team and its
> players by various authors.

7-37   Baseball Confidential. Arthur Mann. David McKay Co. 1951.
Clothbound.

> An account of the 1946 dispute involving Baseball
> Commissioner A.B. Chandler and New York Yankee
> owner Larry MacPhail on one side, and Brooklyn Dod-
> ger president Branch Rickey and manager Leo Durocher

on the other. Events leading to Durocher's suspension, reinstatement, and transfer to the New York Giants.

7-37A   Baseball Journey. Arthur Mann. F.J. Low Co. 1951. Paperbound.

Manuscript edition of 7-37.

7-38   Dodger Daze and Knights. Tommy Holmes. David McKay Co. 1953. Clothbound.

An anecdotal history of the Brooklyn Dodgers.

7-39   The Artful Dodgers. Tom Meany. A.S. Barnes & Co. 1953, 1954, 1958. Clothbound. Grosset & Dunlap. 1963, 1966. Clothbound.

Sketches of contemporary Brooklyn players.

7-40   The Rhubarb Patch. Walter (Red) Barber. Simon & Schuster. 1954. Clothbound and Paperbound.

A pictorial review of the Brooklyn Dodgers since 1940.

7-41   Dodger Fans of the World, Unite. Arthur King. William-Frederick Press. 1957. Paperbound.

A report concerning the purported shift of the Brooklyn Dodger franchise to Los Angeles.

7-42   The Los Angeles Dodgers. Paul Zimmerman. Coward-McCann. 1960. Clothbound.

A history since the franchise transfer from Brooklyn. Records, statistics.

7-43   The Giants and The Dodgers. Lee Allen. G.P. Putnam's Sons. 1964. Clothbound.

The 75-year history of baseball's oldest and fiercest rivalry.

7-44   Every Diamond Doesn't Sparkle. L. Fresco Thompson and Cy Rice. David McKay Co. 1964. Clothbound.

Anecdotes and inside stories of the Dodgers by their vice-president.

7-44A   Inside the Dodgers. L. Fresco Thompson and Cy Rice. Holloway House. 1966. Paperbound.

Revised edition of 7-44.

7-45   The Boys of Summer. Roger Kahn. Harper & Row. 1971. Clothbound.

Interviews with men who played for the Brooklyn
Dodgers in the 1950's. Their recollections of the
game and their lives today. Accounts by the author
of his days as a Dodger fan and a reporter covering
the team.

7-46   The Dogers All-Time Greats: A Pictorial History. Fred Claire.
Los Angeles Dodgers. 1972. Magazine.

A photographic historical sketch of the Brooklyn and
Los Angeles Dodgers.

7-47   The Boston Red Sox. Frederick Lieb. G.P. Putnam's Sons. 1947.
Clothbound.

A narrative history since 1901. Photos.

7-48   The Red Sox, the Bean and the Cod. Al Hirshberg. Waverly
House. 1947. Clothbound.

History of the Boston Red Sox since the time of the
Yawkey purchase in 1933.

7-49   The Boston Red Sox. Tom Meany. A.S. Barnes & Co. 1956.
Clothbound.

A profile of the current team.

7-50   The Washington Senators. Morris Bealle. Columbia Publishing
Co. 1947. Clothbound.

Year-by-year history. All-time records, all-time
player index.

7-51   The Washington Senators. Shirley Povich. G.P. Putnam's Sons.
1954. Clothbound.

A narrative history since the 1860's, including the
record in the National and American Associations.

7-52.   The Pittsburgh Pirates. Frederick Lieb. G.P. Putnam's Sons.
1948. Clothbound.

History since 1876. Photos.

7-53   Pittsburgh Baseball Through the Years. A. (Rowsy) Rowswell. Fort
Pitt Brewing Co. 1952. Booklet.

Capsule history. Records, yearly rosters.

7-54   Forbes Field 60th Birthday: Pittsburgh Pirates Album. Century
Printing Co. 1969. Magazine.

A pictorial sketch of the Pirates since 1909.

7-55   The Cleveland Indians. Franklin Lewis. G.P. Putnam's Sons.

1949. Clothbound.

Narrative history since 1869. Photos.

7-56 The Philadelphia Phillies. Frederick Lieb and Stan Baumgartner.
G.P. Putnam's Sons. 1953. Clothbound.

Narrative history since pre-Civil War days. Photos.

7-57 Phillies Batting, Pitching, Fielding All-Time Records and Rosters.
Lee Allen. Kirsh Publishing Co. 1953. Booklet.

Yearly team and player records, rosters of the Philadelphia Phillies.

7-58 It All Started in 1908 and Ended in 1970. Tri-State Printers.
1970. Booklet.

Issued to commemorate the final year of Shibe Park-
Connie Mack Stadium's existence. A yearly chronology of baseball events in Philadelphia.

7-59 The Psychologist at Bat. Dr. David Tracy. Sterling Publishing
Co. 1951. Clothbound.

Experiences of a psychologist engaged to help the St.
Louis Browns in 1950. A discussion of the psychologi-
cal aspects of baseball.

7-60 A Study in Brown. John Sullivan. 1966. Booklet.

Two volumes. St. Louis Browns' all-time roster and
records.

7-61 The Baltimore Orioles. Frederick Lieb. G.P. Putnam's Sons.
1955. Clothbound.

Narrative history of the St. Louis Browns and Baltimore
Orioles, including the various franchise transfers. Photos.

7-62 The Home Team. James Bready. 1958. Clothbound. 1971.
Clothbound and Paperbound.

Yearly supplemental inserts. A pictorial history of
the Baltimore Orioles.

7-63 One Hundred Years of Baseball in Baltimore. Maryland Historical
Society. 1959. Baseball.

A description of an exhibit by the society in April
1959.

7-64 The New Chicago White Sox. Arch Ward. Henry Regnery Co.
1951. Paperbound.

Review of present and past teams. White Sox Hall
of Fame, World Series history.

7-65   The Chicago White Sox. Warren Brown. G.P. Putnam's Sons.
            1952. Clothbound.

            Narrative history since 1901. Photos.

7-66   The Go-Go White Sox. Dave Condon. Coward-McCann. 1960.
            Clothbound.

            Complete history of the Chicago White Sox, including
            the 1959 pennant winners. All-time records and ros-
            ter.

7-67   Eight Men Out. Eliot Asinof. Holt, Rinehart, Winston. 1963.
            Clothbound. Ace Books. 1970, reissue. Paperbound.

            The story of the Chicago "Black Sox," reconstructed
            from newspapers and personal interviews. Background
            material.

7-68   The Great Baseball Mystery. Victor Luhrs. A.S. Barnes & Co.
            1966. Clothbound.

            An examination of the 1919 Chicago "Black Sox."
            Background, the case for and against the accused
            players, the case against Judge Landis. Detailed
            analysis of the 1919 World Series: composite score,
            play by play, box scores, pitching statistics.

7-69   The New York Giants. Frank Graham. G.P. Putnam's Sons.
            1952. Clothbound.

            Narrative history since 1876. Photos.

7-70   Thrilling True Story of the Baseball Giants. Charles Dexter.
            Fawcett Publishing Co. 1952. Booklet.

            A history in comic book form of the New York Giants.

7-71   The San Francisco Giants. Joe King. Prentice-Hall. 1958.
            Clothbound.

            Recent history, including the franchise transfer from
            New York.

7-72   A Flag for San Francisco. Charles Einstein. Simon & Schuster. 1962,
            1963. Clothbound. J. Lowell Pratt. 1963, reissue. Paperbound.

            History of the San Francisco Giants. Humorous inci-
            dents. The 1963 edition included the account of the
            winning of the 1962 pennant.

7-73   My Giants. Russ Hodges and Al Hirshberg. Doubleday & Co.

1963. Clothbound.

The autobiography of the New York and San Francisco Giants announcer, and the history of the Giants during Hodges' association with them.

7-74   The Giants of San Francisco. Art Rosenbaum and Robert Stevens. Coward-McCann. 1963. Clothbound.

History since 1958. Player sketches, records, statistics.

7-75   The Mets Will Win the Pennant. William R. Cox. G.P. Putnam's Sons. 1964. Clothbound.

A serious analysis of the New York Mets, demonstrating the team's building program for the future.

7-76   The Amazing Mets. Jerry Mitchell. Grosset & Dunlap. 1964. Clothbound. Tempo Books. 1964, reissue. Paperbound. Grosset & Dunlap. 1970. Clothbound.

History of the New York Mets, written in a light vein. Player sketches. Illustrated by Willard Mullin.

7-77   Now Wait a Minute, Casey. Maurey Allen. Doubleday & Co. 1965. Clothbound.

A complete inside history of the New York Mets.

7-78   Backstage at the Mets. Lindsey Nelson and Al Hirshberg. Viking Press. 1966. Clothbound.

The story of the New York Mets as told by their play-by-play announcer. Accounts of broadcasting experiences.

7-79   The Incredible Mets. Maury Allen. Paperback Library. 1969. Paperbound.

A history of the New York Mets through their 1969 championship season.

7-80   Once Upon the Polo Grounds: The Mets That Were. Leonard Schecter. Dial Press. 1969. Clothbound.

The story of the New York Mets' first two seasons.

7-81   The New York Mets: The Whole Story. Leonard Koppett. Macmillan Co. 1970. Clothbound.

The complete record and statistics of every past and present Met player.

7-82   Joy in Mudville. George Vecsey. McCall Books. 1970. Clothbound.

A narrative history of the New York Mets.

7-83   Last to First: The Story of the Mets. Larry Fox. Harper & Row. 1970. Clothbound.

A yearly narrative history of the New York Mets. All-time roster, photos.

7-84   A Decade at the Met: The Twins and Vikings. Minneapolis Chamber of Commerce. 1966. Magazine.

The development of Metropolitan Stadium in Blooming-ton, Minnesota, and a review of the Minnesota Twins.

7-85   Minnesota Twins Baseball Fun. Halsey Hall. Station WCCO. 1967. Booklet.

Anecdotes of baseball in Minneapolis-St. Paul.

7-86   The Great Teams of Baseball. MacLean Kennedy. The Sporting News. 1928. Paperbound.

Stories of 16 great teams. Records, team photos.

7-87   Baseball's Greatest Teams. Tom Meany. A.S. Barnes & Co. 1949. Clothbound. Bantam Books. 1950, reissue. Paperbound.

Stories of 16 teams with player, season, and World Series statistics.

7-88   The Book of Major League Baseball Clubs. Ed Fitzgerald, ed. A.S. Barnes & Co. 1952. Clothbound. Grosset & Dunlap. 1955. Clothbound.

7-88A   The American League.

7-88B   The National League.

History of each team, written by various authors. Compiled from a series appearing in Sport Magazine.

7-89   Baseball in Illinois. Illinois State Historical Society. April 1961. Illinois History. Vol. 14, no. 7.

Articles on major and minor leaguers and leagues.

7-90   Amazing Baseball Teams. Dave Wolf. Random House Little League Library. 1970. Clothbound. Reissued as Major League Library.

Stories of the Cubs, Braves, Cardinals, Indians, Dodg-ers, Mets, and Yankees.

7-91   Great Moments in Baseball. Dave Klein. Cowles Book Co. 1971. Clothbound.

Accounts of outstanding seasons of ten teams.

8. Biographies

8-1   In Memoriam: Aaron Burt Champion. Cincinnati House of Refuge Manual Training School. 1896. Paperbound.

> A tribute to the man who was president of the Cincinnati Red Stockings from 1867-70.

8-2   A Ball Player's Career. Adrian Anson. Era Publishing Co. 1900. Clothbound.

> The autobiography of a pioneer great player and manager. Includes an account of the 1889 world tour.

8-3   The Spectacular Career of Rev. Billy Sunday, Famous Baseball Evangelist. Theodore Frankenberg. McClelland & Co. 1913. Clothbound.

> The biography of a ball player who became a famous evangelist.

8-4   The Real Billy Sunday. Elijah Brown. Fleming H. Revell Co. 1914. Clothbound.

8-5   Billy Sunday. William T. Ellis. John C. Winston Co. 1914. 1936, reissue. Clothbound.

> One chapter devoted to his baseball career.

8-6   Commy. G.W. Axelson. Reilly and Lee. 1919. Clothbound.

> The biography of Charles Comiskey, a pioneer player and owner.

8-7   Christy Mathewson Testimonial. Frederick Lieb, ed. Harry M. Stevens. September 30, 1921. Booklet.

> Articles by various writers paying tribute to Mathewson, who was honored during a game between New York and Boston at the Polo Grounds.

8-8   Playing the Game. Stanley (Bucky) Harris. Frederick A. Stokes Co. 1925. Clothbound.

The autobiography of a player and manager. Unusual
player records.

8-9   Ty Cobb, the Idol of Baseball Fandom. Sverre O. Braathen. Avon-
dale Press. 1928. Clothbound.

A season-by-season account. Records, statistics.

8-10   The Tiger Wore Spikes. John McCallum. A.S. Barnes & Co.
1956. Clothbound.

An informal biography of Ty Cobb. Batting records
versus each team and pitcher.

8-11   My Life in Baseball, The True Record. Ty Cobb and Al Stump.
Doubleday & Co. 1961. Clothbound.

Recollections of other great players, opinions on baseball scandals. World Series stories, instructional chap-
ters.

8-12   Babe Ruth, Idol of the American Boy. Dan Daniel. Whitman Publishing Co. 1930. Clothbound.

An informal biography. Records, photos.

8-13   The Daily Ghost. All-American Board of Baseball. December 17,
1933. Newspaper.

Humorous photos of and anecdotes concerning Babe
Ruth. Issued for the Babe Ruth Dinner at the New
York Athletic Club.

8-14   Adios to Ghosts. Christy Walsh. 1937. Clothbound.

An autobiographical account of Walsh's experiences as
Babe Ruth's ghost writer. Reprinted from a series of
articles in the Cleveland News.

8-15   Babe Ruth. Tom Meany. A.S. Barnes & Co. 1947. Clothbound.
Bantam Books. 1948, reissue. Paperbound.

The story of Ruth's career. Home run records.

8-16   The Babe Ruth Story. Allied Artists. 1948. Paperbound.

Based on the movie script.

8-17   Babe Ruth As I Knew Him. Waite Hoyt. Dell Publishing Co.
1948. Magazine.

Recollections by a former team-mate. Photos, records.

8-18   Babe Ruth. Martin Weldon. Thomas Y. Crowell Co. 1948. Clothbound.

A year-by-year account of Ruth's career.

8-19   The Babe Ruth Story. Babe Ruth and Bob Considine. E.P. Dutton & Co. 1948. Clothbound. Pocket Books. 1948, reissue. Paperbound. Scholastic Book Services. 1963, reissue. Paperbound.

Autobiography. Records, photos.

8-20   The Real Babe Ruth. Dan Daniel. The Sporting News. 1948. 1963, reissue. Paperbound.

Anecdotes, photos. Date of and opposing pitcher allowing each lifetime home run.

8-21   The King of Swat. Father Ted, S.S.P. Society of St. Paul. 1955. Paperbound.

A biography of Babe Ruth.

8-22   I Was with Babe Ruth at St. Mary's. Louis Leisman. 1956. Paperbound.

An account of Ruth's boyhood days at St. Mary's Industrial School in Baltimore, by one who spent six years with him there. Photos.

8-23   The Babe and I. Mrs. Babe Ruth and Bill Slocum. Prentice-Hall. 1959. Clothbound. Avon Books. 1959, reissue. Paperbound.

A personal account of Babe Ruth's career and their life together.

8-24   Babe Ruth, His Story in Baseball. Lee Allen. G.P. Putnam's Sons. 1966. Clothbound.

Anecdotes, little-known facts.

8-25   Babe Ruth. Kenneth Richards. Children's Press. 1967. Clothbound.

For young readers.

8-26   Lou Gehrig, Baseball's Iron Man. Stan Carlson. 1940. Clothbound.

A biography of the immortal New York Yankee firstbaseman. Records, photos.

8-27   Lou Gehrig, Iron Horse of Baseball. Richard Hubler. Houghton-Mifflin Co. 1941. Clothbound.

Career records.

8-28   Lou Gehrig, A Quiet Hero. Frank Graham. G.P. Putnam's Sons. 1942. Clothbound.

8-29   <u>Lou Gehrig, Pride of the Yankees.</u> Paul Gallico. Grosset & Dunlap. 1942. Clothbound.

        Career records. Later reissued in comic book form.

8-30   <u>Lou Gehrig, Iron Man of Baseball.</u> Willard and Celia Luce. Garrard Publishing Co. 1970. Americans All Series. Clothbound.

        A biography for young readers.

8-31   <u>Clowning Through Baseball.</u> Al Schacht. A.S. Barnes & Co. 1941. Clothbound. Bantam Books. 1949, reissue. Paperbound. Finch Press, 1972, reissue. Clothbound.

        The autobiography of the "Clown Prince of Baseball." Humorous anecdotes.

8-32   <u>G I Had Fun.</u> Al Schacht. G.P. Putnam's Sons. 1945. Clothbound.

        An account of Schacht's personal appearance tour of Africa and the Pacific during World War II.

8-33   <u>My Own Particular Screwball.</u> Al Schacht. Doubleday & Co. 1955. Clothbound.

        An informal autobiography. Recollections of star players.

8-34   <u>McGraw of the Giants.</u> Frank Graham. G.P. Putnam's Sons. 1944. Clothbound. Armed Forces Edition. 1944, reissue. Paperbound.

        A biography of John McGraw, the immortal player and manager.

8-35   <u>The Real McGraw.</u> Mrs. John J. McGraw and Arthur Mann. David McKay Co. 1953. Clothbound.

        A comprehensive biography of John McGraw. Reminiscenses, inside stories.

8-36   <u>The Days of Mr. McGraw.</u> Joseph Durso. Prentice-Hall. 1969. Clothbound.

        An account of the 33-year association of John McGraw with the New York Giants as their manager, and of the American mores during those years.

8-37   <u>Connie Mack Golden Anniversary.</u> Philadelphia Athletics. August 4, 1944. Magazine.

        Special issue of the game program, celebrating Mack's fiftieth baseball anniversary. Articles, photos.

8-38   <u>Golden Jubilee of Connie Mack and the A's.</u> Connie Mack Golden Jubilee Committee. Bingham Co. 1950. Cover title: <u>Golden Jubilee of Club and Manager Connie Mack and the A's.</u> Paperbound.

        Issued in honor of Mack's fiftieth year with the Philadelphia Athletics. Articles, records, history, photos.

8-39   <u>Lucky To Be a Yankee.</u> Joe DiMaggio. Rudolph Field. 1946. Paperbound. Bantam Books. 1949. Paperbound. Grosset & Dunlap. 1951. Clothbound.

        Autobiography, playing instructions, records.

8-40   <u>The Thrilling Story of Joe DiMaggio.</u> Gene Schoor. Frederick Fell. 1950. Magazine.

        A pictorial biography. Playing tips, records.

8-41   <u>Joe DiMaggio - His Golden Year.</u> Al Silverman. Prentice-Hall. 1969. Clothbound. Macfadden-Bartell. 1971, reissue. Paperbound.

        An account of DiMaggio's 1941 season, in which he established a record of hitting safely in 56 consecutive games.

8-42   <u>Judge Landis and Twenty-Five Years of Baseball.</u> J.G. Taylor Spink. Thomas Y. Crowell Co. 1947. Clothbound.

        A biography of baseball's first commissioner. Photos.

8-43   <u>Walter Johnson, King of the Pitchers.</u> Roger Treat. Julian Messner, Inc. 1948. Clothbound.

        A biography of the all-time great pitcher.

8-44   <u>Pitchin' Man.</u> Satchel Paige and Hal Liebowitz. 1948. Booklet.

        An anecdotal autobiography. Box scores of outstanding major league games.

8-45   <u>Maybe I'll Pitch Forever.</u> Leroy (Satchel) Paige and David Lipman. Doubleday & Co. 1962. Clothbound. Grove Press. 1963, reissue. Paperbound.

        An anecdotal autobiography of the great Negro pitcher who made the major leagues in the twilight of his career.

8-46   <u>The Dodgers and Me.</u> Leo Durocher. Ziff-Davis. 1948. Clothbound.

        The inside story of Durocher's managerial experiences and internal struggles while manager of the Brooklyn Dodgers.

8-47   Day with the Giants. Laraine Day. Doubleday & Co. 1952. Clothbound.

Inside baseball from the viewpoint of a manager's wife, by the actress and then-wife of Leo Durocher. Humorous anecdotes.

8-48   Jackie Robinson, My Own Story. Jackie Robinson and Wendell Smith. Greenberg. 1948. Clothbound and Paperbound.

The autobiography of the first major league Negro player, written one year after his National League rookie season.

8-49   The Jackie Robinson Story. Arthur Mann. F.J. Low. 1950. Clothbound. Grosset & Dunlap. 1951, reissue. Clothbound.

8-50   Jackie Robinson. Fawcett Publishing Co. 1950. Booklet.

A sketch in comic book form.

8-51   Jackie Robinson, Baseball Hero. Gene Schoor. G.P. Putnam's Sons. 1958. Clothbound.

8-52   Wait Till Next Year. Carl Rowan and Jackie Robinson. Random House. 1960. Clothbound.

The story of Jackie Robinson.

8-53   Breakthrough to the Big League. Jackie Robinson and Alfred Duckett. Harper & Row. 1965. Clothbound.

The story of Robinson's struggle from poverty to the major leagues.

8-54   Jackie Robinson. Kenneth Rudeen. Thomas Y. Crowell Co. 1971. Clothbound.

A sketch for young readers.

8-55   I Never Had It Made. Jackie Robinson and Al Duckett. G.P. Putnam's Sons. 1972. Clothbound.

The public and private life of the first Negro major leaguer.

8-56   Strikeout Story. Bob Feller. A.S. Barnes & Co. 1947. Clothbound. Bantam Books. 1948, reissue. Paperbound. Grosset & Dunlap. Reissue. Clothbound.

The autobiography of an all-time great pitcher.

8-57   Bob Feller - Twenty Years With the Cleveland Indians. Cleveland Indians. September 9, 1956. Booklet.

Biography, photos, records, box scores of important

games. Distributed at the game honoring Feller.

8-58   Bob Feller, Hall of Fame Strikeout Star. Gene Schoor. Doubleday & Co. 1962. Clothbound.

8-59   Player-Manager. Lou Boudreau and Ed Fitzgerald. Little, Brown
& Co. 1949, 1952. Clothbound.

The autobiography of a star shortstop and manager.

8-60   Larry Dobey, Baseball Hero. Charles Dexter. Fawcett Publishing
Co. 1950. Booklet.

A sketch in comic book form.

8-61   Ralph Kiner, Home Run King. Charles Dexter. Fawcett Publishing Co. 1950. Booklet.

A sketch in comic book form.

8-62   Roy Campanella, Baseball Hero. Charles Dexter. Fawcett Publishing Co. 1950. Booklet.

A sketch in comic book form.

8-63   It's Good to Be Alive. Roy Campanella. Little, Brown & Co.
1959. Clothbound.

An autobiography of the former Brooklyn Dodger star
catcher, written after his crippling, near-fatal acci-
dent.

8-64   Roy Campanella, Man of Courage. Gene Schoor. G.P. Putnam's
Sons. 1959. Clothbound.

8-65   Don Newcombe, Baseball Hero. Charles Dexter. Fawcett Publishing Co. 1950. Booklet.

A sketch in comic book form.

8-66   Phil Rizzuto, Baseball Hero. Charles Dexter. Fawcett Publishing
Co. 1951. Booklet.

A sketch in comic book form.

8-67   Baseball and Mr. Spalding. Arthur Bartlett. Straus & Young.
1951. Clothbound.

The story of Albert G. Spalding, one of the foremost
of the baseball pioneers and founder of the A.G.
Spalding Brothers sporting goods company. An account
of his playing, baseball executive, and business careers.

8-68   My Fifty Years in Baseball. Edward G. Barrow and James M.

Kahn. Coward-McCann. 1951. Clothbound.

The autobiography of a long-time general manager of the New York Yankees. All-time player selections, Yankee history.

8-69   Eddie Stanky, Baseball Hero. Charles Dexter. Fawcett Publishing Co. 1951. Booklet.

A sketch in comic book form.

8-70   Yogi Berra, Baseball Hero. Charles Dexter. Fawcett Publishing Co. 1951. Booklet.

A sketch in comic book form.

8-71   Yogi. Yogi Berra and Ed Fitzgerald. Doubleday & Co. 1961. Clothbound.

An autobiography of the star catcher of the New York Yankees.

8-72   Yogi Berra. Joe Trimble. Tempo Books. 1965. Paperbound.

A revised edition of 8-188M.

8-73   My Kind of Baseball. Rogers Hornsby. David McKay Co. 1953. Clothbound.

The autobiography of an all-time great second baseman. Playing instructions.

8-74   The Story of Bobby Shantz. Bobby Shantz and Ralph Bernstein. J.B. Lippincott Co. 1953. Clothbound.

The autobiography of a major league pitching star and winner of the Most Valuable Player Award. An account of how Shantz overcame his small physical stature to become a major leaguer.

8-75   The Mickey Mantle Story. Mickey Mantle and Ben Epstein. Henry Holt & Co. 1953. Clothbound.

The autobiography of a great New York Yankee outfielder. Photos, records.

8-76   Mickey Mantle, Baseball's King. Al Silverman, ed. SI-New Publishing Corp. 1957. Magazine.

Feature stories by various authors, records.

8-77   Mickey Mantle of the Yankees. Gene Schoor. G.P. Putnam's Sons. 1958. Clothbound.

8-78   Mickey Mantle, Mr. Yankee. Al Silverman. G.P. Putnam's Sons. 1963. Clothbound.

8-79 The Mickey Mantle Album. Howard Liss. Hawthorn Books. 1966. Clothbound.

An illustrated biographical sketch.

8-80 The Education of a Baseball Player. Mickey Mantle. Simon & Schuster. 1967. Clothbound. Benco. 1967, reissue. Paperbound. Pocket Books. 1967, reissue. Paperbound.

The autobiography of a star outfielder. Instructional lessons drawn from Mantle's playing experiences.

8-81 The Baseball Life of Mickey Mantle. John Devaney. Scholastic Book Services. 1969. Paperbound.

A biography of an all-time great outfielder.

8-82 Mickey Mantle Slugs It Out. Julian May Dikty, (pseudonym Julian May). Crestwood House. 1972. Clothbound.

A biography for young readers.

8-83 Casey Stengel. Frank Graham. John Day. 1956. Clothbound.

A biography of the great New York Yankee manager and former major league player.

8-84 Casey Stengel's Secret. Clay Felker. Walker & Co. 1961. Clothbound and Paperbound.

An informal biography written after Stengel's forced retirement by the New York Yankees. Photos.

8-85 Casey at the Bat. Casey Stengel and Harry Paxton. Random House. 1961. Clothbound.

An autobiography of the all-time great manager.

8-86 Casey, the Life and Legend of Charles Dillon Stengel. Joseph Durso. Prentice-Hall. 1967. Clothbound.

A biography of the all-time great manager. Appendix, index, photos.

8-87 The Amazing Willie Mays. Famous Funnies. 1954. Booklet.

A sketch in comic book form.

8-88 The Willie Mays Story. Ken Smith. Greenberg. 1954. Clothbound and Paperbound.

A pictorial biography of the star New York Giant outfielder.

8-89 Born to Play Ball. Willie Mays and Charles Einstein. G.P. Putnam's Sons. 1955. Clothbound.

An autobiography of Willie Mays.

8-90   Complete Life of Willie Mays. Mickey Greenman. Pocket Mag-
        azines. 1955. Booklet.

        A biographical sketch. Photos.

8-91   Willie Mays. Hubert Saal. 1960. Paperbound.

        The "Say Hey" Kid grows up.

8-92   Willie Mays, Modest Champion. Gene Schoor. G.P. Putnam's
        Sons. 1960. Clothbound.

8-93   Willie Mays, Coast to Coast Giant. Charles Einstein. G.P.
        Putnam's Sons. 1963. Clothbound.

8-94   The Willie Mays Album. Howard Liss. Hawthorn Books. 1966.
        Clothbound.

        An illustrated biographical sketch.

8-95   Willie Mays: My Life in and out of Baseball. Willie Mays and
        Charles Einstein. E.P. Dutton & Co. 1966, 1972. Clothbound.

        Observations on players, managers, civil rights, his
        marriage, other topics. Career records.

8-96   Willie Mays. Arnold Hano. Grosset & Dunlap. 1966. Cloth-
        bound. Tempo Books. 1970, reissue. Paperbound.

        A revised edition of 8-190E. The biography of an
        all-time great outfielder.

8-97   Six Hundred. Adirondack Industries. 1970. Booklet.

        Sequence photos and descriptions of Willie May's
        600th home run. Career highlights.

8-98   The Baseball Life of Willie Mays. Lee Greene. Scholastic Book
        Services. 1970. Paperbound.

        A biography of an all-time great outfielder.

8-99   Willie Mays-Most Valuable Player. Julian May Dikty, (pseud-
        onym Julian May). Crestwood House. 1972. Clothbound.

        A biography for young readers.

8-100   General Baseball Doubleday. Robert S. Holzman. Longmans,
        Green. 1955. Clothbound.

        The story of baseball and its supposed "inventor."
        Development of the game, baseball during the Civil
        War. Doubleday's career during and after the Civil
        War.

8-101   Fear Strikes Out. Jim Piersall and Al Hirshberg. Atlantic, Little, Brown. 1955. Clothbound. Grosset & Dunlap. 1956, reissue. Clothbound. Bantam Books. 1957, reissue. Paperbound.

An autobiography of the Boston Red Sox star who suffered a nervous breakdown and recovered to return as a player.

8-102   Branch Rickey, American in Action. Arthur Mann. 1957. Houghton-Mifflin Co. Clothbound and Paperbound.

The story of a baseball pioneer, by his long-time assistant.

8-103   Mr. Baseball. David Lipman. G.P. Putnam's Sons. 1966. Clothbound.

The story of Branch Rickey. An account of how he originated the farm system, brought Negroes into the major leagues and spurred the expansion of the major leagues.

8-104   Bob Turley, Fireball Pitcher. Gene Schoor. G.P. Putnam's Sons. 1959. Clothbound.

The biography of a star New York Yankee pitcher and strikeout specialist.

8-105   The Splendid Splinter. Ted Blood. Exposition Press. 1960. Clothbound.

A biographical sketch and spirited defense of Ted Williams. The story of "how the sports writers tried to chop up the Splinter for firewood."

8-106   Ted Williams. Ray Robinson. G.P. Putnam's Sons. 1962. Clothbound.

A biography of the all-time great Boston Red Sox outfielder.

8-107   My Turn at Bat. Ted Williams and John Underwood. Simon & Schuster. 1969. Clothbound. Pocket Books. 1970, reissue. Paperbound.

An autobiography of the all-time star outfielder.

8-108   Ted Williams, the Golden Year. Edwin Pope. Prentice-Hall. 1970. Clothbound.

The story of Williams' 1957 season, in which he won the American League batting championship at the age of 39.

8-109 **What a Baseball Manager Does.** Roy and Spencer Hoopes. John Day. 1970. Clothbound.

   An illustrated account of Ted Williams' activities with the Washington Senators during 1969, his first year as a manager. His performance gained him the Manager of the Year award.

8-110 **Lew Burdette of the Braves.** Gene Schoor. G.P. Putnam's Sons. 1960. Clothbound.

   A biography of the star Milwaukee Braves pitcher and hero of the 1957 World Series.

8-111 **The Red Schoendienst Story.** Gene Schoor. Julian Messner, Inc. 1961. Clothbound.

   A biography of the star infielder who overcame tuberculosis to continue his major league career.

8-112 **Slide, Kelly, Slide.** Alfred Cappio. Passaic County, New Jersey Historical Society. 1962. Booklet.

   An autobiographical sketch of Michael "King" Kelly, famous nineteenth century player.

8-113 **Roger Maris at Bat.** Roger Maris and Jim Ogle. Duell, Sloan & Pearce. 1962. Clothbound. Meredith Press. 1962, reissue. Paperbound.

   An account of the 1961 season, in which Maris hit 61 home runs. An account of each home run and Maris' disputes with the press.

8-114 **Frank Frisch: The Fordham Flash.** Frank Frisch and J. Roy Stockton. Doubleday & Co. 1962. Clothbound.

   An autobiography of the Hall of Fame second baseman. Advice to young players, Frish's all-star teams, reminiscences.

8-115 **Veeck As in Wreck.** Bill Veeck and Ed Linn. G.P. Putnam's Sons. 1962. Clothbound. Doubleday & Co. 1962, reissue. Clothbound. Bantam Books. 1963, reissue. Paperbound.

   The autobiography of a successful club owner and promoter. Pungent observations on the management of the game today.

8-116 **It Pays to Steal.** Maury Wills and Steve Gardner. Prentice-Hall. 1963. Clothbound. Book Co. of America. Reissue. Paperbound.

   The story of baseball's modern speed and base-stealing king.

8-117 Edward Morgan Lewis, Early Career. Hobart L. Morris, Jr. Syra-
cust University. 1964. Clothbound.

A Master of Arts thesis sketching the baseball career
of Ted Lewis, a college graduate who pitched for
Boston from 1896-1901, after which he retired to become a college professor.

8-118 Warren Spahn. JKW Sports Publications. 1964. Magazine.

A pictorial biography of the star pitcher.

8-119 Cy Young. Ralph Romig. Dorrance & Co. 1964. Clothbound.

A biography of the all-time leader in lifetime career
pitching victories. His yearly record with each team.
Photos.

8-120 Stan Musial, Baseball's Durable "Man". Ray Robinson. G.P.
Putnam's Sons. 1964. Clothbound.

A biography of the star St. Louis Cardinal outfielder.

8-121 Stan Musial. Bob Broeg. Doubleday & Co. 1964. Clothbound.

Biography, recollections, observations on the game.
Batting tips, Musial's views on managers and stars of
his day. Records.

8-122 Sandy Koufax, Strike Out King. Arnold Hano. G.P. Putnam's
Sons. 1964. Clothbound.

A biography of the star Dodger pitcher.

8-123 Sandy Koufax. JKW Sports Publications. 1964. Magazine.

A pictorial biography.

8-124 Koufax. Sandy Koufax and Ed Linn. Viking Press. 1966. Clothbound.

An autobiography of the present-day pitching great.
Includes an account of the historic 1966 "double hold-
out" by Koufax and Don Drysdale. Game-by-game
statistics.

8-125 Sandy Koufax. Jerry Mitchell. Grosset & Dunlap. 1966. Clothbound. Tempo Books. 1966, reissue. Paperbound.

Biography, records, box scores of outstanding games.

8-126 The Sandy Koufax Album. Howard Liss. Hawthorn Books. 1966.
Clothbound.

An illustrated biographical sketch.

8-127   The Baseball Life of Sandy Koufax. George Vecsey. Scholastic Book Services. 1968. Paperbound.

The story of an all-time great pitcher.

8-128   So You Want to Be a Major Leaguer? Cy Block. 1964. Paperbound.

The autobiography of a successful insurance executive who spent 14 years in organized baseball, 11 of them in the minors.

8-129   Ken Boyer, Guardian of the Hot Corner. Jack Zanger. Thomas Nelson & Sons. 1965. Clothbound.

The biography of a star third baseman, written for younger readers.

8-130   Ken Boyer. David Lipman. G.P. Putnam's Sons. 1967. Clothbound.

A biography of the star third baseman of the St. Louis Cardinals and New York Mets.

8-131   The Story of Jim Bunning. Jim Bunning and Ralph Bernstein. J. B. Lippincott Co. 1965. Clothbound.

Includes the radio play-by-play account of Bunning's 1964 perfect game, as well as the story of the September 1964 collapse of the Philadelphia Phillies. Pitching observations.

8-132   The Bobby Richardson Story. Bobby Richardson. Fleming H. Revell Co. 1965. Clothbound. Pyramid Publications. 1966, reissue. Paperbound.

An autobiography and statement of Richardson's religious beliefs.

8-133   Don't Knock the Rock. Gordon Cobbledick. World Publishing Co. 1966. Clothbound.

The biography of Rocky Colavito. Childhood, career, romance, and marriage. Opinions on baseball.

8-134   Alston and the Dodgers. Walter Alston and Si Burick. Doubleday & Co. 1966. Clothbound.

An account of Alston's successful major league managing career. Players and events. Photos.

8-135   The Kid from Cuba. James Terzian. Doubleday & Co. 1967. Clothbound.

The story of Zoilo Versalles, star shortstop of the Minnesota Twins.

8-136   <u>My Life and Baseball</u>. Felipe Alou and Herman Weiskopf. Word Books. 1967. Paperbound.

An autobiography and statement of Alou's religious faith.

8-137   <u>You Can't Steal First Base.</u> Jimmy Dykes and Charles Dexter. J.B. Lippincott Co. 1967. Clothbound.

An autobiography of the former player and manager. An account of a 50-year baseball career. Anecdotes, viewpoints.

8-138   <u>Dizzy Dean</u>. Lee Allen. G.P. Putnam's Sons. 1967. Clothbound.

A biography of the Hall of Fame pitcher who was also one of baseball's all-time "characters."

8-139   <u>The High Hard One</u>. Kirby Higbe and Martin Quigley. Viking Press. 1967. Clothbound.

An informal autobiography of the former zany Brooklyn Dodgers pitcher. Humorous incidents, life with the Dodgers, the rough road down.

8-140   <u>A Pitcher's Story</u>. Juan Marichal and Charles Einstein. Doubleday & Co. 1967. Clothbound.

The autobiography of a star pitcher. Experiences in his Dominican Republic homeland, anecdotes of the major leagues, descriptions of the private side of the game.

8-141   <u>Juan Marichal: Mr. Strike.</u> John Devaney. G.P. Putnam's Sons. 1971. Clothbound.

The biography of a star pitcher. Records.

8-142   <u>The All-American Dropout.</u> George F. Twombley. 1967. Clothbound.

The autobiography of a former major leaguer who became the president of a paper firm.

8-143   <u>Yaz.</u> Carl Yastrzemski and Al Hirshberg. Viking Press. 1968. Clothbound. Tempo. 1970, reissue. Paperbound.

The autobiography of a star outfielder.

8-144   <u>Let's Go, Yaz.</u> Robert Jackson. Henry Z. Walck. 1968. Clothbound.

A boys' biography of star outfielder Carl Yastrzemski.

8-145   <u>My Ups and Downs in Baseball.</u> Orlando Cepeda and Charles

Einstein. G.P. Putnam's Sons. 1968. Clothbound.

The star first baseman traces his career from Puerto Rico to the major leagues.

8-146　　"Aaron, r. f." Henry Aaron and Furman Bisher. World Publishing Co. 1968. Clothbound.

The autobiography of an all-time great outfielder and hitter.

8-147　　Henry Aaron: Quiet Super Star. Al Hirshberg. G.P. Putnam's Sons. 1969. Clothbound.

The biography of an all-time great.

8-148　　Hammerin' Hank of the Braves. Joel Cohen. Scholastic Book Services. 1971. Paperbound.

The story of all-time great outfielder Hank Aaron.

8-149　　Hank Aaron Clinches the Pennant. Julian May Dikty, (pseudonym, Julian May). Crestwood House. 1972. Clothbound.

A biography for young readers.

8-150　　Baseball, I Love You. Charlie Grimm and Ed Prell. Henry Regnery Co. 1968. Clothbound.

The autobiography of a famous player and manager.

8-151　　Rhubarb in the Catbird Seat. Red Barber and Robert Creamer. Doubleday & Co. 1968. Clothbound.

The autobiography of an announcer who broadcast baseball for 33 years. Recollections, techniques of announcing, background information on players, owners, and sponsors.

8-152　　The Broadcasters. Red Barber. Dial Press. 1970. Clothbound.

The autobiography of a former baseball announcer. Recollections of the early days of radio and its pioneer announcers.

8-153　　From Ghetto to Glory. Bob Gibson and Phil Pepe. Prentice-Hall. 1968. Clothbound. Popular Library. 1968, reissue. Paperbound.

The story of a star pitcher's rise from poverty to World Series stardom, and his battles with racism along the way.

8-154　　My Life Is Baseball. Frank Robinson and Al Silverman. Doubleday & Co. 1968. Clothbound.

The autobiography of a star outfielder.

8-155   Phil Regan. Phil Regan and James Hefley. Zondervan Publishing House. 1968. Clothbound.

The autobiography of a star relief pitcher.

8-156   Roberto Clemente: Batting King. Arnold Hano. G.P. Putnam's Sons. 1968. Clothbound.

The biography of a star outfielder.

8-157   Thirty-One and Six. Robert Jackson. Henry Z. Walck. 1969. Clothbound.

A biographical sketch of pitcher Denny McLain, who won 31 games for the Detroit Tigers in 1968.

8-158   Hawk. Ken Harrelson and Al Hirshberg. Viking Press. 1969. Clothbound.

An autobiography of Ken Harrelson, a colorful player renowned for his off-the-field exploits.

8-159   The Tommy Davis Story. Patrick Russell. Doubleday & Co. 1969. Clothbound.

The biography of a star hitter.

8-160   The Perfect Game: Tom Seaver and the Mets. Tom Seaver and Dick Schaap. E.P. Dutton & Co. 1970. Clothbound. Bantam Books. 1970, reissue. Paperbound.

An account of Seaver's winning performance in the fourth game of the 1969 World Series. Autobiographical recollections.

8-161   Tom Seaver of the Mets. George Sullivan. G.P. Putnam's Sons. 1971. Clothbound.

The story of a star pitcher.

8-162   Seeing It Through. Tony Conigliaro. Macmillan Co. 1970. Clothbound.

The story of a star outfielder whose career was impaired and finally ended as a result of being struck by a pitch.

8-163   Tony Conigliaro: Up from Despair. Robert Rubin. G.P. Putnam's Sons. 1971. Clothbound.

8-164   Ball Four. Jim Bouton and Leonard Shecter. World Publishing Co. 1970. Clothbound. Dell Publishing Co. 1971, reissue. Paperbound.

A controversial inside look at major league baseball
by a former star pitcher.

8-165   I'm Glad You Didn't Take It Personally.   Jim Bouton and Leonard
Shecter.   William Morrow & Co.   1971.   Clothbound.   Dell Publishing Co.   1972, reissue.   Paperbound.

Bouton tells of his experiences as a result of having
written Ball Four.

8-166   Jim Thorpe.   Donald Clifford Snow, (pseudonym Thomas Fall).
Thomas Y. Crowell Co.   1970.   Clothbound.

A sketch for young readers of the all-time great athlete and major league baseball player.

8-167   Jim Thorpe, All-Around Athlete.   George Sullivan.   Garrard Publishing Co.   1971.   Clothbound.

A biographical sketch for young readers.

8-168   The Pete Rose Story.   Pete Rose.   World Publishing Co.   1970.
Clothbound.

The autobiography of a star outfielder.

8-169   Pete Rose: They Call Him Charlie Hustle.   Bill Libby.   G.P.
Putnam's Sons.   1972.   Clothbound.

The biography of an outstanding hitter and all-around
player.

8-170   Knuckler: The Phil Niekro Story.   Wilfred Binette.   Hallux, Inc.
1970.   Clothbound.

The biography of a successful knuckleball pitcher.

8-171   Iron Man.   Billy Williams.   Regensteiner Publishing Enterprises.
1970.   Clothbound and Paperbound.

The autobiography of a star outfielder for younger
readers.

8-172   Cleon.   Cleon Jones and Ed Hershey.   Coward-McCann.   1970.
Clothbound.

The autobiography of a star outfielder.

8-173   Behind the Mask.   Bill Freehan, Steve Gelman, and Dick Schaap.
World Publishing Co.   1970.   Clothbound.   Popular Library.   1970,
reissue.   Paperbound.

A diary kept during the 1969 season by the Detroit
Tigers' catcher.

8-174   The Way It Is.   Curt Flood and Richard Carter.   Trident Press.

1971. Clothbound. Pocket Books. 1972, reissue. Paperbound.

The autobiography of a star player who refused to be traded to another team and challenged baseball's reserve clause in the courts.

8-175   Rusty Staub of the Expos.   John Robertson.   Prentice-Hall. 1971. Clothbound.

The biography of a star outfielder. English and French editions.

8-176   Johnny Bench.   Robert Jackson.   Henry Z. Walck. 1971. Clothbound.

The biography of a star catcher, for young readers.

8-177   From Behind the Plate.   Johnny Bench.   Prentice-Hall. 1972. Clothbound.

A photographic autobiography of a star catcher. Aspects of catching and hitting.

8-178   Johnny Bench: The Little General.   Bill Libby.   G.P. Putnam's Sons. 1972. Clothbound.

The biography of a star catcher.

8-179   Harmon Killebrew: Baseball's Superstar.   Dr. Wayne J. Anderson. Deseret Book Co. 1971. Clothbound.

The detailed biography of a star hitter.

8-180   Mr. Cub.   Ernie Banks and Jim Enright.   Follett Publishing Co. 1971. Clothbound.

The autobiography of the all-time great Chicago Cubs infielder. Box scores of important games, records.

8-181   Baseball's Great Tragedy.   Bob McGarigle.   Exposition Press. 1972. Clothbound.

The story of Carl Mays, whose pitch caused the death of Ray Chapman, the only fatality in major league history.

8-182   Brooks Robinson: Sports Hero.   Marshall and Sue Burchard.   G.P. Putnam's Sons. 1972. Clothbound.

A biography of the star third baseman for young readers.

8-183   Vida: His Own Story.   Vida Blue and Bill Libby.   Prentice-Hall. 1972. Clothbound.

The autobiography of a star pitcher.

8-184	<u>Vida: Birth of the Blue.</u> Ron Bergman. Coward-McCann. 1972. A biography of star pitcher Vida Blue.
8-185	<u>Vida.</u> Richard Deming. Lancer Books. 1972. Paperbound. The biography of star pitcher Vida Blue.
8-186	<u>Winning!</u> Earl Weaver and John Sammis. William Morrow & Co. 1972. Clothbound. The autobiography of a successful major league manager. Strategy, insights.
8-187	<u>Caught Short.</u> Donald Davidson and Jesse Outlar. Atheneum. 1972. Clothbound. The autobiography of an Atlanta Brave executive who overcame his height of four feet to carve out a successful career.
8-188	<u>A.S. Barnes Biographical Series.</u> A.S. Barnes & Co. Clothbound.
8-188A	<u>Jackie Robinson.</u> Bill Roeder. 1950.
8-188B	<u>Ted Williams.</u> Arthur Sampson. 1950.
8-188C	<u>Yogi Berra.</u> Ben Epstein. 1951.
8-188D	<u>Ewell Blackwell.</u> Lyall Smith. 1951.
8-188E	<u>Jim Konstanty.</u> Frank Yeutter. 1951.
8-188F	<u>Bob Lemon.</u> Ed McAuley. 1951.
8-188G	<u>Joe DiMaggio.</u> Tom Meany. 1951.
8-188H	<u>Stan Musial.</u> Tom Meany. 1951.
8-188I	<u>Ralph Kiner.</u> Tom Meany. 1951.
8-188J	<u>Andy Pafko.</u> John C. Hoffman. 1951.
8-188K	<u>Ted Williams.</u> Tom Meany. 1951.
8-188L	<u>Phil Rizzuto.</u> Joe Trimble. 1951.
8-188M	<u>Yogi Berra.</u> Joe Trimble. 1952, 1956, reissue.
8-188N	<u>Roy Campanella.</u> Dick Young. 1952.
8-188P	<u>Bobby Shantz.</u> Ed Delaney. 1953.
8-188Q	<u>Hank Sauer.</u> John C. Hoffman. 1953.

1951: Small editions, issued as Most Valuable Player Series and grouped as All-Star Library. Paperbound Armed Forces Editions were also published.

8-189   Julian Messner Biographical Series. Julian Messner, Inc. Clothbound.

8-189A   The Jim Thorpe Story. Gene Schoor and Henry Gilfond, 1951. Clothbound. Archway. 1967, reissue. Paperbound.

8-189B   The Story of Ty Cobb. Gene Schoor and Henry Gilfond, 1952, 1966, reissue. Pocket Books. 1967, reissue. Paperbound.

8-189C   Christy Mathewson. Gene Schoor. 1952.

8-189D   Casey Stengel, Baseball's Greatest Manager. Gene Schoor. 1953, 1961.

8-189E   The Ted Williams Story. Gene Schoor. 1954.

8-189F   The Stan Musial Story. Gene Schoor. 1955.

8-189G   The Leo Durocher Story. Gene Schoor. 1955.

8-189H   The Pee Wee Reese Story. Gene Schoor. 1956.

8-189I   Joe DiMaggio, Yankee Clipper. Gene Schoor. 1956.

8-189J   Jackie Robinson of the Brooklyn Dodgers. Milton J. Shapiro. 1957. Archway. 1967, reissue. Paperbound.

8-189K   The Sal Maglie Story. Milton J. Shapiro. 1957.

8-189L   The Yogi Berra Story. Gene Roswell. 1958.

8-189M   The Roy Campanella Story. Milton Shapiro. 1958.

8-189N   The Warren Spahn Story. Milton Shapiro. 1958, 1959.

Spahn instituted an "invasion of privacy" suit over publication of this book.

8-189P   The Phil Rizzuto Story. Milton J. Shapiro. 1959.

8-189Q   The Mel Ott Story. Milton J. Shapiro. 1959.

8-189R   The Billy Martin Story. Joe Archibald. 1959.

8-189S   The Richie Ashburn Story. Joe Archibald. 1960.

8-189T   The Gil Hodges Story. Milton J. Shapiro. 1960.

8-189U	The Willie Mays Story. Milton J. Shapiro. 1960.
8-189V	The Eddie Mathews Story. Al Hirshberg. 1960.
8-189W	The Jackie Jensen Story. Al Hirshberg. 1960, 1961.
8-189X	Red Schoendienst, The Man Who Fought Back. Al Hirshberg. 1961.
8-189Y	The Hank Aaron Story. Milton J. Shapiro. 1961.
8-189Z	From Sandlots to League President. Al Hirshberg. 1962. The story of Joe Cronin.
8-189AA	The Whitey Ford Story. Milton J. Shapiro. 1962.
8-189BB	Mickey Mantle, Yankee Slugger. Milton J. Shapiro. 1962.
8-189CC	The Dizzy Dean Story. Milton J. Shapiro. 1963.
8-189DD	The Duke Snider Story. Irwin Winehouse. 1964.
8-189EE	The Don Drysdale Story. Milton J. Shapiro. 1964.
8-189FF	The Al Kaline Story. Al Hirshberg. 1964.
8-189GG	The Harmon Killebrew Story. Hal Butler. 1966.
8-189HH	The Brooks Robinson Story. Jack Zanger. 1967.
8-189II	The Bob Allison Story. Hal Butler. 1967.
8-189JJ	Stormin' Norman Cash. Hal Butler. 1968.
8-189KK	The Willie Horton Story. Hal Butler. 1970. Clothbound.
8-190	Sport Magazine Biographical Series. Bartholomew House. Paperbound.
8-190A	Stan Musial. Irv Goodman. 1961. Thomas Nelson & Sons. 1961, reissue. Clothbound.
8-190B	Ted Williams. Ed Linn. 1961. Thomas Nelson & Sons. 1961, reissue. Clothbound.
8-190C	Baseball's Best Managers. Harold Rosenthal. 1916. Thomas Nelson & Sons. 1961, reissue. Clothbound.
8-190D	Mickey Mantle. Dick Schaap. 1961.
8-190E	Willie Mays. Arnold Hano. 1961.

8-190F   Warren Spahn. Al Silverman. 1961.

8-190G   Roger Maris. Len Schecter. 1962.

          Lifetime records included.

8-191   Mantle and Maris. Cape Magazine Corp. 1961. Magazine.

          Records, photos, sketches of Mickey Mantle and
          Roger Maris.

8-192   Maris/Mantle. JKW Sports Publications. 1961. Magazine.

          Pictorial biographies of Roger Maris and Mickey Man-
          tle. Records, including Maris' 61 home runs.

8-193   Mantle/Mays. JKW Sports Publications. 1962. Magazine.

          Pictorial biographies of Mickey Mantle and Willie
          Mays. Records.

8-194   Musial/Mays. JKW Sports Publications. 1963. Magazine.

          Pictorial biographies of Stan Musial and Willie Mays.
          Records.

8-195   DiMaggio/Williams. JKW Sports Publications. 1964. Magazine.

          Pictorial biographies of Joe DiMaggio and Ted Williams.
          Records.

8-196   They Played the Game. Harry Grayson. A.S. Barnes & Co.
          1944, 1945. Clothbound. Books for Libraries Press. 1972, re-
          issue. Clothbound.

          Sketches of great stars and teams.

8-197   Famous Names in Baseball. John Carmichael. Hart Schaffner
          and Marx. 1945. Booklet.

          Biographical sketches.

8-198   Grauley All-Stars. S.O. Grauley. Philadelphia Inquirer. 1948.
          Paperbound.

          All-star teams for each decade since 1890 as selected
          by the Inquirer Sports Editor. Records and sketches
          of each player.

8-199   Baseball Personalities. James J. Powers. Rudolph Field. 1949.
          Clothbound.

          Illustrated sketches of more than 50 star players.

8-200   The Best in Baseball. Robert Shoemaker. Thomas Y. Crowell Co.
          1949, 1954, 1959, 1962. Clothbound.

Sketches of twentieth century stars: Simmons, Coch-rane, Boudreau, Feller, Hornsby, Roberts, Dean, Mantle, Maris, Spahn, Hubbell, Cobb, Ruth, J. Di-Maggio, Mays, Newhouser, Gehrig.

8-201   Baseball Stars of 1950. Bruce Jacobs, ed. Lion Books. 1950. Paperbound.

Player biographies by various authors. Player records.

8-201A   Baseball Stars of (date of previous season). Lion Books. 1953-57. Paperbound. Pyramid Books. 1958-to date. Bruce Jacobs. 1953-57. Ray Robinson. 1958-to date. Paperbound.

Continuation of 8-201.

8-202   Baseball's Greatest Players. Tom Meany. A.S. Barnes & Co. 1950, 1951, 1953, 1955. Clothbound. Dell Publishing Co. 1955. Paperbound.

Sketches and statistics of players from Ty Cobb to Willie Mays.

8-203   Baseball's Best. Tom Meany and Tommy Holmes. Franklin Watts. 1964. Clothbound.

Records and sketches of Meany's twentieth century all-star team.

8-204   Heroes of Baseball. Robert Smith. World Publishing Co. 1952, 1953, reissue. Clothbound.

Sketches of great figures from Alexander Cartwright to Jackie Robinson. Emphasis on the nineteenth century.

8-205   Hits, Runs, No Errors. E.G. Patterson. Babe Ruth Foundation. 1952. Booklet.

Great moments and stars of baseball.

8-206   Baseball's Greatest Lineup. Christy Walsh, ed. A.S. Barnes & Co. 1952. Clothbound.

Sketches and records of an all-time team as selected by a poll of sports writers, each sketch by a different writer. Includes Connie Mack's 50 year all-star team.

8-207   Baseball Heroes. Fawcett Publishing Co. 1952. Booklet.

Sketches in comic book form.

8-208   Baseball Extra. Frank Graham. A.S. Barnes & Co. 1954. Cloth-bound.

Biographical sketches of 17 great players.

8-209   <u>Baseball Immortals</u>. Ed Burkholder. Christopher Publishing House. 1955. Clothbound.

        Unusual stories of all-time greats such as John McGraw, Buck Ewing, Jim McAleer, Rube Waddell, Bucky Harris, Rogers Hornsby, George Sisler, Dizzy Dean, and others.

8-210   <u>Book of Baseball Stars</u>. Rawlings Manufacturing Co. 1961. Booklet.

        Sketches, records, photos.

8-211   <u>The Greatest in Baseball</u>. Mac Davis. Scholastic Book Services. 1962. Paperbound.

        The all-time best at each position.

8-212   <u>Pacemakers in Baseball</u>. Mac Davis. World Publishing Co. 1968. Clothbound.

        Sketches of 30 stars.

8-213   <u>Baseball's All-Time Greats</u>. Mac Davis. Bantam Books. 1970. Paperbound.

        Sketches of 50 stars.

8-214   <u>Baseball's Greatest Players Today</u>. Jack Orr, ed. Franklin Watts. 1963. Clothbound. J. Lowell Pratt. 1963, reissue. Paperbound.

        Player biographies by various authors.

8-215   <u>The Quality of Courage</u>. Mickey Mantle. Doubleday & Co. 1964. Clothbound. Sports Book League. 1965, reissue. Clothbound. Bantam Books. 1965, reissue. Paperbound.

        Stories of ballplayers who overcame handicaps to become stars.

8-216   <u>Baseball's Most Valuable Players</u>. George Vecsey. Random House Little League Library. 1966. Clothbound. Reissued as Major League Library.

        Sketches of thirteen winners of the Most Valuable Player award, from Frisch to Versalles. Index, photos.

8-217   <u>The Year They Won the Most Valuable Player Award</u>. Milton J. Shapiro. Julian Messner, Inc. 1966. Clothbound.

        History of the MVP from 1911-65. Key games of 11 award winners. Photos, statistics.

8-218   <u>Baseball's All Stars</u>. J. Lowell Pratt, ed. Doubleday & Co. 1967. Clothbound.

        Reprints of newspaper and magazine articles on nine

outstanding contemporary players. Sketches of 16
additional stars. Records, index.

8-219   Heroes of the Major Leagues. Alexander Peters. Random House
Little League Library. 1967. Clothbound. Reissued as Major
League Library.

Sketches and photos of nine current stars.

8-220   The Greatest American Leaguers. Al Hirshberg. G.P. Putnam's
Sons. 1970. Clothbound.

Sketches of 20 outstanding players: four pitchers and
two players in each of the other eight positions.

8-221   Super Stars of Baseball. Bob Broeg. The Sporting News. 1971.
Clothbound.

Biographical sketches of 40 stars of the past. Career
records.

8-222   Baseball's Zaniest Stars. Howard Liss. Random House. 1971.
Clothbound. Major League Library Series.

Profiles of colorful figures: Waddell, Stengel, Newsom, others.

8-223   Baseball's All-Time Great Stars. Dell Publishing Co. 1971. Magazine.

Records and statistics covering Ruth, Speaker, Williams,
Dean, Feller, Cobb, and Gehrig.

8-224   Meet the Dodger Family Series. Bob Laughlin and Budd Theobold.
Union Oil Co. 1960. Booklet.

A series of booklets containing biographical sketches
of each Los Angeles Dodger player.

8-224A   The New Dodger Family Series. Union Oil Co. 1961. Booklet.

Continuation of 8-224.

8-225   Greatest Giants of Them All. Arnold Hano. G.P. Putnam's Sons.
1967. Clothbound.

Sketches of Mathewson, Hubbell, Ewing, Terry, Ott,
Frisch, Mays, McGraw, others.

8-226   The Greatest Cardinals of Them All. John Devaney. G.P. Putnam's Sons. 1968. Clothbound.

Sketches of 12 players.

8-227   The Greatest Yankees of Them All. Ray Robinson. G.P. Putnam's
Sons. 1969. Clothbound.

Sketches of 15 players.

8-228   The Greatest Dodgers of Them All. Steve Gelman. G.P. Putnam's Sons. 1968. Clothbound.

Sketches of 14 players.

8-229   Baseball's Greatest Hitters. Tom Meany. A.S. Barnes & Co.
1950. Clothbound.

Lifetime records and sketches of the top 20 hitters
since 1900.

8-230   Kings of the Home Run. Arthur Daley. G.P. Putnam's Sons.
1962. Clothbound.

Biographical sketches and records of all-time sluggers
from Ruth to Maris.

8-231   All the Home Run Kings. Arthur Daley. G.P. Putnam's Sons.
1972. Clothbound.

Sketches of 23 players.

8-232   Champions of the Bat. Milton J. Shapiro. Julian Messner, Inc.
1967. Clothbound.

Sketches of baseball's greatest hitters.

8-233   The Fabulous 500. JKW Sports Publications. 1968. Magazine.

Photographic sketches of the players who have hit 500
or more major league home runs.

8-234   Triple-Crown Winners. Howard Liss. Julian Messner, Inc. 1969.
Clothbound.

Sketches of the six triple crown winners.

8-235   Great Hitters of the Major Leagues. Frank Graham, Jr. Random
House Little League Library. 1969. Clothbound. Reissued as
Major League Library.

Sketches of eleven stars.

8-236   Champions at Bat: Three Power Hitters. Ann Finlayson. Garrard
Publishing Co. 1970. Clothbound.

Sketches of Rogers Hornsby, Ted Williams, and Joe
DiMaggio.

8-237   Baseball's Greatest Pitchers. Tom Meany. A.S. Barnes & Co.
1951. Clothbound.

Sketches and lifetime records.

8-238   Baseball's Famous Pitchers. Ira Smith. A.S. Barnes & Co. 1954.

Clothbound.

Records and stories of 53 greats.

8-239   The Fireballers: Baseball's Fastest Pitchers. Jack Newcombe. G.P. Putnam's Sons. 1964. Clothbound.

Sketches of Mathewson, Johnson, Alexander, Waddell, Vance, Grove, Dean, Feller, Vander Meer, Koufax, Drysdale.

8-240   Great Baseball Pitchers. Jim Brosnan. Random House Little League Library. 1965. Clothbound. Reissued as Major League Library.

Ten all-time greats.

8-241   Three Great Pitchers - on the Mound. Robert Reeder. Garrard Publishing Co. 1966. Clothbound.

Sketches of Feller, Hubbell, and Ehmke.

8-242   Heroes of the Bullpen. Milton J. Shapiro. Julian Messner, Inc. 1967. Clothbound.

Sketches of baseball's greatest relief pitchers: Casey, Page, Konstanty, Black, others. Heroes of the future, records.

8-243   Baseball's Greatest Pitchers. Milton J. Shapiro. Julian Messner, Inc. 1969. Clothbound.

Sketches of outstanding pitchers.

8-244   Star Pitchers of the Major Leagues. Bill Libby. Random House. 1971. Clothbound. Major League Library Series.

Sketches of nine stars.

8-245   Great Pitchers Series. Dave Klein. Tempo Books. 1972. Vol. 1. Seaver, McNally, Jenkins, Lolich. Vol. 2. Gibson, Marichal, Blue, Wilhelm. Paperbound.

Sketches, statistics.

8-246   Baseball's Greatest Catchers. Al Hirshberg. G.P. Putnam's Sons. 1966. Clothbound.

Sketches of Berra, Campanella, Dickey, Cochrane, Tebbetts, Crandall, Lopez, Howard, Ruel, Hartnett, ten others.

8-247   Heroes Behind the Mask: America's Great Catchers. Milton J. Shapiro. Julian Messner, Inc. 1968. Clothbound.

Sketches of ten outstanding catchers.

8-248 Great Catchers of the Major Leagues. Jack Zanger. Random House Little League Library. 1970. Clothbound. Reissued as Major League Library.

Sketches of ten outstanding catchers.

8-249 Baseball's Famous First Basemen. Ira Smith. A.S. Barnes & Co. 1956. Clothbound.

Stories and records of 36 outstanding players.

8-250 Heroes of the Hot Corner. Bill Libby. Franklin Watts. 1972. Clothbound.

Sketches of star major league third basemen.

8-251 Great Infielders of the Major Leagues. Dave Klein. Random House. 1972. Clothbound. Major League Library.

Sketches of 12 post-World War II players.

8-252 A History of Baseball's Immortal Outfields. Dan Daniel. Packard Motor Car Co. 1951. Booklet.

Sketches, records, photos.

8-253 Baseball's Famous Outfielders. Ira Smith. A.S. Barnes & Co. 1954. Clothbound.

Records and little-known facts covering 50 stars.

8-254 All-Stars of the Outfield. Milton J. Shapiro. Julian Messner, Inc. 1970. Clothbound.

Sketches of ten stars.

8-255 Speed Kings of the Base Paths. Ray Robinson. G.P. Putnam's Sons. 1964. Clothbound.

Sketches of Cobb, Pepper Martin, Jackie Robinson, Reiser, Wills, Mays, Carey, Aparicio, Eddie Collins. Pictorial instructions on base running.

8-256 Baseball Rookies Who Made Good. Mary G. Bonner. Alfred A. Knopf, Inc. 1954. Clothbound.

Stories, records, statistics of 40 rookies who became stars. Listing of Rookie of the Year awards.

8-257 Great Rookies of the Major Leagues. Jim Brosnan. Random House Little League Library. 1966. Clothbound. Reissued as Major League Library.

Sketches of the winners of the Rookie of the Year award from 1947-64. Photos.

8-258 Young Baseball Champions. Steve Gelman. W.W. Norton & Co.

1966. Clothbound. Scholastic Book Services. 1967, reissue.
Paperbound.

Sketches of Mays, DiMaggio, Aaron, Feller, Ruth,
Mantle, Cobb, Ott, Drysdale, Williams.

8-259   Baseball's Youngest Big Leaguers. John Devaney. Holt, Rinehart,
          & Winston. 1969. Clothbound.

Sketches of players who made the major leagues before their 22nd birthday: Williams, Feller, DiMaggio,
Dean Chance, Yastrzemski, and Mays.

8-260   Great Negro Baseball Stars and How They Made the Major Leagues.
          Andrew S. Young. A.S. Barnes & Co. 1953. Clothbound and
          Paperbound.

Background story of the color line and Branch Rickey's
role in breaking it. Sketches, records, statistics.

8-261   Baseball Has Done It. Jackie Robinson. J.B. Lippincott Co.
          1964. Clothbound.

Interviews with Negro stars concerning integration
problems in and out of baseball. Experiences while
breaking into baseball.

8-262   The Mets from Mobile. Andrew S. (Doc) Young. Harcourt,
          Brace & World. 1970. Clothbound.

Biographies of Cleon Jones and Tommie Agee. Records.

8-263   Major League Baseball Players from Iowa. George S. May. 1955.
          Paperbound. State Historical Society of Iowa. 1955. Paperbound.
          The Palimpsest. Vol. 36, no. 4.

Outfielders: McVey to Lindell. Infielders: Anson
to Dittmer. Pitchers: Hoffer to Feller.

8-264   The Great Baseball Managers. Charles Cleveland. Thomas Y.
          Crowell Co. 1950. Clothbound.

Sketches, photos. Strategy, techniques.

8-265   Baseball's Greatest Managers. Edwin Pope. Doubleday & Co.
          1960. Clothbound.

As selected by a panel of sports writers.

8-266   Baseball's Most Colorful Managers. Ray Robinson. G.P. Putnam's
          Sons. 1969. Clothbound.

Sketches of Durocher, Stengel, Huggins, Mack,
Robinson, and McGraw.

8-267   The Mighty Macs: Three Famous Baseball Managers. Guernsey Van Riper, Jr. Garrard Publishing Co. 1972. Clothbound.

           Sketches of Mack, McGraw, and McCarthy.

8-268   Bat Boy of the Giants. Garth Garreau. Westminster Press. 1948. Clothbound. Pocket Books. 1949, reissue. Paperbound.

           Autobiography, anecdotes, inside view of the New York Giants.

8-269   Yankee Bat Boy. Joe Carrieri and Zander Hollander. Prentice-Hall. 1955. Clothbound.

           Carrieri's account of his experiences as batboy of the New York Yankees.

8-270   Bat Boy of the Braves. Paul Wick and Bob Wolf. Greenberg. 1957. Clothbound.

           Autobiography, anecdotes, inside view of the Milwaukee Braves.

8-271   The Bat Boy. Dominick Ardovino. McGraw-Hill. 1967. Clothbound.

           A week with the batboy of the New York Mets. Photos.

8-272   Big League Batboy. Jerry Gibson and Ed Wilks. Random House. 1970. Clothbound.

           Experiences of a batboy for the St. Louis Cardinals.

A very
Short stop.

9. Instructionals

9-1   Batting and Pitching. John Morrill and Tim Keefe. Wright & Ditson. 1884. Booklet.

  The first instructional. Batting by John Morrill of the Boston Club, pitching by Tim Keefe of the New York Club. Illustrations, sketches and records of Morrill and Keefe.

9-2   Wright & Ditson's Book on Batting, Fielding, Pitching and Base Running. John Morrill and Tim Keefe. Wright & Ditson. 1885. Paperbound.

  Batting by John Morrill of the Boston Club. Pitching by Tim Keefe of the New York Club. Fielding by Joseph Hornung of the Boston Club. Base Running by Michael J. Kelly of the Chicago Club. Enlarged edition of 9-1 Biographical sketches of Hornung and Kelly. Illustrations.

9-3   Wright and Ditson Guide to Baseball. Timothy Murnane. Wright & Ditson. 1913. Paperbound.

  Batting, baserunning, pitching, catching, fielding, signals. Tips by major league stars, photos, rules.

9-4   Spalding Instructional Series. A.G. Spalding & Brothers. Paperbound.

9-4A   The Art of Batting. Henry Chadwick. 1885.

9-4B   The Art of Pitching. Henry Chadwick. 1885.

9-4C   The Art of Baseball Fielding and Base Running. Henry Chadwick. 1885.

9-4D   .The Art of Batting and Base Running. Henry Chadwick. 1886, 1887.

9-4E   The Art of Pitching and Fielding. Henry Chadwick. 1886, 1887.

These were scientific, illustrated treatises. The 1886 and 1887 editions contain player records for the previous seasons.

9-4F   How to Play Baseball. Henry Chadwick. 1889.
        A summary of the 1885-88 editions.

9-4G   Practical Ball Playing. Arthur Irwin. 1895.

9-4H   How to Play Baseball. Walter Camp. 1896.
        Instructions for boys.

9-4I   How to Play Baseball. 1903-35. Timothy H. Murnane. 1903-14. John B. Foster. 1919-35. French edition published in 1919.
        The play of each position by various stars.

9-4J   How to Play First Base. 1905-20. J. Edward Wray. 1905-16. Hal Chase. 1917-20.
        Instructions by various stars. Player records.

9-4K   How to Play Second Base. 1905-20. J. Edward Wray. 1905-16. John Evers. 1917-20.
        Instructions by various stars. Player records.

9-4L   How to Play Third Base. J. Edward Wray. 1905-20.
        Instructions by various stars. Player records.

9-4M   How to Play Short Stop. 1905-20. J. Edward Wray. 1905-19. Art Fletcher. 1920.
        Instructions by various stars. Player records.

9-4N   How to Play the Outfield. J. Edward Wray and Jesse F. Matteson. 1905-20.
        Instructions by various stars. Player records.

9-4P   How to Pitch. 1905-33. John B. Foster. 1905-25. J. Edward Wray. 1926-33.

9-4Q   How to Catch. J. Edward Wray. 1905-20.
        Instructions by various stars. Account of the Washington monument feat by Gabby Street and Billy Sullivan.

9-4R   How to Catch; How to Run Bases. John B. Foster. 1921-35.

9-4S   How to Run Bases. J. Edward Wray. 1905-20.

9-4T   How to Bat. 1905-40. Jesse F. Matteson. 1905-09, 1919.

John B. Foster. 1910-18, 1920-40.

9-4U How to Play the Infield; How to Play the Outfield. John B. Foster. 1921-40.

9-4V How to Umpire; How to Coach; How to Captain; How to Manage; How to Organize a League. Timothy Murnane. 1905-06.

>   Instructions by various officials, managers, umpires.

9-4W How to Umpire; How to Coach; How to Captain; How to Manage; How to Organize a League; Technical Terms of Baseball. 1907-18. Timothy H. Murnane. 1907-15. J. Edward Wray. 1916-18.

9-4X How to Umpire. W.G. (Billy) Evans. 1917-40.

>   The 1917 edition included knotty problems.

9-4Y How to Organize a League, Manage a Team, Captain a Team, Coach a Team, Score a Game, Arrange Signals; Technical Terms of Baseball. J. Edward Wray. 1919, 1920.

9-4Z How to Organize a League, Manage a Team, Captain a Team, Coach a Team, Score a Game, Arrange Signals; How to Lay Out a League Diamond; Technical Terms of Baseball. J. Edward Wray. 1921-36. "How A Big League Keeps Its Records," by Ernest Lanigan.

9-4AA How to Organize a League, Manage a Team, Captain a Team, Coach a Team, Score a Game, Arrange Signals; How to Lay Out a League Diamond. 1937.

9-4BB How to Score a Baseball Game. Joseph M. Cummings. 1911-20.

9-4CC Baseball for Beginners. 1920-27, 1930, 1935. John Sheridan. 1920-27. John B. Foster. 1930, 1935.

9-5 Baseball, How to Become a Player. John Montgomery Ward. Athletic Publishing Co. 1888, 1889. Clothbound. Penn Publishing Co. 1889, reissue. Paperbound.

>   Origin, history, and explanation of the game by a star player. Playing instructions. Cover titles vary.

9-6 Scientific Ball. N. Fred Pfeffer. 1889. Clothbound.

>   General advice and instructions on the play of each position by a star player. Chapter on pitching by Tim Keefe. Biographical sketch of Pfeffer, anecdotes.

9-7 Baseball and How to Play It. Edward J. Prindle. 1896, 1902, 1906, reissue. Booklet.

A general handbook of instructions covering every
department of the game. Remedies for headache and
rheumatism.

9-8   How to Play Baseball. Connie Mack. Drexel Biddle. 1903,
1908. Paperbound.

Pitching, batting, catching, running, fielding, bunting.
Coaching, teamwork strategy. History of baseball. By
a future Hall of Fame manager.

9-9   Connie Mack's Baseball Book. Connie Mack. Alfred A. Knopf,
Inc. 1950. Clothbound.

General instructions, the play of each position by an
all-time great manager. Records, terminology, general discussion of the game.

9-9A   From Sandlot to Big League. Connie Mack. Alfred A. Knopf,
Inc. 1960. Clothbound.

Reissue of 9-9.

9-10   Practical Hints on Baseball Practice. Jay M. Fisher. Gazette
Publishing Co. 1905. Booklet.

The fine points of the game in systematic and progres-
sive order.

9-11   Baseball Instruction Book. Jay M. Fisher. Spirit Publishing Co.
1916. Paperbound.

Philosophy of the game, advice, photos.

9-12   Letters from a Baseball Fan to His Son. S. Dewitt Clough. Back-
bone Publishing Co. 1910. Paperbound.

General advice on training, playing, conduct.

9-13   Book on Baseball. Henry J. Wehman. 1910. Baseball.

Rules, player duties, playing advice.

9-14   The Baseball Coacher. Lee A. Seamster. Benton County Sun
Print. 1911. Booklet.

The play of each position.

9-15   The Battle of Baseball. C.H. Claudy. Century Co. 1911, 1912,
reissue. Clothbound.

General instructions on all phases of the game. A
chapter on "How I Became A Big-League Pitcher,"
by Christy Mathewson. Official rules.

9-16   How to Play Baseball. By the Greatest Baseball Players. Sprague

Publishing Co. 1912. Clothbound. Thomas Y. Crowell Co.
1913, reissue. Clothbound.

Instructions by Stanage, Coombs, Schulte, Chance,
Collins, Lord, Bush, Speaker, Cobb. Umpiring by
Evans. Full-page photos.

9-17   Learn Major League Baseball. John J. Troy. Troy & Engel.
1915. Baseball.

Advice from and reminiscences of an old-time player.

9-18   Modern Baseball Science. Edward B. Rankin. National Baseball
Registration Bureau. 1915. Paperbound.

Rules, instructions on batting, pitching, fielding,
running, and training. General information.

9-19   Baseball, Individual Play and Team Play in Detail. William J.
Clarke and Frederick T. Dawson. Charles Scribner's Sons. 1915,
1924. Paperbound. 1927. Clothbound.

Illustrations, photos, and diagrams.

9-20   Baseball Notes for Coaches and Players. Elmer Berry. American
Physical Education Association. 1916, 1922, 1924, 1927, 1930,
1931. Clothbound.

Batting, bunting, running and stealing, the play of
each position. Offense and defense, battery strategy,
training, the structure of organized baseball.

9-21   How to Play Baseball. Eagle Printing Co. 1921. Paperbound.

Reprints of newspaper articles appearing in the Brooklyn
Daily Eagle. Instructions by Cobb, Alexander, Sisler,
Speaker, Collins, Robinson, O'Neill. Records, statis-
tics, schedules, World Series.

9-22   Science of Baseball. Byrd Douglas. Thomas E. Wilson & Co.
1922. Clothbound.

Playing and coaching "inside" baseball.

9-23   Wilson Instructional Series. John Griffith and George (Potsy)
Clark. Thomas E. Wilson & Co. 1923. Booklet.

9-23A   Baseball Defense.

9-23B   Baseball Offense.

9-23C   How to Pitch, Catch and Play All Positions.

9-23D   Training of a Baseball Team.

9-24   Fundamentals of Baseball. Charles Wardlaw. Charles Scribner's
        Sons. 1924. Clothbound.

        Batting, pitching, catching, throwing, running,
        coaching. The mechanics of baseball. Full-page
        action photos.

9-25   Baseball, How to Play It. Stanley (Bucky) Harris. Frederick
        Stokes & Co. 1925. Clothbound.

        By a major league star player and manager. Practical
        instruction for each position. Strategy and tactics.

9-26   Reach Playing Pointers. A.J. Reach & Co., Wright & Ditson,
        Inc. 1925-32. Booklet.

        The play of each position, game situations, a discus-
        sion of the rules.

9-27   Secrets of Baseball. Mitchell Charnley, ed. D. Appleton & Co.
        1927. Clothbound.

        Instructions by Hornsby, Gehrig, Collins, Traynor,
        Speaker, Hartnett, Sisler, others.

9-28   Making the Big League. Rawlings Manufacturing Co. 1927. Book-
        let.

        Instructions by various players. Pitching, batting,
        fielding, running.

9-29   Baseball, How to Play It and How to Watch It. Alan Monk.
        Haldeman-Julius Publications. 1927. Little Blue Book Series.
        Booklet.

        Batting, running, fielding. Theory, terms.

9-30   How to Play Baseball. Babe Ruth. Cosmopolitan Book Corp.
        1930, 1931, reissue. Clothbound.

        Pitching, batting, running, defense. Catching strategy,
        coaching, signals, play of each position. Full-page
        action photos of Ruth.

9-31   Babe Ruth's Baseball Book for 1932. Christy Walsh, ed. Syndi-
        cate Publishing Co. 1932. Magazine.

        Playing instructions by Ruth and other major league
        players. Review of the 1931 World Series by John
        McGraw. Autobiographical sketch of Ruth.

9-32   Babe Ruth's Big Book of Baseball. Babe Ruth. Quaker Oats Co.
        1935. Paperbound.

        Tips on batting, fielding, pitching. Ruth's records.

9-33　　Babe Ruth's Baseball Advice. Babe Ruth. Rand, McNally. 1936.
　　　　Paperbound.

　　　　　　Full-page photos of Ruth demonstrating baseball tech-
　　　　　　niques.

9-34　　How to Play Baseball and Inside Baseball. Jess W. Orndorff.
　　　　National Baseball School. 1930, 1935. Booklet.

　　　　　　Baseball as played by the professionals.

9-35　　The Fundamentals of How to Play Baseball. Jesse Orndorff. Na-
　　　　tional Baseball School. 1936. Paperbound.

　　　　　　How to play in six lessons.

9-36　　Baseball. Kellogg Co. 1934. Booklet.

　　　　　　Pitching, fielding, batting, running, all-time records.

9-37　　What's What in Baseball. Lew Fonseca. Great Western Athletic
　　　　Goods Co. 1935. Booklet.

　　　　　　The play of each position by a former major league
　　　　　　player and manager.

9-38　　Play Ball. Lew Fonseca. Kellogg Co. 1938. Booklet.

　　　　　　How to play, facts for fans, rules.

9-39　　Baseball Coaching Aids. H.S. DeGroat. 1935. Booklet.

9-39A　Vol. 1. Battery Men.

9-39B　Vol. 2. First Basemen.

9-39C　Vol. 3. Second Basemen.

9-39D　Vol. 4. Third Basemen.

9-39E　Vol. 5. Shortstops.

9-39F　Vol. 6. Outfielders.

9-39G　Vol. 7. Signal System.

9-40　　Baseball! How to Play and Coach It. Charles G. Doak. Men-
　　　　denhall's Print Shop. 1936. Paperbound.

　　　　　　Historical background, defense, offense, training. By
　　　　　　a college coach.

9-41　　Baseball and How to Play It. Frank Shaughnessy. Canada Starch
　　　　Co. Ltd. 1936. Booklet.

Published in Canada. How to play each position.
Records and photos.

9-42   How to Play Better Baseball. Lloyd Percival. Sports College.
1948. Booklet.

Instructions for Canadian players.

9-43   Know Your Baseball. George (Specs) Toporcer. Hamco Coke.
1953. Booklet.

Instructions and explanations for Canadian players and
fans.

9-44   Tips from the Whips. Canada Safeway, Ltd. 1960. Booklet.

The play of each position as described by members of
the Winnipeg Whips.

9-45   Fundamentals, Techniques and Strategy of Baseball. Chicago Park
District. 1938. Paperbound.

Playing instructions illustrated with slow-motion pictures of Chicago Cub players in action.

9-46   Major League Baseball. Ethan Allen. Macmillan Co. 1938.
Clothbound.

Technique and tactics. General and individual instructions by a major leaguer.

9-47   Baseball, Major League Techniques and Tactics. Ethan Allen.
Macmillan Co. 1953. Clothbound.

Revised edition of 9-46.

9-48   Winning Baseball. Ethan Allen. McGraw-Hill. 1942. Paperbound. A.S. Barnes & Co. 1956. Clothbound.

Pictorial analysis of baseball fundamentals. Demon-
strations by leading players, action photos.

9-49   Baseball Techniques Illustrated. Ethan Allen and Tyler Michaleau.
A.S. Barnes & Co. 1951. Clothbound.

Diagrammed instructions.

9-50   Baseball Play and Strategy. Ethan Allen. Ronald Press. 1959,
1964, reissue, 1968. Clothbound.

Fundamentals, instructions on each position. Photos
of major leaguers in action.

9-51   Baseball, Individual Play and Team Strategy. John Coombs. Prentice-Hall. 1938, 1939, 1947, 1949, 1951. Clothbound.

By a former major league star, now a college coach.
A batter-by-batter instructional account of a nine-
inning game. Offense, defense, the play of each
position, coaching.

9-52   Jack Coombs' Baseball. Danny Litwhiler, ed. Prentice-Hall.
1966. Clothbound.

Revised edition of 9-51.

9-53   Baseball Notes. Bill Anderson. 1938. Paperbound.

Privately-printed playing instructions.

9-54   Rogers Hornsby Instructional Series. Rogers Hornsby. 1939. Booklet.

9-54A   How to Become a Batter.

9-54B   How to Become a Pitcher.

9-54C   How to Become a Catcher.

9-54D   How to Become an Outfielder.

9-54E   How to Play First Base.

9-54F   How to Play Second Base.

9-54G   How to Play Third Base.

9-54H   How to Play Shortstop.

9-55   How to Play Baseball. Rogers Hornsby. National Sports Almanac.
1956. Booklet.

The eight booklets of the 9-54 series in one volume.

9-56   Chicago Daily News Instructional Series. Rogers Hornsby. Chicago Daily News. 1945. Booklet.

9-56A   How to Hit and Play First.

9-56B   How to Hit and Play Second.

9-56C   How to Hit and Play Third.

9-56D   How to Hit and Play Short.

9-56E   How to Hit and Play the Outfield.

9-56F   How to Hit and Pitch.

9-57   Baseball. Dan Jessee. A.S. Barnes & Co. 1939. Clothbound.
        Diagrammed instructions by a long-time college coach,
        covering all aspects of play.

9-58   How to Play Baseball the Professional Way. Jimmy Reese and
        Bob Gibson. New York Yankees. 1939, 1940, reissue. Paper-
        bound.
        Instructions by New York Yankee scouts. Records,
        facts, photos.

9-59   Quaker Oats Instructional Series. Quaker Oats Co. Booklet.

9-59A   How to Knock Home Runs. Babe Ruth. 1939.

9-59B   How to Play the Outfield. Babe Ruth. 1939.

9-59C   How to Play the Infield. Babe Ruth. 1939.

9-59D   How to Throw Curves. Babe Ruth. 1939. Title page: Pitching.

9-59E   How to Play Baseball. Ethan Allen. 1954.

9-60   How to Play Baseball. J. Gordon Bennet, ed. International
        Baseball School. 1939. Eight volumes. Paperbound.
        Action photos of major league players.

9-60A   Catching.

9-60B   Pitching.

9-60C   First Base.

9-60D   Third Base.

9-60E   Second Base.

9-60F   Shortstop.

9-60G   Outfield.

9-60H   Batting and Baserunning.

9-61   All-Star Series. William J. Webb, ed. International Baseball
        School. 1941. Paperbound.
        Instructions by major league stars. Action photos.

9-61A   How to Catch. Mickey Cochrane and Gabby Hartnett.

9-61B   How to Pitch. Carl Hubbell and Gabby Hartnett.

9-61C   How to Play First Base. Hank Greenberg and Jimmy Foxx.

9-61D   How to Play Second Base. Charlie Gehringer and Billy Herman.

9-61E   How to Play Third Base. Red Rolfe and Maike Higgins.

9-61F   How to Play Shortstop. Luke Appling and Dick Bartell.

9-61G   How to Play the Outfield. Earl Averill and Paul Waner.

9-61H   How to Bat and Run Bases. Joe Medwick and Jimmy Dykes.

9-62   Ulrich's Baseball Manual. Walter Ulrich. William P. Ulrich.
         1941. Paperbound.

             The play of each position. Training, general obser-
             vations.

9-63   How to Play Baseball. The Sporting News. 1941, 1945, 1951,
         1953, 1955, 1968. Cover title: How to Play. 1941. Paper-
         bound. Don Weiskopf, ed. 1968.

             Each position covered by a different major league
             star. Player records.

9-64   How to Enjoy Baseball. Charles (Gabby) Street. Hyde Park Brew-
         eries. 1941. Booklet.

             Instructions and explanations by a former player and
             manager.

9-65   How to Play Baseball. Luke Sewell. Esquire Magazine. 1945.
         Booklet.

             Written by a major league player and manager for
             candidates for Esquire's annual All-America Boys
             Baseball Game. Batting, pitching and fielding in-
             structions.

9-66   Baseball. U.S. Rubber Co. 1945. Booklet.

             Instructions covering all phases and each position.

9-67   Play Ball. Frank Frisch. U.S. Rubber Co. 1945. Booklet.

             Batting, pitching, catching, fielding. Action photos.
             By a Hall of Fame player.

9-68   How to Play Baseball Like a Big Leaguer. Gary Schumacher.
         New York Giants. 1945. Paperbound.

             Instructions by Hubbell, Mort Cooper, Walters, Lopez,
             McQuinn, Gutteridge, Marion, Hack, Ott, Dixie
             Walker.

9-69 Ziff-Davis Instructional Series. 1948. Clothbound. 1949, reissue. Paperbound.

9-69A Covering the Outfield. Terry Moore.

9-69B Good Infield Play. Lou Boudreau.

9-69C Pitching to Win. Hal Newhouser.

9-69D Secrets of Pitching. Ewell Blackwell.

     Action photos of each author.

9-70 Baseball for Everyone. Joe DiMaggio. Whittlesey House. 1948.
Clothbound. Signet. 1949, reissue. Paperbound. Grosset &
Dunlap. 1952, reissue. Clothbound.

     Instructions for general play and individual positions
     by a future Hall of Fame player. Baseball from sand-
     lot to big leagues. Pitching and running, coaching
     and signs, slumps. "How to Score" by Red Barber.
     Tips for fans.

9-71 Beginning Baseball. Dick Siebert and Otto Vogel. Athletic Institute. 1948. Seven volumes. Booklet.

9-71A The Game.

9-71B Throwing.

9-71C Fielding.

9-71D Hitting.

9-71E Baserunning.

9-71F Pitching.

9-71G Catching.

9-72 How to Improve Your Baseball. Otto Vogel and Dick Siebert.
Athletic Institute. 1952. Paperbound.

     Sequence photos. By two college coaches.

9-73 Learning How......Baseball. Dick Siebert. Athletic Institute.
1961. Paperbound. Creative Educational Society. 1968. Clothbound.

     Fundamentals, strategy, game situations, drills. Pho-
     tos, diagrams. By a former major league star.

9-74 Baseball. Dick Siebert and Otto Vogel. Athletic Institute. Sterling Publishing Co. 1965, 1968. Clothbound.

Revised editions of the 1961 edition of 9-73.

9-75   Playing the Giants Game. Leo Durocher. New York Giants. 1949. Paperbound.

Instructions by the manager of the New York Giants.

9-76   Facts on American Sports and Health. Health Publications Institute. 1950. Baseball edition. Booklet.

Baseball facts interspersed with health information.

9-77   How to Play Big League Baseball. Malcolm Child. Harcourt, Brace. 1951. Clothbound.

The play of each position by Brecheen, Campanella, Kell, Gordon, Rizzuto, others.

9-78   American Baseball Academy Library. Malcolm Child. A.S. Barnes & Co. 1953. Clothbound.

9-78A   Vol. 1. Pitching.

9-78B   Vol. 2. Catching.

9-78C   Vol. 3. Batting.

9-78D   Vol. 4. Fielding.

9-79   How the Majors Play Baseball. Stan Musial and Bob Broeg. Rawlings Manufacturing Co. 1952, 1955, 1962. Booklet.

With Musial's playing records.

9-80   How to Play Winning Baseball. Arthur Mann. Grosset & Dunlap. 1953. Clothbound.

Pitching, catching, infield and outfield play, batting, running. Coaching, umpiring, scouting, training, building a team. Major league anecdotes.

9-81   Baseball, from Back Yard to Big League. George (Specs) Toporcer. Sterling Publishing Co. 1954. Clothbound. 1961, reissue. Paperbound.

The play of each position by a former major leaguer. Defensive tactics, qualifications of a good hitter, running. Signals, coaching, training. Glossary.

9-82   Sisler on Baseball. George Sisler. David McKay Co. 1954. Clothbound.

A manual for players and coaches. Personal recollections of the major leagues by a Hall of Fame player.

9-83   How to Play Championship Baseball. Oscar Fraley. A.A. Wynn, Inc. 1954. Paperbound.

A pictorial instructional with sequence action photos of Reynolds, Breecheen, Maglie, Musial, Kiner, Mantle, others.

9-84   Pictorial Baseball Instructor. Lamont Buchanan. E.P. Dutton & Co. 1954. Clothbound.

The play of each position as demonstrated by action photos. Sections on major league, college and Little League play.

9-85   The Dodgers' Way to Play Baseball. Al Campanis. E.P. Dutton & Co. 1954. Clothbound.

Instructions by the field supervisor and assistant field director of the Brooklyn Dodgers.

9-86   Boston Red Sox Manual for Baseball Coaches. John Murphy and Neil Mahoney. Boston Red Sox. 1955. Paperbound.

The play of each position, batting, baserunning.

9-87   Baseball Fundamentals. G.E. Bolin. Ozark Baseball Camp. 1955. Paperbound.

Comparisons of the greatest all-time players at each position.

9-88   Instructors' Baseball Guide. 1955. Paperbound.

9-89   Modern Baseball Strategy. Paul Richards. Prentice-Hall. 1955. Clothbound.

By a successful manager, developer of young players and accomplished strategist. Handling pitchers, pitching, catching, running. Signs, bunts, squeeze plays, defense.

9-90   The Game Plays of Baseball. Al Niemiec. Al Niemiec and Ned Stickle. 1956. Paperbound.

Techniques and strategy.

9-91   Grandstand Rookie. Interstate Bakeries. 1956. Booklet.

Playing instructions, explanations of the game.

9-92   You Can Play Better Baseball. Lew Watts. 1956. Booklet.

Strategy, game situations, playing tips from Musial, Hubbell, Campanella, Jackie Robinson, Dressen.

9-93   The Fine Art of Baseball. Lew Watts. Prentice-Hall. 1964. Clothbound.

A complete guide to strategy, skills and system.

9-94   Playing Major League Baseball. Mickey Mantle. Karo Syrup. 1957. Booklet.

Playing instructions by various major league stars.

9-95   Coaching Baseball. New York Yankees. 1958, 1963. Paperbound.

A general guide for amateur, high school and college coaches.

9-96   Union Oil Instructional Series. Union Oil Co. Booklet.

9-96A   Fine Points of Batting. Duke Snider. 1958.

9-96B   Fine Points of Baseball Pitching. Bob Lemon. 1958.

9-96C   Fine Points of Infield Play. Red Schoendienst. 1958.

9-96D   Fine Points of Baseball Strategy. Bill Rigney. 1958.

9-96E   Fine Points of Hitting. Ernie Banks. 1959.

Instructions by major league stars.

9-97   How to Play and Enjoy Baseball. Lou Chapman and Chuck Capaldo. Kalmbach Publishing Co. 1958. Magazine.

Instructions by stars of the Milwaukee Braves.

9-98   Milwaukee Braves Instruction Book. Ford Motor Co. 1963. Booklet.

Playing tips by Milwaukee players.

9-99   Handbook of Baseball Drills. Archie Allen. Prentice-Hall. 1959. Clothbound.

Offense, defense, conditioning, indoor drills. By a college coach.

9-100   Big League Secrets. Phillies Cigars. 1959. Reprinted from a series in Sports Illustrated. Booklet.

Playing instructions by Maglie, Sievers, Ashburn, McDougald, Crandall.

9-101   Sports Illustrated Book of Baseball. Sports Illustrated. J.B. Lippincott Co. 1960, 1966. Clothbound.

Pictorial instructions by major league stars.

9-101A   Sports Illustrated Baseball.   Sports Illustrated.   J.P. Lippincott Co.   1972.   Paperbound.

               Continuation of 9-101.

9-102   Baseball.   Frank F. DiClemente.   Creative Educational Society. 1960, 1962.   Clothbound.

               Instructions, playing techniques, play situations, coaching, and strategy.   Full-page color photos of major league action.   Origin and early history of baseball.

9-103   Baseball the Major League Way.   Don Weiskopf.   Ronald Press. 1962.   Clothbound.

               Hitting, fielding, and pitching instructions by Mantle, Koufax, Frank Robinson, others.   Action photos.

9-104   Baseball.   Robert R. Spackman, Jr.   U.S. Naval Institute.   1963. Clothbound.

               Playing instructions, conditioning.

9-105   Baseball Coach's Guide to Drills and Skills.   Danny Litwhiler. Prentice-Hall.   1963, 1964, 1965, 1966, 1967.   Clothbound.

               By a former major leaguer, now a college coach. Training, conditioning, drills, practice, organization.

9-106   Coaching Baseball.   Virgil Ledbetter.   William C. Brown.   1964. Clothbound.

               Defense, offense, team and field management.

9-107   Baseball: How to Play It and Understand It.   Don Schiffer.   Cornerstone Library.   1964.   Paperbound.

               Step-by-step illustrated instructions.

9-108   Grand Slam.   Jim Bunning, Whitey Ford, Mickey Mantle, Willie Mays.   Viking Press.   1965.   Clothbound.

               Secrets of power baseball by major league stars.   Pitching techniques, power hitting, base running, throwing. Physical conditioning, "baseball brains."   Anecdotes, photos.

9-109   Personality Scores!   Roy B. Deal.   Naylor Co.   1966.   Clothbound.

               The philosophy of coaching and managing a winner.

9-110   Baseball Coach's Complete Handbook.   Donald Edwards.   Parker Publishing Co.   1966.   Clothbound.

               Psychology, the play of each position, pitching.   Offense, defense, signals. Coaching, practice, conditioning.

9-111   Baseball Secrets Revealed. Max Carey. B.B. Associates. 1966. Paperbound.

Fundamentals of batting, baserunning, and fielding. Fifty "musts." By a former major league star.

9-112   Comparative Baseball Strategy. S. Charles Irace. Burgess Publishing Co. 1967. Paperbound.

Skills, strategy, and tactics from Little League to major league.

9-113   Concentrated Baseball. Ray Merkle and Bobby Shantz. Whitmore Publishing Co. 1967. Clothbound and Paperbound.

The official training manual for Baseball Clinic, U.S.A. Fundamentals for players and coaches.

9-114   My Secrets of Playing Baseball. Willie Mays and Howard Liss. Viking Press. 1967. Clothbound. Barnes & Noble. 1970, reissue. Paperbound.

Offensive and defensive techniques by a major league star. An analysis of percentage baseball. Sequence photos.

9-115   The Name of the Game Is Baseball. Prudential Insurance Co. 1968. Booklet.

Conditioning and playing pointers by major leaguers. Photos.

9-116   Championship Baseball. Hank Bauer. Doubleday & Co. 1968. Clothbound.

Hitting, fielding, running, and pitching instructions by a former manager and player.

9-117   Practice Sessions, Scouting and Game Strategy for Baseball. Hugh Bateman. Davis Brothers Publishing Co. 1969. Paperbound. Marty Karo National Baseball Improvement Service. 1970. Paperbound.

Baseball Improvement Series. Fundamentals, drills.

9-118   Teaching and Performing Individual Skills in Baseball. Hugh Bateman. Davis Brothers Publishing Co. 1969. Paperbound. Marty Karow. National Baseball Improvement Service. 1970. Paperbound. Marty Karow and Loyal Park. McClure Enterprises. 1972. Paperbound.

Baseball Improvement Series. Fundamentals, drills.

9-119   Baseball Improvement Series. Marty Karow and Loyd Park. Mc-Clure Enterprises. 1972. Paperbound.

9-119A   How to Pitch.

9-119B   How to Catch.

9-119C   How to Play First Base.

9-119D   How to Play Second Base.

9-119E   How to Play Third Base.

9-119F   How to Play Shortstop.

9-119G   How to Play the Outfield.

9-119H   How to Hit, Run Bases and Slide.

9-120   Tips from the Champs. Stroh Brewing Co. 1969. Booklet.

         Instructions by the 1968 champion Detroit Tigers.

9-121   Detroit Tigers Baseball Instruction Handbook. Detroit Tigers. No date. Booklet.

         Fundamentals of pitching, catching, fielding, and hitting.

9-122   Inside Baseball. Dell Bethel. Reilly & Lee. 1969. Clothbound and Paperbound.

         How to play and coach baseball. By a high school and college coach. Hitting, bunting, running, pitching, fielding.

9-123   The Game of Baseball. Gil Hodges and Frank Slocum. Crown Publishers, Inc. 1969. Clothbound. 1970. Paperbound.

         Recollections and playing advice by a former star player and present manager. The 1970 edition includes the 1969 championship season.

9-124   Baseball As We Played It. Boys Life. G.P. Putnam's Sons. 1969. Clothbound.

         Players of the past tell how they played the game. Playing instructions, advice.

9-125   Winning Baseball, Science and Strategies. Jim Kaat and Daryl Siedentop. Scott, Foresman. 1971. Clothbound.

         Playing, coaching, strategy, practice. By a major league pitcher.

9-126   Mickey Mantle, Bobby Bragan Big League Baseball Book. Sports Program of America, Inc. 1971. Booklet.

Playing instructions by various major league players.

9-127   How to Organize and Coach Winning Baseball. Ken Dugan. Parker Publishing Co. 1971. Clothbound.

Management, offense, defense.

9-128   What Research Tells the Coach about Baseball. Guy G. Reiff. American Association for Health, Physical Education, and Recreation. 1971. Paperbound.

Scientific research literature applied to principles of batting, pitching, and strategy.

9-129   Baseball Coaching Techniques. Walter J. Nitardy. A.S. Barnes & Co. 1972. Clothbound.

Philosophy, techniques, batting, pitching, fielding, running, building a team, preparation, strategy. By a college coach.

9-130   The Complete Baseball Handbook. Walter Alston and Donald Weiskopf. Allyn & Bacon. 1972. Clothbound.

Strategies and techniques by a successful major league manager.

9-131   Complete Baseball Play Book. Jim Trainor. Doubleday & Co. 1972. Paperbound.

Techniques, strategy, position play, offense, defense. Photos.

9-132   How to Play Better Baseball. Bud Harrelson and Joel H. Cohen. Atheneum. 1972. Clothbound and Paperbound.

Fielding, batting, and running instructions by a major league shortstop.

9-133   Power Baseball: Dynamic Techniques of Winning. Mel Didier and Gerry Arbic. Prentice-Hall. 1972. Paperbound.

Conditioning, defense, offense by a former player and coach. English and French editions.

9-134   Baseball. Joe Archibald. Follett Publishing Co. 1972. Clothbound.

Batting, pitching, position play.

9-135   A Guide to Better Baseball. George H. McQuinn. 1972. Paperbound.

Diagrammatic instructions for players and coaches by a former major league star.

9-136   Fundamentals of Baseball. Leslie Mann. Feltus Printing Co. No date. Booklet.

An explanatory text accompanying a stereoptican picture instructional series.

9-137   How to Play Better Baseball. J.C. Higgins Co. No date. Booklet.

Instructions by major league stars.

Pitching

9-138   Hecker's Guide to the Art of Pitching. Guy Hecker. Hecker Baseball Supply Co. 1885. Paperbound.

Instructions by a major league pitching star of the 1880's. Illustrations.

9-139   The Art of Curved Pitching. Edward J. Prindle. A.J. Reach & Co. 1886, 1888. Booklet.

Theory, practice, hints for beginners. Illustrations.

9-139A   The Art of Curve Pitching. Edward J. Prindle. A.J. Reach & Co. 1890, 1894, 1909, 1911. Cover title: Reach Art of Curve Pitching. Booklet.

Continuation of 9-139.

9-140   The Art of Zig-Zag Curve Pitching. Edward J. Prindle. A.J. Reach & Co. 1890, 1895, 1910. Booklet.

Theory and practice for amateur and professional players. Illustrations.

9-141   Scientific Baseball Pitching. James W. Smith. American Authors' Publishing Co. 1894. Booklet.

9-142   How to Pitch Curves. Mordecai Brown. W.D. Boyce. 1913. Paperbound.

By an all-time pitching great.

9-143   Pitching. Baseball Correspondence League of America. 1913. Paperbound.

Instructions by major league stars.

9-144   Pitching Course. Irwin Howe, ed. Baseball Correspondence

League of America. Max Stearns Sons. 1914. Booklet.

Instructions by Mathewson, Johnson, Rucker, Walsh, White, and Wood.

9-145   Secrets of Pitching. Burt L. Standish. Street & Smith. 1914. Paperbound.

A practical treatise on the science of curve pitching.

9-146   How to Pitch Real Curves. Henry Buser. B & N Publishing Co. 1924. Paperbound.

9-147   How to Pitch. Grover C. Alexander. Stall & Dean. 1927. Booklet.

Illustrated instructions on throwing various pitches, by an all-time great pitcher.

9-148   How to Pitch. Rube Marquard. 1932. Paperbound.

Ten lessons by a future Hall of Fame pitcher.

9-149   How I Pitch. Lefty Grove. Cunningham Sports Series. 1933. Booklet.

Instructions, anecdotes, photos.

9-150   How to Throw Curves. Charles Paulsen. Warp Publishing Co. 1934, 1936. Booklet.

How to throw various types of breaking pitches. Discussion of principles of physics involved in pitching curves.

9-150A   Baseball Curves. Charles Paulsen. 1957, 1959. Booklet.

Continuation of 9-150.

9-151   The Craft of Pitching. John F. Fraser. 1940. Paperbound.

Instructions on how to throw various pitches.

9-152   How to Pitch Baseball. Lew Fonseca. Little Technical Library. 1942. Clothbound.

The play of the other eight positions in relation to the pitcher. Sequence photos. By a former major leaguer.

9-153   A Cinematographic and Mechanical Analysis of Major League Baseball Pitchers. James L. Breen. University of Illinois. 1948. Paperbound.

A Master of Science thesis.

9-154   How to Pitch. Bob Feller. A.S. Barnes & Co. 1948. Clothbound.

Full-page action photos of Feller and various batters.

9-155 Pitching to Win. Bob Feller. Grosset & Dunlap. 1952. Cloth-bound.

Enlarged edition of 9-151.

9-156 The Art of Baseball Pitching. W.E. Swanson, Jr. Wesmore Book Co. 1954. Paperbound.

A detailed manual for high school players.

9-157 The Road to Successful Pitching. Bert Thiel. Washington Senators. 1960. Booklet.

Instructions by a minor league pitching coach.

9-158 How to Pitch. Warren Spahn and Neal Russo. Rawlings Manufacturing Co. 1962, 1964, reissue. Paperbound.

How to throw different pitches, fielding, batting.

9-159 The Making of a Big League Pitcher. Ed Richter. Chilton Co. 1963. Clothbound.

The fine points of pitching.

9-160 The Art of Pitching. Lloyd Davids. Pageant Press. 1964. Paperbound.

For amateur players.

9-161 Bob Turley's Pitching Secrets. Bob Turley. G.P. Putnam's Sons. 1965. Clothbound.

General advice, solving problems, things to remember.

9-162 Insight Pitching. Frederick Fober. Fober Films. 1965, 1968. Paperbound.

Detailed mechanics of pitching for right and left-handers. Designed for coaches, fathers, and high school players.

9-163 How to Develop the Successful Pitcher. Ron Squire. Prentice-Hall. 1965. Clothbound.

Scouting, environment, instructional techniques, motivation.

9-164 How to Pitch. Major League Baseball Players Association. Grosset & Dunlap. 1971. Major League Baseball Player Guide Series. Clothbound.

Instructions by 13 major league pitchers.

9-165 Pitching to Win. Tom Seaver. Lion Press. 1971. Clothbound.

Instructions by a major league star.

9-166   Pitching. Bob Shaw. Viking Press. 1972. Clothbound.

Basic fundamentals and mechanics. By a former major
league pitcher.

9-167   Inside Pitching. Ferguson Jenkins and Dave Fisher. Henry Regnery Co. 1972. Clothbound and Paperbound.

Fundamentals and techniques by a star pitcher. Photos.

Catching

9-168   Catching. Elston Howard. Viking Press. 1966. Clothbound.

Secrets of catching by a major league star. Studying
hitters, handling pitchers. Action photos.

9-169   Jim Hegan's Secrets of Catching. Jim Hegan. G.P. Putnam's
Sons. 1968. Clothbound.

Advice for young players by a former major league
catcher.

Defense

9-170   Want to Be a Baseball Champion? Lew Fonseca. General Mills.
1945. Booklet.

The defensive game. By a former major leaguer.

9-171   On Your Toes in Baseball. F.C. (Babe) Herman. 1954. Paperbound.

How to execute the various defensive plays, by a
former major leaguer. Illustrations.

9-172   Coach's Guide to Defensive Baseball. Archie Allen. Prentice-
Hall. 1960. Clothbound.

Individual and team defense, strategy, and fundamentals.
Pitching techniques. Diagrams. By a college coach.

9-173   The Chicago Cubs System of Defensive Plays. Robert Whitlow.
Chicago Cubs. 1963. Paperbound.

For players in the Cubs organization, by the general
manager.

9-174   Defensive Baseball. Michael J. Frederick. 1963. Booklet.

9-175   <u>Defensive Baseball</u>. MacGregor Sporting Goods Co. 1964, 1971. Booklet.

         Playing tips by various players.

9-176   <u>Defensive Positioning and Actions in Every Batted Ball Situation</u>. Hugh Bateman. Davis Brothers Publishing Co. 1969. Paperbound. Marty Karow. National Baseball Improvement Service. 1970. Paperbound.

         Baseball Improvement Series. The placement of fielders to cover different game situations.

9-177   <u>How to Play the Infield</u>. Major League Baseball Players Association. Grosset & Dunlap. 1972. Major League Baseball Player Guide Series. Clothbound.

         Instructions by 17 stars.

9-178   <u>How to Play the Outfield</u>. Major League Baseball Players Association. Grosset & Dunlap. 1972. Major League Baseball Players Guide Series. Clothbound.

         Instructions by 17 stars.

Batting

9-179   <u>How Not to Strike Out</u>. Jay M. Fisher. Gazette Publishing Co. c1890. Paperbound.

         "By one who has not struck out."

9-180   <u>Art of Batting</u>. Edward J. Prindle. A.J. Reach & Co. 1890, 1904, reissue, 1909, reissue. Booklet.

         Theory, practice, hints for beginners. Illustrations.

9-181   <u>The Winning Punch</u>. John Sheridan. Hillerich & Bradsby. 1923. Booklet.

         Batting instructions by major leaguers. Care of the bat, records, photos.

9-181A   <u>The Knack of Batting</u>. Hillerich & Bradsby. 1924-34. Booklet.

         Continuation of 9-181.

9-182   <u>How to Select and Care for Your Bat</u>. Hillerich & Bradsby. 1934. Booklet.

         Descriptions of various types of bats, instructions on hitting.

9-183   <u>Batting</u>. Frank C. Lane. Baseball Magazine. 1925. Paperbound.

         One thousand expert opinions. Descriptions of great hitters.

9-184   How I Bat. Jimmy Foxx. Cunningham Sports Series. 1933.
         Booklet.

         Instructions, anecdotes, photos.

9-185   The "Ins and Outs" of Inside Baseball. W.W. Mouch. American
         National Game. 1934, 1945, 1946. Paperbound.

         Offensive plays, the science of batting. Anecdotes,
         records, photos.

9-186   Want to Be a Baseball Champion? Ethan Allen. General Mills.
         1946. Booklet.

         The offensive game. By a former major leaguer.

9-187   Batting and Bunting. Ethan Allen. Coca Cola Co. Prentice-
         Hall. 1961. Booklet. Scholastic Book Services. 1968. Paper-
         bound.

         Illustrated instructions.

9-188   Batting As Major Leaguers Do It. Clifford W. and Ralston B.
         Brown. Vantage Press. 1953. Clothbound.

         Form, stride, exercise. Wrist action, timing, place
         hitting.

9-189   How to Hit. Johnny Mize and Murray Kaufman. Holt, Rinehart
         & Winston. 1953. Clothbound.

         How to become a player, selecting a bat, the grip,
         place-hitting, bunting, hitting curves, slumps. Mize's
         records, photos.

9-190   How I Hit. Mickey Mantle. Mickey Mantle Enterprises. 1956.
         Booklet.

         Various aspects of batting by a major league star.
         Baserunning, stealing, fielding.

9-191   How to Be a Better Hitter. Ted Williams. Hillerich & Bradsby.
         1957. Booklet.

         Instructions by an all-time great.

9-192   Batting Tips From Ted. Sears, Roebuck. 1967. Booklet.

         How to become a better hitter, by Ted Williams.

9-193   The Science of Hitting. Ted Williams and John Underwood.
         Simon & Schuster. 1971. Clothbound. Pocket Books. 1972,
         reissue. Paperbound.

         A guide to batting by a Hall of Fame outfielder.
         Photos of great hitters.

9-194   Big League Batting Secrets. Harvey Kuenn and Jack Smilgoff.

Prentice-Hall. 1958. Clothbound.

Action photos of Kuenn and other major leaguers.

9-195 The Secret of Power Hitting. B. Barrett. 1961. Paperbound.
Illustrated.

9-196 Hitters' Handbook. 1962. Paperbound.

Wrist action, bunting, hit and run place-hitting,
breaking a slump. Photos.

9-197 Paul Waner's Batting Secrets. Paul Waner. B.B. Associates.
1962. Booklet.

With tips to Little Leaguers. By a Hall of Fame star.

9-198 How to Bat. Harry Walker and Tom Meany. McGraw-Hill.
1963. Clothbound.

Instructions by Walker and other major league stars.

9-199 Offensive Baseball. MacGregor Sporting Goods Co. 1964. Booklet.

Playing tips by various players.

9-200 Baseball Coach's Handbook of Offensive Strategy and Techniques.
Archie Allen. Prentice-Hall. 1964. Clothbound.

Batting fundamentals, bunting, baserunning, and sliding.
Strategy, batting order, signals, baseline coaching,
drills. Recognizing faults, keeping records. By a
college coach.

9-201 Gene Woodling's Secrets of Batting. Gene Woodling. G.P. Putnam's Sons. 1967. Clothbound.

Fundamentals, bunting, conditioning. How to use the
bat, outwitting the catcher.

9-202 Where Are Baseball's 400 Hitters of the Dead Ball Era? Archer
W. Zamloch, Sr. and Frank (Lefty) O'Doul. 1967. Paperbound.

Comments and opinions on batting.

9-203 Secrets of Power Hitting. Reggie Jackson. Lion Press. 1970.
Clothbound.

Instructions by an outstanding slugger.

9-204 How to Hit and Run the Bases. Major League Baseball Players
Association. Grosset & Dunlap. 1971. Major League Baseball
Player Guide Series. Clothbound.

Tips on hitting and running by 15 players.

9-205 <u>Batting.</u> Carl Yastrzemski and Al Hirshberg. Viking Press. 1972. Clothbound.

   Basics and fine points by a three-time American League batting champion.

9-206 <u>Correct Offensive Plays for Every Situation in Baseball.</u> Marty Karow and Loyal Park. McClure Enterprises. 1972. Baseball Improvement Series. Paperbound.

   Fundamentals, drills.

Baserunning

9-207 <u>The Art of Base Running.</u> Edward J. Prindle. A.J. Reach & Co. 1890. Booklet.

   Theory, practice, hints for beginners. Illustrations.

9-208 <u>Frank Crosetti's Secrets of Base Running and Infield Play.</u> Frank Crosetti. G.P. Putnam's Sons. 1966. Clothbound.

   By a long-time New York Yankee player and coach. Cartoon illustrations.

For Young Players

9-209 <u>How to Play Baseball.</u> John McGraw. Harper & Brothers. 1913, 1914, reissue. Clothbound. Finch Press. 1972, reissue. Clothbound.

   A manual for boys by an all-time great player and manager. Illustrations of major league stars. The play of each position, batting, running, teamwork, how to control various pitches.

9-210 <u>The Baseball Coacher for the Young Player.</u> Reed Publishing Co. 1921. Booklet.

   Batting, pitching, fielding.

9-211 <u>Baseball.</u> Carl Lundgren. 1928. Paperbound.

   Instructions for high school and college coaches.

9-212 <u>How to Play Baseball.</u> Martin J. McManus. 1935. Paperbound.

   Instructions for young boys on all phases of the game by a former major leaguer. Records of star players.

9-213 <u>How to Play Better Baseball.</u> Ralph Henry Barbour and LaMarr Sarra. Appleton-Century. 1935, 1936, reissue, 1942, reissue,

1946, reissue. Clothbound.

For junior players and their coaches.

9-214   Baseball for British Youth. Eric Whitehead. Link House. 1939.
Paperbound.

Explanations and playing instructions.

9-215   Play Ball! Charles Chapman and Henry Severeid. Harper &
Brothers. 1941. Clothbound.

Advice for young players. Fundamentals, offense,
and defense. Major league recollections.

9-216   Play Ball, Son! Bert Dunne. Serra Publishing Co. 1945. Clothbound. Ford Motor Co. 1947, reissue. Booklet.

Instructions for boys. Photos. The 1947 edition contains excerpts from the 1945 edition.

9-216A   Play Ball! Bert Dunne. Doubleday & Co. 1947. Clothbound.

Reissue of the 1945 edition of 9-216.

9-217   Batter Up. Bert Dunne. Standard Oil Co. of California. 1948.
Booklet.

General instructions for boys.

9-218   Terry and Bunky Play Baseball. Richard M. Fischel & Clair G.
Hare. G.P. Putnam's Sons. 1947. Clothbound.

An instructional in the form of a children's story.

9-219   Grantland Rice's Baseball Strategy. Jack Coombs. Wells Publishing Co. 1949. Booklet.

A manual for boys. Strategy, fundamentals, play
diagrams and text.

9-220   Hal Schumacher's Baseball Strategy. Hal Schumacher. Wells Publishing Co. 1949. Booklet.

Same as 9-219.

9-221   First Book of Baseball. Franklin Folsom, (pseudonym Benjamin
Brewster). Don Schiffer, ed. Franklin Watts. 1950, 1956, 1958,
1963. Clothbound.

Terms, equipment, position. Instructions, scoring.

9-222   Baseball. Franklin Folsom, (pseudonym Benjamin Brewster.) Franklin Watts. 1970. Clothbound.

Revised edition of 9-221.

9-223   The Real Book about Baseball. Franklin Folsom, (pseudonym
Lyman Hopkins). Garden City Books. 1951, 1958, 1962. Cloth-

bound.

Instructions for boys. Major league anecdotes.

9-224 The Way to Better Baseball. Tommy Heinrich and A.L. Plaut. Exposition Press. 1951. Clothbound.

A guide for young players and their coaches by a star player. How to coach high school baseball.

9-225 Skill on the Diamond. Carol R. Gast. Douglas Publishing Co. 1953. Paperbound.

Successful baseball for the young player and his coach.

9-226 Baseball. Loren E. Taylor. Children's Enterprises. 1953. Paperbound.

A handbook for teachers, recreation leaders, and beginning players. Baseball vocabulary, great stars.

9-227 Championship Baseball. William (Buck) Lai. Prentice-Hall. 1954. Clothbound.

From Little League to big league. Techniques for the player and coach.

9-228 How to Play Baseball. Mary G. Bonner. Alfred A. Knopf, Inc. 1955. Clothbound.

For boys.

9-229 Baseball for Boys. John McCallum, ed. Prudential Insurance Co. 1955. Booklet.

Instructions by major league stars: Batting - Eddie Mathews, Pitching - Robin Roberts, Infield - Harvey Kuenn, Outfield - Duke Snider.

9-230 Baseball for Boys. George Digby and John McCallum. Follet Publishing Co. 1960. Paperbound.

Enlarged edition of 9-229.

9-231 Winning High School Baseball. James Smilgoff. Prentice-Hall. 1956. Clothbound.

Batting, drills, offense, defense. Illustrations.

9-232 Baseball for Young Champions. Ralph Antonacci and Jene Barr. Whittlesey House. 1956. Clothbound.

Pitching, catching, hitting, infield, and outfield play. Equipment, game preparation.

9-233 Play Baseball, Boys. J. Carl Trimble. Comet Press. 1957. Paperbound.

Basic skills, catching, pitching, infield, and outfield play, running.

9-234   Better Baseball for Boys. David Cooke. Dodd, Mead & Co. 1959, 1965, reissue. Clothbound.

Illustrated by action photos of Little Leaguers.

9-235   Baseball for Boys. John Rosenburg. Oceana Publications, Inc. 1960. Clothbound. 1965, reissue. Paperbound.

Basic skills, offense, defense, organization, and development.

9-236   Make the Team in Baseball. Clary Anderson. Grosset & Dunlap. 1960, 1966, reissue. Clothbound.

For school players. Action photos of major leaguers.

9-237   How to Star in Baseball. Herman Masin. Scholastic Book Services. 1960. Paperbound. Four Winds Press. 1966, reissue, 1968, reissue. Clothbound.

A step-by-step guide for young players. Sequence photos.

9-238   I Want to Be a Baseball Player. Carla Greene. Children's Press. 1961. Clothbound.

An instructional in the form of a children's story.

9-239   Detroit Tigers Baseball Handbook. Detroit Tigers. Detroit Free Press. 1961. Booklet.

Advice to young ballplayers. Hitting, pitching, and fielding fundamentals.

9-240   Finer Points of Baseball for Everyone. Wm. C. Popper & Co. 1961. 12 volumes. Booklet.

Illustrated instructions for Little League, Junior League, Midget League, and Babe Ruth League players.

9-240A   Baseball, Finer Points for Everyone.

9-240B   How to Bat.

9-240C   How to Run Bases.

9-240D   How to Use Baseball Signals.

9-240E   How to Play First Base.

9-240F   How to Play Second Base.

9-240G   How to Play Third Base.

9-240H   How to Play Shortstop.

9-240I   <u>How to Catch.</u>

9-240J   <u>How to Play the Outfield.</u>

9-240K   <u>How to Pitch.</u>

9-240L   <u>Rules for Umpires.</u>

9-241   <u>Bernie McCay's Baseball Manual.</u> Bernie McCay. 1962. Paperbound.

         For boys.

9-242   <u>The Boy's Baseball Book.</u> Mickey Owen and Frank Farmer. Prentice-Hall. 1963. Clothbound.

         Playing tips, techniques, strategy by a former major leaguer.

9-243   <u>How to Play Better Baseball.</u> C. Paul Jackson. Thomas Y. Crowell Co. 1963. Clothbound. 1965, reissue. Paperbound. Scholastic Books. 1971. Paperbound.

         A basic primer for boys. Glossary, illustrations.

9-244   <u>How to Play Baseball.</u> Robert Fitzsimmons and Martin Iger. Doubleday & Co. 1963. Clothbound.

         For boys.

9-245   <u>The Young Sportsman's Guide to Baseball.</u> Clary Anderson. Thomas Nelson & Sons. 1963. Clothbound.

         General description, playing instructions.

9-246   <u>Secrets of Big League Play.</u> Robert Smith. Random House Little League Library. 1965. Clothbound. Reissued as Major League Library.

         Inside tips from major league stars.

9-247   <u>Basic Baseball Strategy.</u> Serge H. Freeman. Doubleday & Co. 1965. Clothbound.

         For boys, their coaches, and parents.

9-248   <u>To The Young Ballplayer.</u> Dee Phillips. Baltimore Baseball Club. 1965. Booklet.

         Advice on playing better baseball by a Baltimore Orioles scout.

9-249   <u>Yogi Berra's Baseball Guidebook.</u> Yogi Berra. McGraw-Hill. 1966. Paperbound.

         The ins and outs of baseball for boys 9-13. How to warm up, pitch, catch, bunt, throw, field.

9-250   Illustrated Guide to Championship Baseball. John Herbold. Parker Publishing Co. 1967. Clothbound.

For high school players. Hitting, fielding, running, bunting. The play of each position, coaching.

9-251   Baseball and Your Boy. Al Rosen. World Publishing Co. 1967. Clothbound. Funk & Wagnalls, 1968, reissue. Paperbound.

A parents' guide to boys' baseball by a former major league star.

9-252   Basic Baseball. Bragg Stockton. 1967. Paperbound.

Conditioning, pitching, position play, hitting, running, game situations.

9-253   Baseball Tips for Boys 19 and Under. Edsel B. Martz. 1969. Paperbound.

Batting, pitching, baserunning, fielding, coaching, strategy. By a scout for the Pittsburgh Pirates.

9-254   The Father and Son Baseball Book. Howard Liss. Harper & Row. 1969. Clothbound.

A description and analysis of the various aspects of the game. Designed to enable fathers to explain and teach the fundamentals of the game to their sons.

9-255   Strike Zone. Bob Gibson. Sport Specials. 1970. Paperbound.

Instructions for boys on how to pitch curves, sliders, and fastballs. Batting and fielding. By a star pitcher.

9-256   Winning Baseball. Carl Yastrzemski. Sport Specials. 1970. Paperbound.

Instructions for boys on batting, pitching, and fielding by a star outfielder.

9-257   Pitching, Hitting and Throwing Tips. Major League Baseball Promotions, Inc. Phillips Petroleum Co. 1970, 1971. Booklet.

Rules for the annual pitch, hit and throw competition. Playing instructions.

9-257A   Pitch, Hit and Throw Tips. Major League Baseball Promotion Corp. Phillips Petroleum Co. 1971-to date. Booklet.

Continuation of 9-257.

9-258   Baseball Bonanza. Baseball Associates. No date. Booklet.

Conditioning, illustrated playing tips.

9-259   Tips on Baseball. Ed Hamman. Baseball Associates. No date. Booklet.

Batting, pitching, fielding, running.

9-260   One Hundred Tips by 100 Big Leagurers. Baseball Associates.
         No date. Booklet.

         Miscellaneous advice.

9-261   Baseball Associates Instructional Series. Ed Hamman. Baseball
         Associates. No date. Booklet.

         Seven volumes.

9-261A   How to Play First Base.

9-261B   How to Play Second Base.

9-261C   How to Play Third Base.

9-261D   How to Play Shortstop.

9-261E   How to Play Outfield.

9-261F   How to Pitch.

9-261G   How to Catch.

10. Anthologies

10-1   My Greatest Day in Baseball. John Carmichael, ed. A.S. Barnes & Co. 1945, 1950, reissue. Clothbound. Bantam Books.
1948, reissue. Paperbound. Grosset & Dunlap. 1951, reissue,
1963. Clothbound. Tempo Books. 1968, reissue. Paperbound.

      Accounts of 47 stars as written by noted sportswriters.

10-2   My Greatest Baseball Game. Don Schiffer, ed. A.S. Barnes &
Co. 1950. Clothbound.

      Accounts of 34 present-day stars, written by leading
sportscasters. Lifetime records.

10-3   The Baseball Reader. Ralph Graber, ed. A.S. Barnes & Co.
1951. Clothbound.

      A collection of fiction and non-fiction by Lardner,
Runyon, Van Loan, Standish, Grey, others.

10-4   Crack of the Bat. Phyllis Fenner, ed. Alfred A. Knopf, Inc.
1952. Clothbound.

      Stories of baseball. Fact and fiction.

10-5   The Best of Baseball. Sidney Offit, ed. G.P. Putnam's Sons.
1956. Clothbound.

      Selections from Baseball Magazine. The game's im-
mortal men and moments.

10-6   The Fireside Book of Baseball. Charles Einstein, ed. Simon &
Schuster. 1956. Clothbound.

      A selection of essays, short-stories, poetry, and news-
paper articles by various authors. Index.

10-7   The Second Fireside Book of Baseball. Charles Einstein, ed.
Simon & Schuster. 1958. Clothbound.

      A selection of essays, short stories, poetry, and news-
paper articles by various authors. Index.

10-8   The Third Fireside Book of Baseball. Charles Einstein, ed. Simon & Schuster. 1968. Clothbound.

A selection of essays, short stories, poetry, and newspaper articles by various authors. Index.

10-9   Mostly Baseball. Tom Meany. A.S. Barnes & Co. 1958. Clothbound.

A collection of Meany's magazine articles from the past 20 years.

10-10   Baseball Stories. Parke Cummings, ed. Hill & Wang. 1959. Clothbound.

An anthology of stories by various authors.

10-11   Baseball Wit and Wisdom. Frank Graham and Dick Hyman, eds. David McKay Co. 1962. Clothbound. Scholastic Book Services. 1965, reissue. Paperbound.

An anthology of baseball folklore. The 1965 edition is abridged.

10-12   Baseball Research Journal. L. Robert Davids, ed. Society for American Baseball Research. 1972. Paperbound.

Statistical and historical research articles by various authors.

11. Periodicals

11-1   The New York Clipper. New York. 1853-1924. Newspaper.
        Weekly. Other sports covered.

11-2   Spirit of the Times. New York. 1856-92. Newspaper.
        Weekly. Scores, game resumes, articles. Other
        sports covered.

11-3   The Ball Players' Chronicle. Name changed during 1868 to
        American Chronicle of Sports and Pastimes. Henry Chadwick, ed.
        Thompson & Pearson. New York. June 6, 1867 - July 23,
        1868. Newspaper.
        A weekly journal devoted to the interests of the
        American game of baseball. The first periodical de-
        voted exclusively to baseball.

11-4   The Sporting Times. Boston. 1867-72. New York. 1884-92.
        Newspaper.
        Weekly. Other sports covered.

11-5   The New England Baseballist. Boston. August 6 - December 31,
        1868. Newspaper.
        Weekly.

11-6   The National Chronicle. Journal of American Sports and Pastimes.
        Boston. January 9, 1869 - June 18, 1870. Newspaper.
        Weekly. Other sports covered.

11-7   The New York Mercury. New York. 1875-80. Newspaper.
        Weekly. Other sports covered.

11-8   Our Boys. N.L. Munro. 1877, 1878. Newspaper.
        A weekly sporting paper for boys.

11-9   The Met. Henry Chadwick. Pinckney & Jackson. New York.
        1882-84. Newspaper.

Weekly. Other sports covered. A journal of the Polo Grounders for fans.

11-10   The Sporting Life. Francis Richter. Sporting Life Publishing Co. Philadelphia. 1883-1917. Newspaper.

The first long-run baseball weekly. Articles, box scores, averages, coverage of each team.

11-11   American Sports Weekly. Chicago. 1883. Newspaper.

Comprehensive baseball coverage.

11-12   Mirror of American Sports. Chicago. 1884-85. Newspaper.

Weekly. Other sports covered.

11-13   American Roller and Baseball Journal. F.W. Walsh. Boston. 1885. Newspaper.

Weekly.

11-14   Official Baseball Record. New York. July - October 1885; April - October 1886. Newspaper.

Daily. Statistics, standings.

11-15   Inter-Ocean. Chicago. 1886-87. Newspaper.

Daily. Other coverage.

11-16   The Sporting News. C.C. Spink & Son. St. Louis. March 17, 1886-to date. Newspaper. No edition for the week of May 30, 1946.

The oldest continuous baseball publication. Major and minor league averages, standings, articles. Weekly coverage of each major league team. A reprint of the first issue was issued in 1970.

11-17   The National Daily Baseball Gazette. New York. April 16, 1887- April 28, 1887. Newspaper.

Articles, box scores.

11-18   The Baseball Tribune. New York. 1887. Newspaper.

Daily.

11-19   Baseball Magazine. Baseball Magazine Co. May 1908 - September 1957; November, December 1964; January - April 1965. Magazine.

Prospectus issued December 1907. Articles, photos, statistics, previous reviews. Issued monthly through 1951. 1952: ten issues. 1953: eight issues. 1954

and 1955: four issues. 1956: five issues. 1957:
two issues. Smaller editions were issued during the
1910's for sale at ball parks.

11-20   National Baseball Weekly. 1915. Newspaper.

11-21   Baseball World. Chicago. Baseball World, Inc. 1915-30. News-
           paper.

11-21A   Collyer's Eye. Chicago. 1929-30. Newspaper.

           Continuation of 11-21.

11-22   Weekly Baseball Guide. April - October 1925. Newspaper.

11-23   The Fans' Baseball League Magazine. The Fans' Baseball League,
           Inc. May 1926 - ? Magazine.

11-24   Sport. September 1927 - ? Magazine.

           Vol. 1, no. 1 of a monthly sports pictorial. This is-
           sue was devoted to baseball.

11-25   Colored Baseball and Sports Monthly. Nat Trammel, ed. Colored
           Baseball and Sports Publishing Co. September 1, 1934 - ? Mag-
           azine.

           Reviews, player sketches, articles.

11-26   The Base Hit. Howard Gray, ed. Northern California Baseball
           Managers Association. 1935. Paperbound.

           A monthly journal covering the American, National,
           and Pacific Coast League and also semi-pro and ama-
           teur baseball.

11-27   Fan and Family. Fan and Family, Inc. Chicago. August - Oc-
           tober 1935. Newspaper.

           Coverage of Chicago White Sox and Cubs.

11-28   Baseball Digest. Herbert Simons, ed. Baseball Digest Co. Aug-
           ust 1942 - to date. Paperbound.

           Best stories of the month collected from newspapers
           around the country. Rosters, original statistical tables.
           1942: August, October, November, December.
           1943, 1953-to date: ten issues. 1944-47: nine is-
           sues. 1948-52: 11 issues. Annual roster booklets
           issues separately, 1947-49.

11-29   The Blearcherite. 1945. Newspaper.

           Monthly.

11-30 Baseball Parade. 1945-46. Newspaper.

     Semi-monthly.

11-31 The Sports Exchange. New York. January 1945 - December
     1945. Newspaper.

     Monthly. Baseball articles, coverage of sports col-
     lecting.

11-31A The Trading Post. January 1946 - December 1950. Newspaper.

     Continuation of 11-31.

11-32 Sportland Baseball Magazine. St. Joseph's, Missouri. Sportland
     Co. 1946. Magazine.

     Monthly.

11-33 The Baseball News. Jack Rossiter. Springfield, Illinois. 1948.
     Newspaper.

11-34 The Baseball World. 1948-57. Newspaper.

11-35 Complete Baseball. Bruce Jacobs, ed. Classic Syndicate, Inc.
     Spring 1949 - Winter 1953. Magazine.

     1949: Spring. 1950: Spring, April, Fall, Winter.
     1951: Spring, Summer, Fall, Winter. 1952: Spring,
     July, September, November. 1953: February, April,
     Summer, September, December, Winter. Articles,
     records, statistics, team analyses.

11-36 The Baseball Journal. Norman Paulson. September 1950-52.

     Articles, notes.

11-37 Grandstand Manager. Brooklyn. March 1950 - March 1956.
     Newspaper.

     Monthly. Emphasis on the New York Giants. Cover-
     age of sports collecting.

11-38 Baseball Thrills. Bob Feller, ed. Approved Comics. 1951. Book-
     let.

     Two issues published. A comic book featuring stories
     on a variety of baseball topics.

11-39 The Bat. R.W. Glass. Lexington, Kentucky. February 1951 -
     ? Magazine.

11-40 Inside Baseball. Weiser Publishing Co. July 1952 - February
     1954. Magazine.

     Monthly. Stories on players, managers, teams.

11-41   Baseball: Dreyer's Weekly Averages.   D. Dreyer.   4/18/52 – 4/9/52.   Booklet.

Weekly player statistics covering the American, National, Pacific Coast, and California Leagues.

11-42   Home Run.   Magazine Enterprises.   1953.   Booklet.

Three issues published.   A comic book featuring stories on a variety of baseball topics.

11-43   Los Angeles Baseball News.   1961-to date.   Newspaper.

Semi-weekly during the season.

11-44   Mickey Mantle's Baseball Magazine.   Inside Sports.   H.S. Publications.   1962.   Magazine.

Issued three times during the spring and summer.   Photos, stories, records.

11-45   Baseball Monthly.   BRS Publishing Co.   March-June, 1962.   Magazine.

Articles, photos, statistics.   Coverage of sports collecting.

11-46   Mickey Owen's Hit.   Mickey Owen Publishing Co.   December 1962-1968.   Monthly.   Booklet.

Articles on a variety of topics.

11-47   Baseball Scoreboard.   Green's Southern California Sport Service.   1963-65.   Booklet.

Issued monthly.   Schedules, pitching statistics.

11-48   American League News.   The American League.   December 1966 – to date.   Newspaper.

Six issues per year.   Separate editions published by each American League team with articles of local interest.

Team Newspapers

Issued, usually monthly, to fans.   Dates are approximate.

11-49   Giants Jottings.   New York and San Francisco Giants.   1936-to date.

11-50   Cub News.   Chicago Cubs.   1936-to date.

11-51   News from the Phillies. Philadelphia Phillies. 1938, 1939. Weekly.

11-52   The Phillies Scorecard. Philadelphia Phillies. June 1943-to date.

11-53   News of the Reds. Cincinnati Reds. 1945-to date.

11-54   Pirate Pickin's. Pittsburgh Pirates. 1946-to date.

11-55   Dodger Doings. Brooklyn Dodgers. 1938-42.

11-56   Line Drives from the Dodgers. Brooklyn and Los Angeles Dodgers. 1947-to date.

11-57   Braves Bulletin. Milwaukee Braves. 1953-67.

11-58   Braves Pow-Wow. Atlanta Braves. 1968-69.

11-59   Braves Fun Kit. Atlanta Braves. 1970-to date.

11-60   Cardinal News. St. Louis Cardinals. 1954-to date.

11-61   The Colt 45's. Houston Colts. 1962-64.

11-62   Astrographs. Houston Astros. 1965-to date.

11-63   Mets Fan Fare. New York Mets. 1966-to date.

11-64   Red Sox Ramblings. Boston Red Sox. 1946-to date.

11-65   Along the Elephant Trail. Philadelphia Athletics. 1946-54.

11-66   Detroit Tiger Tales. Detroit Tigers. May 1947 - November 1966.

11-67   Tiger News. Detroit Tigers. December 1966 - to date.

11-68   Indian News. Cleveland Indians. 1947-to date.

11-69   White Sox Yarns. Chicago White Sox. 1948-to date.

11-70   Chicago White Sox Farm Club News. Chicago White Sox. 1948-to date.

11-71   Browns Express. St. Louis Browns. 1953.

11-72   The Oriole-Gram. Baltimore Orioles. 1955-69.

11-73   Bird Hits. Baltimore Orioles. 1970-to date.

11-74   The Senator. Washington Senators. 1960-71.

11-75   <u>Angel Angles.</u> Los Angeles and California Angels. 1961-to date.

11-76   <u>Seattle Pilots Log.</u> Seattle Pilots. 1969.

Suggestion for an inexpensive
but effective battery.

12. Fiction

12-1   WILLIAM EVERETT

12-1A   Changing Base. Lee & Shepard. 1868.

        The first known novel incorporating baseball activity. Two and one-half chapters devoted to a boys' baseball match, remainder of the book to schoolboy adventures.

12-1B   Double Play. Lee & Shepard. 1870.

        Baseball activity interspersed with boys' adventures.

12-1C   Thine Not Mine. Robert Brothers. 1890.

        Several chapters devoted to baseball.

*　　*　　*

12-2   NOAH BROOKS

12-2A   The Fairport Nine. Charles Scribner's Sons. 1880. 1898, reissue. Clothbound.

        First and last chapters devoted to accounts of games, remainder of book to the adventures of the Fairport Boys.

12-2B   The Boys of Fairport. Charles Scribner's Sons. 1898. 1903, reissue. Clothbound.

        Revised edition of 12-2A. Baseball chapters unchanged, non-baseball content enlarged.

12-2C   Our Baseball Club. E.P. Dutton & Co. 1884, 1896, reissue. Clothbound.

        The first novel devoted exclusively to baseball.

*　　*　　*

12-3   CHARLES M. SHELDON

12-3A   The Captain of the Orient Baseball Nine. 1882. Paperbound.

               A short story by the future author of In His Steps.

*   *   *

12-4   BEADLE DIME NOVELS

12-4A   High Hat Harry, the Baseball Detective. Edward Wheeler. Beadle
              & Co. 1885. Paperbound.

12-4B   Double Curve Dan, the Pitcher Detective. George Jenks. 1888.
              Paperbound.

12-4C   Double Curve Dan, the Pitcher Detective's Foil. George Jenks.
              188?.

*   *   *

12-5   TOM TEASER

12-5A   Muldoon's Baseball Club in Philadelphia. Tousey Wide-Awake Dime
              Library. 1890. Paperbound.

                  Muldoon's Irish Baseball Club vs. the Germantown
                  Guzzlers, Harry Wright's Athletics and others.

*   *   *

12-6   NICHOLS

12-6A   Baseball, a Fairy Story. 1890. Booklet.

               A short story with cartoon sketches.

*   *   *

12-7   BILLY BOXER

12-7A   Yale Murphy, the Great Short. New York Five Cent Library.
              1894. Paperbound.

               About the little midget of the New York Giants.

*   *   *

12-8   EVERETT TOMLINSON

12-8A   Ward Hill, the Senior. A.J. Rowland. 1898. Clothbound.

12-8B   The Pennant. Griffith & Rowland Press. 1912. Clothbound.

136

12-9   WORK AND WIN WEEKLY

12-9A   Fred Fearnot's Home Run. June 23, 1899. Booklet.
            Or, "The Second Tour of His Nine."

                        *   *   *

12-10   GILBERT PATTEN (* pseudonym Burt L. Standish)

12-10A   *Frank Merriwell's Baseball Victory. Street & Smith. 1899.
            Paperbound.

12-10B   *The Rockspur Nine. Street & Smith. 1900. Paperbound.

12-10C   *Frank Merriwell's Schooldays. Gilbert Patten. Street & Smith.
            1901. Paperbound. David McKay Co. 1901, reissue. Cloth-
            bound. Street & Smith Publishers. 1971, reissue. Paperbound.

12-10D   *Dick Merriwell's Day. Street & Smith. 1904. Paperbound.

12-10E   *Dick Merriwell's Setback. Street & Smith. 1904. Paperbound.

12-10F   *Dick Merriwell's Great Struggle. Street & Smith. 1904. Pa-
            perbound.

12-10G   *Frank Merriwell's Phenom. Street & Smith. 1908. Paperbound.

12-10H   Clif Sterling, Captain of the Nine. David McKay Co. 1910.
            Clothbound.

12-10I   *Dick Merriwell, Captain of the Varsity. Gilbert Patten. Street
            & Smith. 1910. Paperbound.

12-10J   *Dick Merriwell's Varsity Nine. Gilbert Patten. Street & Smith.
            1912. Paperbound.

12-10K   The College Rebel. Barse & Hopkins. 1914. Clothbound.

12-10L   *Brick King, Backstop. Barse & Hopkins. 1914. Clothbound.

12-10M   *Lefty O' the Bush. Barse & Hopkins. 1914. Clothbound.

12-10N   *Lefty O' the Blue Stockings. Barse & Hopkins. 1914. Cloth-
            bound.

12-10P   *Lefty O' the Training Camp. Barse & Hopkins. 1914. Cloth-
            bound.

12-10Q   *Lefty O' the Big League. Barse & Hopkins. 1914. Clothbound.

12-10R   *Lefty Locke, Pitcher-Manager. Barse & Hopkins. 1915. Cloth-
          bound.

12-10S   *Courtney O' the Center Garden. Barse & Hopkins. 1915.
          Clothbound.

12-10T   *Covering the Look-In Corner. Barse & Hopkins. 1915. Cloth-
          bound.

12-10U   *Guarding the Keystone Sack. Barse & Hopkins. 1915. Cloth-
          bound.

12-10V   *The Making of a Big Leaguer. Barse & Hopkins. 1915. Cloth-
          bound.

12-10W   The Call of the Varsity. Gilbert Patten. Barse & Hopkins.
          1920. Clothbound.

12-10X   *The Man on First. Barse & Hopkins. 1920. Clothbound.

12-10Y   *Lego Lamb, Southpaw. Barse & Hopkins. 1923. Clothbound.

12-10Z   Sons of Old Eli. Barse & Hopkins. 1923. Clothbound.

12-10AA   *Grip of the Game. Barse & Hopkins. 1924. Clothbound.

12-10BB   *Lefty Locke, Owner. Barse & Hopkins. 1925. Clothbound.

12-10CC   *Lefty Locke Wins Out. Barse & Hopkins. 1926. Clothbound.

12-10DD   *Crossed Signals. Barse & Hopkins. 1928. Clothbound.

12-10EE   *Lefty O' the Big League. Barse & Hopkins. No date. Cloth-
          bound.

          Combined edition of 12-10M, 12-10N, 12-10P, and
          12-10Q.

                         *   *   *

12-11   RALPH HENRY BARBOUR

12-11A   Weatherly's Inning. D. Appleton & Co. 1903. Clothbound.

12-11B   Double Play. D. Appleton & Co. 1909. Clothbound.

12-11C   Finkler's Field. D. Appleton & Co. 1911. Clothbound.

12-11D   Lucky Seventh. Small, Maynard & Co. 1913. Books for Libra-
          ries Press. 1970, reissue. Clothbound.

12-11E   The Purple Pennant. D. Appleton & Co. 1916. Clothbound.

12-11F Winning His Game. D. Appleton & Co. 1917. Clothbound.

12-11G Tod Hale on the Nine. Dodd, Mead & Co. 1921. Clothbound.

12-11H Three Base Benton. D. Appleton & Co. 1921. Clothbound.

12-11I Nid and Nod. Ralph Henry Barbour. D. Appleton & Co. 1923. Clothbound.

12-11J Infield Rivals. D. Appleton & Co. 1924. Clothbound.

12-11K Bases Full. D. Appleton & Co. 1925. Clothbound.

12-11L Relief Pitcher. Little, Brown & Co. 1927. Clothbound.

12-11M Lovell Leads Off. D. Appleton & Co. 1928. Clothbound.

12-11N Grantham Gets On. D. Appleton & Co. 1929. Clothbound.

12-11P Squeeze Play. D. Appleton & Co. 1931. Clothbound.

12-11Q Danby's Error. Cosmopolitan Book Corp. 1931. Clothbound.

12-11R Cub Battery. D. Appleton & Co. 1932. Clothbound.

12-11S Southworth Scores. D. Appleton-Century. 1934. Clothbound.

12-11T Merritt Leads the Nine. D. Appleton-Century. 1936. Clothbound.

12-11U The Score Is Tied. D. Appleton-Century. 1937. Clothbound.

12-11V Rivals on the Mound. D. Appleton-Century. 1938. Clothbound.

12-11W Ninth Inning Rally. D. Appleton-Century. 1940. Clothbound.

12-11X Infield Twins. D. Appleton-Century. 1941. Clothbound.

*   *   *

12-12 ALBERTUS TRUE DUDLEY

12-12A Making the Nine. Lee & Shepard. 1904. Clothbound.

12-12B With Mask and Mitt. Lothrop, Lee & Shepard. 1906.

12-12C At the Home Plate. Lothrop, Lee & Shepard. 1910.

*   *   *

12-13   MAXWELL STEVENS

12-13A   <u>Jack Lightfoot's Decision.</u>   Street & Smith.   1905.   Paperbound.

12-13B   <u>Jack Lightfoot in the Box.</u>   Street & Smith.   1905.   Paperbound.

*   *   *

12-14   EDWARD STRATEMEYER (* pseudonym Captain Ralph Bonehill, ** pseudonym Lester Chadwick)

12-14A   *<u>The Winning Run.</u>   A.S. Barnes & Co.   1905.

12-14B   <u>The Baseball Boys of Lakeport.</u> Lothrop, Lee & Shepard Co.   1908. Republication of 12-16A

12-14C   <u>The Rival Pitchers.</u>   Cupples & Leon.   1910.

12-14D   **<u>Batting to Win.</u>   Cupples & Leon.   1911.

12-14E   **<u>Baseball Joe on the School Nine.</u>   Cupples & Leon.   1912.

12-14F   **<u>Baseball Joe of the Silver Stars.</u>   Cupples & Leon.   1912.

12-14G   **<u>Baseball Joe at Yale.</u>   Cupples & Leon.   1913.

12-14H   **<u>Baseball Joe in the Central League.</u>   Cupples & Leon.   1914.

12-14I   **<u>Baseball Joe in the Big League.</u>   Cupples & Leon.   1915.

12-14J   **<u>Baseball Joe on the Giants.</u>   Cupples & Leon.   1916.

12-14K   **<u>Baseball Joe in the World Series.</u>   Cupples & Leon.   1916.

12-14L   **<u>Baseball Joe around the World.</u>   Cupples & Leon.   1918.

12-14M   **<u>Baseball Joe, Home Run King.</u>   Cupples & Leon.   1922.

12-14N   **<u>Baseball Joe, Saving the League.</u>   Cupples & Leon.   1923.

12-14P   **<u>Baseball Joe, Captain of the Team.</u>   Cupples & Leon.   1924.

12-14Q   **<u>Baseball Joe, Champion of the League.</u>   Cupples & Leon.   1925.

12-14R   **<u>Baseball Joe, Pitching Wizard.</u>   Cupples & Leon.   1928.

*   *   *

12-15   LESLIE QUIRK

12-15A   "Midget" Blake, Pitcher.   McLoughlin Brothers.   1906.   Clothbound.

12-16   WINN STANDISH

12-16A   Jack Lorimer's Champions. A.L. Burt Co. 1970. Clothbound.

                          *   *   *

12-17   WILLIAM D. MOFFAT

12-17A   The Crimson Banner. Goldsmith Publishing Co. 1907. Cloth-
          bound.

12-17B   Belmont College. World Publishing Co. No date. Clothbound.

                          *   *   *

12-18   C.B. BURLEIGH

12-18A   Raymond Benson at Krampton. Lothrop, Lee & Shepard. 1907.
          Clothbound.

                          *   *   *

12-19   ZANE GREY

12-19A   The Shortstop. A.C. McClurg & Co. 1909. Clothbound. Gros-
          set & Dunlap. 1914, reissue. Clothbound.

12-19B   The Young Pitcher. Harper & Brothers. 1911. Clothbound.
          Grosset & Dunlap. 1911, reissue. Clothbound.

12-19C   The Red-Headed Outfield and Other Baseball Stories. Grosset &
          Dunlap. 1915. Clothbound.

                          *   *   *

12-20   HARRIE I. HANCOCK

12-20A   The High School Pitcher. Henry Altemus Co. 1910. Clothbound.

                          *   *   *

12-21   FRANK CHANCE

12-21A   The Bride and the Pennant. Laird & Lee. 1910. Paperbound.

               By a major league star player and manager. Sketch
               of Chance and baseball terminology.

                          *   *   *

12-22   OWEN JOHNSON

12-22A   The Hummingbird. Baker & Taylor. 1910, 1938, reissue. Clothbound.

School boy fiction.

* * *

12-23   CHRISTY MATHEWSON

12-23A   Won in the Ninth. R.J. Bodner Co. 1910. Clothbound. New York Book Co. 1916, reissue. Clothbound.

With a chapter on pitching.

12-23B   Pitcher Pollack. Dodd, Mead & Co. 1914. Clothbound. Grosset & Dunlap. 1914, reissue. Clothbound.

12-23C   Catcher Craig. Dodd, Mead & Co. 1915. Clothbound. Grosset & Dunlap. 1915, reissue. Clothbound.

12-23D   First Base Faulkner. Dodd, Mead & Co. 1916. Clothbound. Grosset & Dunlap. 1916, reissue. Clothbound.

12-23E   Second Base Sloan. Dodd, Mead & Co. 1917. Clothbound. Grosset & Dunlap. 1917, reissue. Clothbound.

These were ghost-written by John Wheeler.

* * *

12-24   ARTHUR PIER

12-24A   The Crashaw Brothers. Houghton Mifflin Co. 1910. Clothbound.

12-24B   The Rigor of the Game. Houghton Mifflin Co. 1929. Clothbound.

12-24C   The Captain. Penn Publishing Co. 1929. Clothbound.

12-24D   The Cheerleader. Penn Publishing Co. 1930. Clothbound.

* * *

12-25   ALLEN CHAPMAN

12-25A   Fred Fenton, Pitcher. Cupples & Leon. 1911. Clothbound.

* * *

12-26   ALLEN SANGREE

12-26A   The Jinx. G.W. Dillingham Co. 1911. Clothbound.

Seven stories of the diamond.

12-27   GRAHAM FORBES

12-27A   <u>Frank Allen, Pitcher.</u> Garden City Books. 1911. Clothbound.

12-27B   <u>Frank Allen in Camp.</u> Garden City Books. 1926. Clothbound.

*   *   *

12-28   MATTHEW COLTON

12-28A   <u>Frank Armstrong's Second Team.</u> Hurst & Co. 1911. Clothbound.

12-28B   <u>Frank Armstrong, Captain of the Nine.</u> Hurst & Co. 1913. Clothbound.

*   *   *

12-29   BETH BRADFORD GILCHRIST (* pseudonym John P. Earl)

12-29A   *<u>The School Team on the Diamond.</u> Penn Publishing Co. 1911. Clothbound.

12-29B   *<u>The School Team in Camp.</u> Penn Publishing Co. 1937. Clothbound.

*   *   *

12-30   WILLIAM HEYLIGER (* pseudonym Hawley Williams)

12-30A   <u>Bartley, Freshman Pitcher.</u> D. Appleton & Co. 1911. Clothbound. Grosset & Dunlap. 1911, reissue. Clothbound.

12-30B   <u>Captain of the Nine.</u> D. Appleton & Co. 1912. Clothbound.

12-30C   *<u>Batter Up!</u> D. Appleton & Co. 1912. Clothbound.

12-30D   <u>Strike Three!</u> D. Appleton & Co. 1913. Clothbound.

12-30E   *<u>Johnson of Lansing.</u> D. Appleton & Co. 1914. Clothbound.

12-30F   <u>Against Odds.</u> D. Appleton & Co. 1915. Clothbound.

12-30G   <u>Captain Fair and Square.</u> D. Appleton & Co. 1916. Clothbound.

12-30H   <u>County Pennant.</u> D. Appleton & Co. 1917. Clothbound.

12-30I   <u>Fighting for Fairview.</u> D. Appleton & Co. 1918. Clothbound.

12-30J   <u>Bean Ball Bill, and Other Stories.</u> Grosset & Dunlap. 1920. Clothbound.

12-30K   Macklin Brothers. D. Appleton & Co. 1928. Clothbound.

12-30L   The Gallant Crosby. D. Appleton & Co. 1933. Clothbound.

12-30M   Big Leaguer. Goldsmith Publishing Co. 1936. Clothbound.

12-30N   The Loser's End. Goldsmith Publishing Co. 1937. Clothbound.

*   *   *

12-31   CHARLES VAN LOAN

12-31A   The Big League. Small, Maynard & Co. 1911. Books for Libraries. 1971, reissue. Clothbound.

12-31B   The $10,000 Arm and Other Tales of the Big League. Small, Maynard & Co. 1912.

12-31C   The Lucky Seventh. Small, Maynard & Co. 1913. Books for Libraries. 1970, reissue. Clothbound.

      These consist of short stories--tales of the big leagues.

12-31D   Score by Innings. George H. Doran. 1919.

      Humorous short stories.

*   *   *

12-32   RAYMOND STONE

12-32A   Tommy Tiptop and His Baseball Nine. Graham & Matlack. 1912. Paperbound.

*   *   *

12-33   J.W. DUFFIELD

12-33A   Bert Wilson's Fadeaway Ball. Sully & Kleinteich. 1913. Paperbound.

*   *   *

12-34   MORGAN SCOTT

12-34A   The New Boys at Oakdale. Hurst & Co. 1913. Clothbound.

*   *   *

12-35   WALTER CAMP

12-35A   Captain Danny. D. Appleton & Co. 1914. Clothbound.

      By a famous football coach.

12-36   GEORGE BARTON

12-36A   The Bell Haven Nine. John C. Winston. 1914. Clothbound.

*   *   *

12-37   JAMES HOPPER

12-37A   Coming Back with the Spitball. Harper & Brothers. 1914. Clothbound.

A pitcher's romance.

*   *   *

12-38   HARRY HALE

12-38A   Jack Race's Baseball Nine. Hearst's International Library Co. 1915. Clothbound.

*   *   *

12-39   HUGH FULLERTON

12-39A   Jimmy Kirkland of the Shasta Boys' Team. John C. Winston Co. 1915. Clothbound.

12-39B   Jimmy Kirkland of the Cascade College Team. John C. Winston Co. 1915. Clothbound.

12-39C   Jimmy Kirkland and the Plot for a Pennant. John C. Winston Co. 1915. Clothbound.

*   *   *

12-40   GORDON BRADDOCK

12-40A   Rex Kingdon Behind the Bat. Hurst & Co. 1916. Clothbound.

*   *   *

12-41   FRANK WARNER

12-41A   Bobby Blake on the School Nine. Barse & Hopkins. 1917. Clothbound.

*   *   *

12-42   H.C. WITWER

12-42A   From Baseball to Boches. Small, Maynard & Co. 1918. Clothbound. Grosset & Dunlap. 1918, reissue. Clothbound.

12-43   DONALD FERGUSON

12-43A   Chums of Scranton High Out for the Pennant.   World Publishing
             Co. 1919. Clothbound.

                              *   *   *

12-44   BABE RUTH

12-44A   The Home Run King. H.K. Fly Co. 1920. Clothbound. A.L.
             Burt Co. 1920, reissue. Clothbound.

                              *   *   *

12-45   GERALD BEAUMONT

12-45A   Hearts and the Diamond. Dodd, Mead & Co. 1920, 1921, re-
             issue. Clothbound.

                  Eleven stories based on the author's observations while
                  serving as an official scorer for the Pacific Coast
                  League.

                              *   *   *

12-46   EARL REED SILVERS

12-46A   Dick Arnold of the Varsity. D. Appleton & Co. 1921. Cloth-
             bound.

12-46B   Jackson of Hillsdale High. D. Appleton & Co. 1923. Cloth-
             bound.

12-46C   Team First. D. Appleton & Co. 1929. Clothbound.

                              *   *   *

12-47   EVERETT (DEACON) SCOTT

12-47A   Third Base Thatcher. Dodd, Mead & Co. 1923. Clothbound.
             Grosset & Dunlap. 1948, reissue. Clothbound.

                              *   *   *

12-48   HEYWOOD BROWN

12-48A   The Sun Field. G.P. Putnam's Sons. 1923. Clothbound.

                              *   *   *

12-49   DAVID STONE

12-49A   Yank Brown, Pitcher. Barse & Hopkins. 1924. Clothbound.

*   *   *

12-50   PEGGY GRIFFITH

12-50A   The New Klondike. Jacobsen-Hodgkinson. 1926. Paperbound.
               A story of a southern baseball training camp. Based
               on a motion picture script.

*   *   *

12-51   GEORGE B. CHADWICK

12-51A   Chuck Blue of Sterling. Century Co. 1927. Clothbound.

*   *   *

12-52   CHARLES MULLER

12-52A   The Baseball Detective. Harper & Brothers. 1928. Clothbound.

*   *   *

12-53   HAROLD M. SHERMAN (* Home Run Series)

12-53A   *Bases Full. Grosset & Dunlap. 1928. Clothbound.

12-53B   *Hit by Pitcher. Grosset & Dunlap. 1928. Clothbound.

12-53C   *Safe. Grosset & Dunlap. 1928. Clothbound.

12-53D   *Hit and Run. Grosset & Dunlap. 1929. Clothbound.

12-53E   *Batter Up. Grosset & Dunlap. 1930. Clothbound.

12-53F   *Strike Him Out. Goldsmith Publishing Co. 1931. Clothbound.

12-53G   Double Play, and Other Baseball Stories. Grosset & Dunlap.
           1932. Clothbound.

*   *   *

12-54   ELMER DAWSON

12-54A   The Pickup Nine. Grosset & Dunlap. 1930. Clothbound.

12-54B   Buck's Winning Hit. Grosset & Dunlap. 1930. Clothbound.

12-54C   Larry's Fadeaway. Grosset & Dunlap. 1930. Clothbound.

12-54D   <u>Buck's Home Run Drive</u>. Grosset & Dunlap. 1931. Clothbound.

12-54E   <u>Larry's Speed Ball</u>. Grosset & Dunlap. 1932. Clothbound.

*   *   *

12-55   DONALD HAINES

12-55A   <u>The Southpaw</u>. Rinehart & Co. 1931. Clothbound.

*   *   *

12-56   NOEL SAINSBURY (* pseudonym Charles Lawton)

12-56A   <u>Cracker Stanton</u>. Cupples & Leon. 1934. Clothbound.

12-56B   <u>Clarksville Battery</u>. Cupples & Leon. 1937. Clothbound.

12-56C   *<u>Home Run Hennessy</u>. Cupples & Leon. 1941. Clothbound.

12-56D   *<u>Stirring Baseball Stories</u>. Cupples & Leon. No date.
           Combined edition of 12-55A, 12-55B and 12-55C.

*   *   *

12-57   COURTNEY FITZSIMMONS

12-57A   <u>Death on the Diamond</u>. Frederick A. Stokes Co. 1934. Clothbound. Grosset & Dunlap. 1934, reissue. Clothbound.
           A baseball mystery.

*   *   *

12-58   FRANK HART

12-58A   <u>Speed Boy</u>. Lakewood House. 1938. Clothbound and Paperbound.

*   *   *

12-59   JULIAN DEVRIES

12-59A   <u>The Strikeout King</u>. World Publishing Co. 1940. Clothbound.

*   *   *

12-60   MACK CORBERT

12-60A   <u>Play the Game</u>. Frederick A. Stokes Co. 1940. Clothbound.
           W.P.A. New Reading Materials Program. For boys.

12-61   JOHN R. TUNIS

12-61A   The Kid from Tompkinsville. Harcourt, Brace & Co. 1940.
         Clothbound. Berkeley Books. 1964, reissue. Paperbound.

12-61B   World Series. Harcourt, Brace & Co. 1914. Clothbound.

12-61C   Keystone Kids. Harcourt, Brace & Co. 1943. Clothbound.

12-61D   Rookie of the Year. Harcourt, Brace & Co. 1944. Clothbound.

12-61E   The Kid Comes Back. William Morrow & Co. 1946. Cloth-
         bound. Tab Books. 1958, reissue. Paperbound.

12-61F   High Pockets. William Morrow & Co. 1948. Clothbound. Tab
         Books. 1958, reissue. Paperbound.

12-61G   Young Razzle. William Morrow & Co. 1949. Clothbound.

12-61H   Buddy and the Old Pro. William Morrow & Co. 1955. Cloth-
         bound.

12-61I   Schoolboy Johnson. William Morrow & Co. 1958. Berkeley
         Books. 1963, reissue. Paperbound.

*   *   *

12-62   WILLARD H. TEMPLE

12-62A   Pitching for Pawling. Farrar & Rinehart. 1940. Clothbound.

*   *   *

12-63   FRANKLIN RECK

12-63A   Varsity Letter. Thomas Y. Crowell Co. 1942. Clothbound.

*   *   *

12-64   JACKSON V. SCHOLZ

12-64A   Soldiers at Bat. William Morrow & Co. 1942. Clothbound.

12-64B   Batter Up. William Morrow & Co. 1946. Clothbound.

12-64C   Fielder from Nowhere. William Morrow & Co. 1948. Clothbound.

12-64D   Keystone Kelly. William Morrow & Co. 1950. Clothbound.

12-64E   Deep Short. William Morrow & Co. 1952. Clothbound.

12-64F   Base Burglar. William Morrow & Co. 1955. Clothbound.

12-64G   <u>Man in a Cage</u>. William Morrow & Co. 1957. Clothbound.

12-64H   <u>Bench Boss.</u> William Morrow & Co. 1958. Clothbound.

12-64I   <u>The Perfect Game</u>. William Morrow & Co. 1959. Clothbound.

12-64J   <u>Little League Town</u>. William Morrow & Co. 1959. Clothbound.

12-64K   <u>Dugout Tycoon</u>. William Morrow & Co. 1963. Clothbound.

12-64L   <u>Sparkplug at Short</u>. William Morrow & Co. 1966. Clothbound.

12-64M   <u>The Big Mitt</u>. William Morrow & Co. 1968. Clothbound.

12-64N   <u>Hot Corner Hank</u>. William Morrow & Co. 1970. Clothbound.

*   *   *

12-65   MARION RENICK (* written with James L. Renick)

12-65A   <u>*Steady.</u> Charles Scribner's Sons. 1942. Clothbound.

12-65B   <u>The Dooleys Play Ball.</u> Charles Scribner's Sons. 1949. Clothbound.

12-65C   <u>Pete's Home Run.</u> Charles Scribner's Sons. 1952. Clothbound.

12-65D   <u>The Heart for Baseball.</u> Charles Scribner's Sons. 1953. Clothbound.

12-65E   <u>Boy at Bat.</u> Charles Scribner's Sons. 1961. Clothbound.

*   *   *

12-66   H. ALLEN SMITH

12-66A   <u>Rhubarb.</u> Doubleday & Co. 1946. Clothbound. Sun Dial Press. 1947, reissue. Clothbound.

         A humorous novel about the Brooklyn Dodgers. Made into a motion picture. Later reissued in comic book form.

*   *   *

12-67   JOHN R. COOPER (* Mel Martin Baseball Stories)

12-67A   <u>Mystery at the Ball Park.</u> Cupples & Leon. 1947. Garden City Books. 1952, reissue.

12-67B   <u>Southpaw's Secret.</u> Cupples & Leon. 1947. Garden City Books. 1952, reissue.

12-67C   Phantom Homer. Garden City Books. 1952.

12-67D   *First Base Jinx. Garden City Books. 1952.

12-67E   *Fighting Shortstop. Garden City Books. 1953.

12-67F   *College League Mystery. Garden City Books. 1953.

* * *

12-68   DUANE DECKER (* pseudonym Richard Wayne)

12-68A   Good Field, No Hit. M.S. Mill Co. 1947.

12-68B   Starting Pitcher. M.S. Mill Co. and William Morrow & Co. 1948.

12-68C   Hit and Run. M.S. Mill Co. and William Morrow & Co. 1949.

12-68D   Catcher from Double A. William Morrow & Co. 1950.

12-68E   *Clutch Hitter. Macrae-Smith. 1951.

12-68F   Fast Man on a Pivot. William Morrow & Co. 1951.

12-68G   Big Stretch. William Morrow & Co. 1952.

12-68H   Wrong Way Rookie. Macrae-Smith. 1952.

12-68I   Switch Hitter. William Morrow & Co. 1953.

12-68J   Mister Shortstop. William Morrow & Co. 1954.

12-68K   Long Ball to Left Field. William Morrow & Co. 1958.

12-68L   Third Base Rookie. William Morrow & Co. 1959.

12-68M   Showboat Southpaw. William Morrow & Co. 1960.

12-68N   Rebel in Right Field. William Morrow & Co. 1961.

* * *

12-69   MARY G. BONNER

12-69A   Out to Win. Alfred A. Knopf, Inc. 1947.

12-69B   Base Stealer. Alfred A. Knopf, Inc. 1951.

12-69C   Dugout Mystery. Alfred A. Knopf, Inc. 1953.

12-69D   Two-Way Pitcher. Lantern Press. 1958.

12-69E <u>Spray Hitter.</u> Lantern Press. 1959.

* * *

12-70 PHILIP HARKINS

12-70A <u>Southpaw from San Francisco.</u> William Morrow & Co. 1948. Clothbound.

12-70B <u>Double Play.</u> Holiday House. 1951. Clothbound.

* * *

12-71 ROBERT S. BOWEN (* pseudonym J.R. Richard)

12-71A <u>The Winning Pitch.</u> Lothrop, Lee & Shepard. 1948. Clothbound.

12-71B <u>Player, Manager.</u> Lothrop, Lee & Shepard. 1949. Clothbound.

12-71C <u>Ball Hawk.</u> Lothrop, Lee & Shepard. 1950. Clothbound.

12-71D *<u>The Club Team.</u> Lothrop, Lee & Shepard. 1950. Clothbound. Grosset & Dunlap. 1951, reissue.

12-71E <u>Hot Corner.</u> Lothrop, Lee & Shepard. 1951. Clothbound.

12-71F <u>Pitcher of the Year.</u> Lothrop, Lee & Shepard. 1952. Clothbound.

12-71G <u>Behind the Bat.</u> Lothrop, Lee & Shepard. 1953. Clothbound.

12-71H <u>Infield Spark.</u> Lothrop, Lee & Shepard. 1954. Clothbound.

12-71I <u>The Big Inning.</u> Lothrop, Lee & Shepard. 1955. Clothbound.

12-71J <u>The Fourth Out.</u> Lothrop, Lee & Shepard. 1956. Clothbound.

12-71K <u>No-Hitter.</u> Lothrop, Lee & Shepard. 1957. Clothbound.

12-71L <u>The Big Hit.</u> Lothrop, Lee & Shepard. 1956. Clothbound.

12-71M <u>Triple Play.</u> Lothrop, Lee & Shepard. 1959. Clothbound.

12-71N <u>Pennant Fever.</u> Lothrop, Lee & Shepard. 1960. Clothbound.

12-71P <u>Million Dollar Rookie.</u> Lothrop, Lee & Shepard. 1961. Clothbound.

12-71Q <u>Bat Boy.</u> Lothrop, Lee & Shepard. 1962. Clothbound.

12-71R <u>Perfect Game.</u> Lothrop, Lee & Shepard. 1963. Clothbound.

12-71S   <u>Hot Corner Blues.</u> Lothrop, Lee & Shepard. 1964. Clothbound.

12-71T   <u>Rebel Rookie.</u> Lothrop, Lee & Shepard. 1965. Clothbound.

12-71U   <u>Man on First.</u> Lothrop, Lee & Shepard. 1966. Clothbound.

12-71V   <u>Lightning Southpaw.</u> Lothrop, Lee & Shepard. 1967. Clothbound.

12-71W   <u>Infield Flash.</u> Lothrop, Lee & Shepard. 1969. Clothbound.

*   *   *

12-72   ED FITZGERALD

12-72A   <u>Turning Point.</u> A.S. Barnes & Co. 1948. Clothbound.

12-72B   <u>College Slugger.</u> A.S. Barnes & Co. 1950. Clothbound.

12-72C   <u>Yankee Rookie.</u> A.S. Barnes & Co. 1952. Clothbound.

12-72D   <u>The Ballplayer.</u> A.S. Barnes & Co. 1957. Clothbound.

*   *   *

12-73   WILFRED McCORMICK (* Bronc Burnett Series, ** Rocky McClune Series, *** Bronc Burnett and Rocky McClune Series)

12-73A   *<u>The Three and Two Pitch.</u> G.P. Putnam's Sons. 1948. Clothbound. Grosset & Dunlap. 1956, reissue.

12-73B   *<u>Legion Tourney.</u> G.P. Putnam's Sons. 1948. Clothbound. Grosset & Dunlap. 1956, reissue.

12-73C   *<u>Fielder's Choice.</u> G.P. Putnam's Sons. 1949. Clothbound. Grosset & Dunlap. 1956, reissue.

12-73D   *<u>Bases Loaded.</u> G.P. Putnam's Sons. 1950. Clothbound. Grosset & Dunlap. 1958, reissue.

12-73E   *<u>Grand Slam Homer.</u> G.P. Putnam's Sons. 1951. Clothbound. Grosset & Dunlap. 1958, reissue.

12-73F   **<u>The Man on the Bench.</u> David McKay Co. 1955.

12-73G   <u>The Big Ninth.</u> G.P. Putnam's Sons. 1958. Clothbound. Grosset & Dunlap. 1960, reissue.

12-73H   **<u>The Hot Corner.</u> David McKay Co. 1958. Clothbound.

12-73I   ***<u>The Proud Champions.</u> David McKay Co. 1959. Clothbound.

12-73J   The Last Put-Out. G.P. Putnam's Sons. 1960. Clothbound. Grosset & Dunlap. 1961, reissue.

12-73K   *One O'Clock Hitter. David McKay Co. 1960. Clothbound. Grosset & Dunlap. 1961, reissue.

12-73L   **The Automatic Strike. David McKay Co. 1960. Clothbound.

12-73M   *The Bluffer. David McKay Co. 1961. Clothbound. Grosset & Dunlap. 1963, reissue.

12-73N   *The Double Steal. David McKay Co. 1961. Clothbound.

12-73P   *Rebel with a Glove. David McKay Co. 1962. Clothbound. Grosset & Dunlap. 1964, reissue.

12-73Q   **Home Run Harvest. David McKay Co. 1962. Clothbound.

12-73R   **The Phantom Shortstop. David McKay Co. 1963. Clothbound.

12-73S   The Starmaker. Robert Speller. 1963. Clothbound.

12-73T   *Once a Slugger. David McKay Co. 1963. Clothbound. Grosset & Dunlap. 1965, reissue.

12-73U   **The Long Pitcher. Duell, Sloan & Pearce. 1964. Clothbound.

12-73V   *The Throwing Catcher. David McKay Co. 1964. Clothbound. Grosset & Dunlap. 1966, reissue.

12-73W   **Wild on the Bases. Duell, Sloan & Pearce. 1965. Clothbound.

12-73X   *The Go-Ahead Runner. David McKay Co. 1965. Clothbound.

12-73Y   *Tall at the Plate. Bobbs-Merrill. 1966. Clothbound.

12-73Z   Rookie on First. G.P. Putnam's Sons. 1967. Clothbound.

12-73AA   ***The Incomplete Pitcher. Bobbs-Merrill. 1967. Clothbound.

*   *   *

12-74   FRANK O'ROURKE

12-74A   Flashing Spikes. A.S. Barnes & Co. 1948. Clothbound.

12-74B   The Team. A.S. Barnes & Co. 1949. Clothbound.
         Based on the 1949 Philadelphia Phillies.

12-74C   Bonus Rookie. A.S. Barnes & Co. 1950. Clothbound.

Based on the 1950 Phillies.

12-74D   The Greatest Victory and Other Baseball Stories. A.S. Barnes &
          Co. 1950. Clothbound.

12-74E   The Heavenly World Series and Other Baseball Stories. A.S.
          Barnes & Co. 1952. Clothbound.

12-74F   Nine Good Men. A.S. Barnes & Co. 1952. Clothbound.

12-74G   Never Come Back. A.S. Barnes & Co. 1952. Clothbound.

12-74H   The Catcher and the Manager. A.S. Barnes & Co. 1953. Cloth-
          bound.

                            *   *   *

12-75   RUSSELL G. EMERY

12-75A   High, Inside. Macrae-Smith. 1948. Clothbound.

12-75B   Relief Pitcher. Macrae-Smith. 1953. Clothbound.

12-75C   Action at Third. Macrae-Smith. 1957. Clothbound.

                            *   *   *

12-76   VALENTINE DAVIES

12-76A   It Happens Every Spring. Farrar, Straus. 1949. Clothbound.
                Light-hearted novel, later made into a motion picture.

                            *   *   *

12-77   GUERNSEY VAN RIPER, JR.

12-77A   Lou Gehrig, Boy of the Sandlots. Bobbs-Merrill. 1949, 1959,
          reissue. Clothbound.
                A fictionalized account of Gehrig's boyhood.

12-77B   Babe Ruth, Baseball Boy. Bobbs-Merrill. 1954. Clothbound.
                A fictionalized account of Ruth's boyhood.

                            *   *   *

12-78   CLAIR BEE

12-78A   Strike Three! Grosset & Dunlap. 1949. Clothbound.

12-78B   Clutch Hitter. Grosset & Dunlap. 1949. Clothbound.

12-78C   <u>Pitchers' Duel</u>. Grosset & Dunlap. 1950. Clothbound.

12-78D   <u>Dugout Jinx</u>. Grosset & Dunlap. 1952. Clothbound.

12-78E   <u>Fence Busters</u>. Grosset & Dunlap. 1953. Clothbound.

12-78F   <u>Pay-Off Pitch</u>. Grosset & Dunlap. 1958. Clothbound.

12-78G   <u>No-Hitter</u>. Grosset & Dunlap. 1959. Clothbound.

12-78H   <u>Home Run Feud</u>. Grosset & Dunlap. 1964. Clothbound.

12-78I   <u>Hungry Hurler</u>. Grosset & Dunlap. 1966. Clothbound.

*   *   *

12-79   MARION RENICK

12-79A   <u>The Dooleys Play Ball</u>. Charles Scribner's Sons. 1949. Clothbound.

12-79B   <u>Pete's Home Run</u>. Charles Scribner's Sons. 1952. Clothbound.

12-79C   <u>The Heart for Baseball</u>. Charles Scribner's Sons. 1953. Clothbound.

12-79D   <u>Bats and Gloves of Glory</u>. Charles Scribner's Sons. 1956. Clothbound.

12-79E   <u>Boy at Bat</u>. Charles Scribner's Sons. 1961. Clothbound.

*   *   *

12-80   FRANCIS WALLACE

12-80A   <u>Big League Rookie</u>. Westminster Press. 1950. Clothbound.

*   *   *

12-81   HOWARD BRIER

12-81A   <u>Shortstop Shadow</u>. Random House. 1950. Clothbound.

*   *   *

12-82   LUCY KENNEDY

12-82A   <u>The Sunlit Field</u>. Crown Publishers. 1950. Clothbound.
        A story of baseball in Brooklyn during the 1950's.

*   *   *

12-83   MURRELL EDMUNDS

12-83A   Behold, Thy Brother. Beechhurst Press. 1950. Clothbound.

The story of a Negro player's struggle against pre-
judice while breaking into the major leagues.

*   *   *

12-84   C. PAUL JACKSON (* pseudonym Colin Lochlons, ** written
with O.B. Jackson, *** written as Cary Jackson)

12-84A   Rookie First Baseman. Thomas Y. Crowell Co. 1950. Clothbound.

12-84B   *Squeeze Play. Thomas Y. Crowell Co. 1950. Clothbound.

12-84C   *Three and Two Pitcher. Thomas Y. Crowell Co. 1951. Clothbound.

12-84D   Shorty at Shortstop. Wilcox & Follett. 1951. Clothbound.

12-84E   *Triple Play. Thomas Y. Crowell Co. 1952. Clothbound.

12-84F   Little Leaguer's First Uniform. Thomas Y. Crowell Co. 1952.
Clothbound.

12-84G   Clown at Second Base. Thomas Y. Crowell Co. 1952. Clothbound.

12-84H   Giant in the Midget League. Thomas Y. Crowell Co. 1953.
Clothbound.

12-84I   *Barney of the Babe Ruth League. Thomas Y. Crowell Co. 1954.
Clothbound.

12-84J   **Hillbilly Pitcher. Whittlesey House. 1956. Clothbound.

12-84K   Little League Tournament. Hastings House. 1959. Clothbound.

12-84L   World Series Rookie. Hastings House. 1960. Clothbound.

12-84M   Bullpen Bargain. Hastings House. 1961. Clothbound.

12-84N   ***A Uniform for Harry. Follett Publishing Co. 1962. Clothbound.

A reading primer.

12-84P   Little Major Leaguer. Hastings House. 1963. Clothbound.

12-84Q   **High School Backstop. Whittlesey House. 1963. Clothbound.

12-84R   Pee Wee Cook of the Midget League. Hastings House. 1964. Clothbound.

12-84S   Minor League Shortstop. Hastings House. 1965. Clothbound.

12-84T   Rookie Catcher with the Atlanta Braves. Hastings House. 1966. Clothbound.

12-84U   Midget League Catcher. Follett Publishing Co. 1966. Clothbound.

12-84V   Bud Baker, High School Pitcher. Hastings House. 1967. Clothbound.

12-84W   Big Play in the Small League. Hastings House. 1968. Clothbound.

12-84X   Second Time Around Rookie. Hastings House. 1968. Clothbound.

12-84Y   Pennant Stretch Drive. Hastings House. 1969. Clothbound.

12-84Z   Bud Baker, College Pitcher. Hastings House. 1970. Clothbound.

12-84AA   Tim Mosely, Midget Leaguer. Hastings House. 1971. Clothbound.

12-84BB   Fifth Inning Fadeout. Hastings House. 1972. Clothbound.

*   *   *

12-85   ARNOLD HANO

12-85A   The Big Out. A.S. Barnes & Co. 1951. Clothbound.

*   *   *

12-86   CURTIS K. BISHOP

12-86A   Banjo Hitter. Steck Co. 1951.

12-86B   Larry of the Little League. Steck Co. 1953.

12-86C   Larry Leads Off. Steck Co. 1954.

12-86D   Larry Comes Home. Steck Co. 1955.

12-86E   Little Leaguer. Steck Co. 1956.

12-86F   The Little League Way. Steck Co. 1957.

12-86G   Lank of the Little League. J.B. Lippincott, Inc. 1958.

12-86H   Little League Little Brother. J.B. Lippincott, Inc. 1960, 1968, reissue.

12-86I   Little League Heroes. J.B. Lippincott, Inc. 1960.

12-86J   Little League Double Play. J.B. Lippincott, Inc. 1962.

12-86K   The Big Game. J.B. Lippincott, Inc. 1963.

12-86L   Little League Amigo. J.B. Lippincott, Inc. 1964.

12-86M   Little League Stepson. J.B. Lippincott, Inc. 1965.

12-86N   Little League Visitor. J.B. Lippincott, Inc. 1966.

12-86P   Little League Victory. J.B. Lippincott, Inc. 1967.

*   *   *

12-87   WILLIAM HEUMAN

12-87A   Wonder Boy. William Morrow & Co. 1951. Clothbound. Scholastic Book Services. 1964, reissue. Paperbound.

12-87B   Little League Champions. J.B. Lippincott, Inc. 1953. Clothbound.

12-87C   Strictly from Brooklyn. William Morrow & Co. 1956. Clothbound.

12-87D   Rookie Backstop. Dodd, Mead & Co. 1962. Clothbound.

12-87E   The Horse that Played the Outfield. Dodd, Mead & Co. 1964. Clothbound.

12-87F   Hillbilly Hurler. Dodd, Mead & Co. 1966. Clothbound.

12-87G   Horace Higby and the Scientific Pitch. Dodd, Mead & Co. 1968. Clothbound.

12-87H   The Goofer Pitch. Dodd, Mead & Co. 1969. Clothbound.

12-87I   Home Run Henri. Dodd, Mead & Co. 1970. Clothbound.

12-87J   Little League Hot Shots. Dodd, Mead & Co. 1972. Clothbound.

*   *   *

12-88   BURGESS LEONARD

12-88A   Rookie Southpaw. J.B. Lippincott, Inc. 1951. Clothbound.

12-88B   Second Base Jinx. J.B. Lippincott, Inc. 1953. Clothbound.

12-88C   The Rookie Fights Back. J.B. Lippincott, Inc. 1954. Clothbound.

12-88D   Stretch Bolton Comes Back. J.B. Lippincott, Inc. 1958. Clothbound.

12-88E   Stretch Bolton's Rookies. J.B. Lippincott, Inc. 1961. Clothbound.

12-88F   Stretch Bolton, Mr. Shortstop. J.B. Lippincott, Inc. 1963. Clothbound.

*   *   *

12-89   FRANK WALDMAN (* pseudonym Joe Webster)

12-89A   Bonus Pitcher. Houghton Mifflin Co. 1951. Clothbound.

12-89B   *Dodger Doubleheader. Ariel Books. 1952. Clothbound.

12-89C   *The Rookie from Junction Flats. Ariel Books. 1952. Clothbound.

12-89D   Delayed Steal. Houghton Mifflin Co. 1952. Clothbound.

12-89E   Lucky Bat Boy. World Publishing Co. 1956. Clothbound.

*   *   *

12-90   BERNARD MALAMUD

12-90A   The Natural. Farrar, Straus & Cudahy. 1952. Clothbound. Noonday Press. 1961, reissue. Paperbound. Dell. 1971, reissue. Paperbound.

                An allegorical novel. First work of a subsequent Pulitzer Prize winner.

*   *   *

12-91   ADOLPH C. REGLI (* pseudonym Addison Rand)

12-91A   Southpaw Flyhawk. Longmans Green. 1952. Clothbound.

*   *   *

12-92   ARTHUR MANN (* pseudonym A.R. Thurman)

12-92A   Bob White: Bonus Player. David McKay Co. 1952. Clothbound.

12-92B   Bob White: Farm Club Player. David McKay Co. 1952. Clothbound.

12-92C   *Money Pitcher. David McKay Co. 1952. Clothbound.

12-92D   Bob White: Spring Terror. David McKay Co. 1953. Cloth-
          bound.

                    *   *   *

12-93   EARL SCHENK MIERS

12-93A   Monkey Shines. World Publishing Co. 1952. Clothbound.

12-93B   The Kid Who Beat the Dodgers, and Other Sports Stories. World
          Publishing Co. 1954. Clothbound.

12-93C   Ball of Fire. World Publishing Co. 1956. Clothbound.

                    *   *   *

12-94   ISADOR S. YOUNG

12-94A   A Hit and a Miss. Wilcox & Follett. 1952. Clothbound.

12-94B   Carson at Second. Wilcox & Follett. 1966. Clothbound.

                    *   *   *

12-95   JOHN F. GARTNER

12-95A   Ace Pitcher. Dodd, Mead & Co. 1953. Clothbound.

                    *   *   *

12-96   EDD WINFIELD PARKS

12-96A   Safe on Second. Bobbs, Merrill. 1953. Clothbound.

                    *   *   *

12-97   JACK WEEKS

12-97A   The Hard Way. A.S. Barnes & Co. 1953. Clothbound.

                    *   *   *

12-98   BOB ALLISON and FRANK E. HILL

12-98A   The Kid Who Batted 1,000. Doubleday & Co. 1953. Cloth-
          bound. Scholastic Book Services. 1972, reissue. Paperbound.

                    *   *   *

12-99   ROBERT SMITH

12-99A   Little League Catcher.   A.S. Barnes & Co.   1953.   Clothbound.

*   *   *

12-100   MARK HARRIS

12-100A   The Southpaw.   Bobbs, Merrill.   1953.   Clothbound.   Permabooks. 1954, reissue.   Paperbound.

> First of the Henry Wiggins trilogy. The story of the successful major league debut of a rookie pitcher from a rural background.

12-100B   Bang the Drum Slowly.   Alfred A. Knopf, Inc.   1956.   Clothbound. Anchor Books.   1962, reissue.   Paperbound.

> Before the start of the season Wiggins learns that a teammate and friend has an incurable illness.

12-100C   Ticket for a Seamstitch.   Alfred A. Knopf, Inc.   1956, 1957, reissue.   Clothbound.

> A female fan travels cross-country to see Wiggins and her favorite team in action.

*   *   *

12-101   CHARLES EINSTEIN (* pseudonym D.J. Michael)

12-101A   * Win or Else.   Lurton Blassingame.   1954.   Paperbound.   Lion Books.   1954, reissue.   Paperbound.

> A story of gambling and baseball.

12-101B   The Only Game in Town.   Dell Publishing Co.   1954.   Paperbound.

> A story of the major league comeback of a minor league player-manager.

*   *   *

12-102   DOUGLAS WALLOP

12-102A   The Year the Yankees Lost the Pennant.   W.W. Norton & Co. 1954, 1964, reissue.   Clothbound.

> The fantasy upon which Damn Yankees was based. How Satan turned a Washington Senator fan into a ballplayer and enꚻled him to lead the Senators to the pennant.

*   *   *

12-103   CHARLES COOMBS

12-103A   <u>Young Infield Rookie.</u> Lantern Press. 1954. Clothbound.

12-103B   <u>Sleuth at Shortstop.</u> Lantern Press. 1955. Clothbound.

12-103C   <u>Young Readers Baseball Mystery.</u> Grosset & Dunlap. 1958.
           Clothbound.

           Reissue of 12-103B.

                        *   *   *

12-104   MATTHEW F. CHRISTOPHER

12-104A   <u>The Lucky Baseball Bat.</u> Little, Brown & Co. 1954. Cloth-
           bound.

12-104B   <u>Baseball Pals.</u> Little, Brown & Co. 1956. Clothbound.

12-104C   <u>Slide, Danny, Slide.</u> Steck Co. 1958. Clothbound.

12-104D   <u>Two Strikes on Johnny.</u> Little, Brown & Co. 1958. Clothbound.

12-104E   <u>Little Lefty.</u> Little, Brown & Co. 1959. Clothbound.

12-104F   <u>Long Stretch at First Base.</u> Little, Brown & Co. 1960. Cloth-
           bound.

12-104G   <u>Challenge at Second Base.</u> Little, Brown & Co. 1962. Cloth-
           bound.

12-104H   <u>Baseball Flyhawk.</u> Little, Brown & Co. 1963. Clothbound.

12-104I   <u>Catcher with a Glass Arm.</u> Little, Brown & Co. 1964. Cloth-
           bound.

12-104J   <u>Too Hot to Handle.</u> Little, Brown & Co. 1965. Clothbound.

12-104K   <u>The Reluctant Pitcher.</u> Little, Brown & Co. 1966. Clothbound.

12-104L   <u>Miracle at the Plate.</u> Little, Brown & Co. 1967. Clothbound.

12-104M   <u>The Year Mom Won the Pennant.</u> Little, Brown & Co. 1968.
           Clothbound.

12-104N   <u>Hard Drive to Short.</u> Little, Brown & Co. 1969. Clothbound.

12-104P   <u>Shortstop from Tokyo.</u> Little, Brown & Co. 1970. Clothbound.

12-104Q   <u>Look Who's Playing First Base.</u> Little, Brown & Co. 1971.
           Clothbound.

12-104R   <u>The Kid Who Only Hit Homers.</u> Little, Brown & Co. 1972.
           Clothbound.

                        *   *   *

Fiction

12-105   DICK FRIENDLICH

12-105A   Baron of the Bullpen. Westminister Press. 1954. Clothbound.

12-105B   Cleanup Hitter. Westminster Press. 1956. Clothbound.

12-105C   Leadoff Man. Westminster Press. 1959. Clothbound.

12-105D   Backstop Ace. Westminster Press. 1961. Clothbound.

12-105E   Relief Pitcher. Westminster Press. 1964. Clothbound. Scholastic Book Services. 1966, reissue. Paperbound.

12-105F   Pinch Hitter. Westminster Press. 1965. Clothbound.

12-105G   The Sweet Swing. Doubleday & Co. 1968. Clothbound.

*   *   *

12-106   JOSEPH OLGIN

12-106A   Little League Champions. E.P. Dutton & Co. 1954. Clothbound.

12-106B   Battery Feud. Houghton Mifflin Co. 1959. Clothbound.

*   *   *

12-107   NELS L. JORGENSEN

12-107A   Dave Palmer's Diamond Mystery. Cupples & Leon. 1954. Clothbound.

*   *   *

12-108   AL HIRSHBERG

12-108A   Battery for Madison High. Little, Brown & Co. 1955. Clothbound.

12-108B   Varsity Double Play. Little, Brown & Co. 1956. Clothbound.

*   *   *

12-109   LILLIAN GARDNER

12-109A   Somebody Called Booie. Franklin Watts. 1955. Clothbound.

*   *   *

12-110   AMELIA ELIZABETH WALDEN

12-110A   Three Loves Has Sandy. McGraw-Hill. 1955. Clothbound.

Scholastic Book Services. 1966, reissue. Clothbound.

12-111   ELIOT ASINOF

12-111A   Man on Spikes. McGraw-Hill. 1955. Clothbound.
          The story of a minor league player.

                    *   *   *

12-112   JOE ARCHIBALD

12-112A   Double Play Rookie. Macrae-Smith. 1955. Clothbound.

12-112B   Full Count. Macrae-Smith. 1956. Clothbound.

12-112C   Circus Catch. Macrae-Smith. 1957. Clothbound.

12-112D   Mr. Slingshot. Macrae-Smith. 1957. Clothbound.

12-112E   Catcher's Choice. Macrae-Smith. 1958. Clothbound.

12-112F   Bonus Kid. Macrae-Smith. 1959. Clothbound.

12-112G   First Base Hustler. Macrae-Smith. 1960. Clothbound.

12-112H   Outfield Orphan. Macrae-Smith. 1961. Clothbound.

12-112I   Shortstop on Wheels. Macrae-Smith. 1962. Clothbound.

12-112J   Big League Busher. Macrae-Smith. 1963. Clothbound.

12-112K   Old Iron Glove. Macrae-Smith. 1964. Clothbound.

12-112L   The Easy Out. Macrae-Smith. 1965. Clothbound.

12-112M   Southpaw Speed. Macrae-Smith. 1965. Clothbound.

12-112N   Mitt Maverick. Macrae-Smith. 1968. Clothbound.

12-112P   Two-Time Rookie. Macrae-Smith. 1969. Clothbound.

12-112Q   Payoff Pitch. Macrae-Smith. 1971. Clothbound.

12-112R   Right Field Runt. Macrae-Smith. 1972. Clothbound.

                    *   *   *

12-113   WALTER R. BROOKS

12-113A   Freddy and the Baseball Team from Mars. Alfred A. Knopf, Inc.
          1955. Clothbound.

          The story of a baseball-playing pig.

                              *   *   *

12-114   LAWRENCE KEATING

12-114A   Kid Brother. Westminster Press. 1956. Clothbound.

12-114B   Freshman Backstop. Westminster Press. 1957. Clothbound.

12-114C   Senior Challenge. Westminster Press. 1959. Clothbound.

                              *   *   *

12-115   ED KEY

12-115A   Phyllis. E.P. Dutton & Co. 1957. Clothbound.

          Humorous story of a sparrow who builds her nest in the
          Philadelphia Phillies park.

                              *   *   *

12-116   BURGESS FITZPATRICK

12-116A   Casey's Redemption. Greenwich Book Publishing Co. 1958.
          Clothbound.

          A prose sequel to Casey at the Bat.

                              *   *   *

12-117   LEGRAND HENDERSON (* pseudonym LeGrand)

12-117A   How Baseball Began in Brooklyn. Abingdon Press. 1958. Cloth-
          bound.

          A fictionalized account of a baseball rivalry between
          the Indians and Dutch settlers.

                              *   *   *

12-118   BEMAN LORD

12-118A   The Trouble with Francis. Henry Z. Walck. 1958. Clothbound.

12-118B   Bats and Balls. Henry Z. Walck. 1962. Clothbound.

12-118C   The Perfect Pitch. Henry Z. Walck. 1965. Clothbound.

12-119   SIDNEY OFFIT

12-119A   The Boy Who Won the World Series. Lothrop, Lee & Shepard. 1960. Clothbound.

12-119B   Soupbone. St. Martin's Press. 1963. Clothbound. Archway. 1968, reissue. Paperbound.

*   *   *

12-120   STEVE GELMAN

12-120A   Baseball Bonus Kid. Doubleday & Co. 1961. Clothbound.

*   *   *

12-121   ROBERT LECKIE (* pseudonym Mark Porter)

12-121A   Winning Pitcher. Grosset & Dunlap. 1962. Clothbound. Tempo Books. 1962, reissue. Clothbound.

*   *   *

12-122   ALL-STAR BASEBALL SERIES

12-122A   Fighting Southpaw. Whitey Ford and Jack Lang. Argonaut, Inc. 1962, 1963. Clothbound. J. Lowell Pratt. 1964, reissue. Paperbound.

12-122B   Behind the Plate. Yogi Berra and Til Ferndenzi. Argonaut, Inc. 1962. Clothbound. J. Lowell Pratt. 1963, reissue. Paperbound.

12-122C   Slugger in Right. Roger Maris and Jack Ogle. Argonaut, Inc. 1963. Clothbound.

12-122D   Danger in Center Field. Willie Mays and Jeff Harris. Argonaut, Inc. 1963. Clothbound. J. Lowell Pratt. 1964, reissue. Paperbound.

12-122E   New Blood at First. Bill Skowron and Jack Lang. Argonaut Inc. 1963. Clothbound.

          Playing tips, Hall of Fame.

*   *   *

12-123   TEX MAULE

12-123A   The Shortstop. David McKay Co. 1962. Clothbound.

12-123B   Beatty of the Yankees. David McKay Co. 1963. Clothbound.

12-123C   The Last Out. David McKay Co. 1964. Clothbound.

*   *   *

12-124   WILLIAM R. COX

12-124A   Wild Pitch. Dodd, Mead & Co. 1963. Clothbound.

12-124B   Big League Rookie. Dodd, Mead & Co. 1965. Clothbound.

12-124C   Big League Sandlotters. Dodd, Mead & Co. 1971. Clothbound.

*   *   *

12-125   HELEN D. FRANCIS

12-125A   Big Swat. Follett Publishing Co. 1963. Clothbound.

*   *   *

12-126   DAVID MALCOLMSON

12-126A   London: The Dog Who Made the Team. Duell, Sloan & Pearce. 1963. Clothbound.

         The story of a pitcher and his talented dog.

*   *   *

12-127   JEAN BETHELL

12-127A   Barney Beagle Plays Baseball. Grosset & Dunlap. 1963. Clothbound.

         First grade reader.

*   *   *

12-128   BILL KNOTT (* pseudonym Bill J. Carol)

12-128A   Circus Catch. Steck-Vaughn. 1963. Clothbound.

12-128B   Junk Pitcher. Follett Publishing Co. 1963. Clothbound. Signet. 1966, reissue. Paperbound.

12-128C   Clutch Single. Steck-Vaughn. 1964. Clothbound.

12-128D   Hit Away. Steck-Vaughn. 1965. Clothbound.

12-128E   Hard Smash to Third. Steck-Vaughn. 1966. Clothbound.

12-128F   Lefty's Long Throw. Steck-Vaughn. 1967. Clothbound.

12-128G   <u>Lefty Finds a Catcher.</u> Steck-Vaughn. 1968. Clothbound.

12-128H   <u>Lefty Plays First.</u> Steck-Vaughn. 1969. Clothbound.

12-128I   <u>Sandy Plays Third.</u> Steck-Vaughn. 1970. Clothbound.

12-128J   <u>Squeeze Play.</u> Steck-Vaughn. 1971. Clothbound.

12-128K   <u>High Fly to Center.</u> Steck-Vaughn. 1972. Clothbound.

*   *   *

12-129   JACK ZANGER

12-129A   <u>Baseball Sparkplug.</u> Doubleday & Co. 1964. Clothbound.

*   *   *

12-130   PAUL MOLLOY

12-130A   <u>A Pennant for the Kremlin.</u> Doubleday & Co. 1964. Clothbound. Avon Books. 1965, reissue. Paperbound.

> A humorous novel concerning the inheriting of the Chicago White Sox by the Soviet Union.

*   *   *

12-131   GEORGE KRAMER

12-131A   <u>The Left Hander.</u> G.P. Putnam's Sons. 1964. Clothbound.

12-131B   <u>Kid Battery.</u> G.P. Putnam's Sons. 1968. Clothbound.

*   *   *

12-132   NORVIN PALLAS

12-132A   <u>The Baseball Mystery.</u> I. Washburn. 1964. Clothbound.

*   *   *

12-133   O.B. JACKSON

12-133A   <u>Southpaw in the Mighty Mite League.</u> McGraw-Hill. 1965. Clothbound.

*   *   *

12-134   MARTIN QUIGLEY

12-134A   <u>Today's Game.</u> Viking Press. 1965. Clothbound.

A detailed account of a crucial major league game.

* * *

12-135   LEONARD KESSLER

12-135A   Here Comes the Strikeout. Harper & Row. 1965. Clothbound.

* * *

12-136   MONTREW DUNHAM

12-136A   Abner Doubleday. Bobbs, Merrill. 1965. Clothbound.
            A fictionalized account of the boyhood of the supposed
            "inventor" of baseball.

* * *

12-137   MIKE FREDERIC

12-137A   Frank Merriwell Returns. Award Books. 1965. Paperbound.

* * *

12-138   SCOTT CORBETT

12-138A   The Baseball Trick. Little, Brown & Co. 1965. Clothbound.

12-138B   The Baseball Bargain. Little, Brown & Co. 1970. Clothbound.

* * *

12-139   JAY HEAVILIN

12-139A   Fastball Pitcher. Doubleday & Co. 1965. Clothbound.

* * *

12-140   GENE OLSEN

12-140A   Three Men on Third. Westminster Press. 1965. Clothbound.
            Tempo Books. 1966, reissue. Paperbound.
            About a high school team composed of and coached
            by misfits.

* * *

12-141   DON CREIGHTON

12-141A   A Little League Giant. Steck Co. 1965. Clothbound.

12-141B   The Secret Little Leaguer. Steck Co. 1966. Clothbound.

12-141C   Little League Old-Timers. Steck Co. 1967. Clothbound.

12-141D   Little League Ball Hawk. Steck-Vaughn. 1968. Clothbound.

*   *   *

12-142   EDMUND O. SCHOLEFIELD

12-142A   Tiger Rookie. World Publishing Co. 1966. Clothbound.

12-142B   Li'l Wildcat. World Publishing Co. 1967. Clothbound.

12-142C   Maverick on the Mound. World Publishing Co. 1968. Clothbound.

*   *   *

12-143   ALFRED SLOTE

12-143A   Stranger on the Ball Club. J.B. Lippincott, Inc. 1966. Clothbound.

12-143B   Jake. J.B. Lippincott, Inc. 1971. Clothbound. Dell Publishing Co. 1972, reissue. Paperbound.

12-143C   Biggest Victory. J.B. Lippincott, Inc. 1972. Clothbound.

12-143D   My Father, The Coach. J.B. Lippincott, Inc. 1972. Clothbound.

*   *   *

12-144   K.L. GRANTHAM

12-144A   Baseball's Darkest Days. Exposition Press. 1966. Clothbound.

A story of an attempt to rig the World Series by electronic means.

*   *   *

12-145   LES ETTER

12-145A   Bull Pen Hero. Bobbs, Merrill. 1966. Clothbound.

The story of a rookie relief pitcher in the major leagues.

*   *   *

12-146   CHARLES M. SCHULTZ

12-146A   Charlie Brown's All-Stars. World Publishing Co. 1966. Cloth-
          bound.
              An account of the "Peanuts" baseball team.

                          *   *   *

12-147   MIKE NEIGOFF

12-147A   Two on First. Albert Whitman & Co. 1967. Clothbound.
              The story of a team pulling together against adversity.

                          *   *   *

12-148   CLEM PHILBROOK

12-148A   Ollie's Team and the Baseball Computer. Hastings House. 1967.
          Clothbound.

12-148B   Ollie's Team Plays Biddy Baseball. Hastings House. 1970.
          Clothbound.

                          *   *   *

12-149   WILLIAM C. GAULT

12-149A   The Lonely Mound. E.P. Dutton & Co. 1967. Clothbound.
              A pitcher's eye-view of the world.

12-149B   Stubborn Sam. E.P. Dutton & Co. 1969. Clothbound.

                          *   *   *

12-150   ROBERT WEAVER

12-150A   Nice Guy, Go Home. Harper & Row. 1968. Clothbound.
              An Amishman's experiences and conflicts in baseball
              and in the civil rights movement.

                          *   *   *

12-151   SYD HOFF

12-151A   Baseball Mouse. G.P. Putnam's Sons. 1969. Clothbound.
              The story of an infielder-mouse.

                          *   *   *

12-152   HAL HIGDON

12-152A   The Horse that Played Center Field. Holt, Rinehart & Winston.
           1969. Clothbound.

                              *   *   *

12-153   WILLIAM MACKELLAR

12-153A   Mound Menace. Follett Publishing Co. 1969. Clothbound.

                              *   *   *

12-154   ROBERT COOVER

12-154A   The Universal Baseball Association, Inc: J. Henry Waugh, Prop.
           Random House. 1968. Clothbound. Signet. 1969, reissue.
           Paperbound.

                   The story of a man who becomes obsessed by an in-
                   tricate baseball game which he has invented.

                              *   *   *

12-155   E.L. KONIGSBURG

12-155A   About the B'nai Bagels. Atheneum. 1969. Clothbound.

                   An amusing story about a woman Little League manager.

                              *   *   *

12-156   A.W. HARMON

12-156A   Base Hit. J.B. Lippincott, Inc. 1970. Clothbound.

                   A Little League pitcher is caught between his father's
                   ambitions for him and his own feelings.

                              *   *   *

12-157   HARRY FOREMAN

12-157A   Awk. Westminster Press. 1970. Clothbound.

                              *   *   *

12-158   RICHARD SUMMERS

12-158A   Ball-Shy Pitcher. Steck-Vaughn. 1970. Clothbound.

                              *   *   *

12-159   MORRIE TURNER

12-159A   <u>Nipper.</u> Westminster Press. 1970. Clothbound.

         A humorous cartoon story of a boys' baseball team.

*   *   *

12-160   LOUISE M. FOLEY

12-160A   <u>Somebody Stole Second.</u> Delacorte Press. 1972. Clothbound.

*   *   *

12-161   FICTION HOUSE

12-161A   <u>Baseball Stories.</u> 1939-53. Paperbound.

         Pulp magazine. Novels, novellettes, short stories, factual articles.

*   *   *

12-162   STANDARD MAGAZINES

12-162A   <u>Popular Baseball.</u> 1941-51. Paperbound.

         Pulp magazine. Novels, novelettes, short stories, factual articles.

*   *   *

12-163   FRANK OWEN, Ed.

12-163A   <u>Baseball Stories.</u> Lantern Press. 1948. Clothbound. Lantern Pocketbooks. 1964, reissue. Paperbound.

         A fiction anthology.

12-163B   <u>Teen-Age Baseball Stories.</u> Lantern Press. 1948. Clothbound. Grosset & Dunlap. 1948, reissue. Clothbound.

         A fiction anthology.

*   *   *

12-164   LEO MARGULIES

12-164A   <u>Baseball Roundup.</u> Cupples & Leon. 1948. Clothbound.

         A fiction anthology.

*   *   *

12-165   ABRAHAM L. FURMAN (pseudonym David Thomas)

12-165A   Teen-Age Stories of the Diamond. Lantern Press. 1950. Clothbound. Grosset & Dunlap. 1950, reissue. Clothbound.

             A fiction anthology.

*   *   *

12-166   CHARLES COOMBS, Ed.

12-166A   Young Readers' Baseball Stories. Lantern Press. 1950. Clothbound.

             An anthology of short stories.

12-166B   Young Readers' Stories of the Diamond. Lantern Press. 1950.
Clothbound. Grosset & Dunlap. 1950, reissue. Clothbound.

             Reissue of 12-166A.

*   *   *

12-167   EDITORS OF BOYS' LIFE

12-167A   Boys' Life Book of Baseball Stories. Random House. 1965.
Clothbound and Paperbound.

             A fiction anthology collected from Boys' Life magazine.

*   *   *

13. Humor

13-1   A Stitch in Time Saves the Nine. Wallace Peck. 1888. Booklet.

         Humorous illustrated descriptions of the players at each position.

13-2   The Krank: His Language and What It Means. Thomas W. Lawson. Rand, Avery Co. 1888. Booklet.

         "With covers made of the skin of a baseball." First "literary" work. Humorous sketches, verses, and glossary.

13-3   Crazy Baseball Stories. Robert Whitting. J.S. Ogilvie Publishing Co. 1902. Paperbound.

         Humorous anecdotes.

13-4   Humorous Stories of the Ball Field. Ted Sullivan. M.A. Donohue & Co. 1903. Paperbound.

         Amusing anecdotes of major league baseball.

13-5   Baseball Jokes, Stories and Poems. James Sullivan. Arthur Westbrook Co. 1906. Paperbound.

         Stories, anecdotes, humor.

13-6   Around the World with the Baseball Bugs. Jack Regan and Will E. Stahl. J. Regan & Co. 1910. Booklet.

         A collection of anecdotes and humor.

13-7   You Know Me, Al. Ring Lardner. Charles Scribner's Sons. 1916. Clothbound. 1925, reissue. Clothbound. World Publishing Co. 1945, reissue. Clothbound.

         Humorous fictional letters from a country boy turned major league pitcher.

13-8   Lose with a Smile. Ring Lardner. Charles Scribner's Sons. 1933. Clothbound.

Humorous correspondence between a ballplayer and his sweetheart covering spring training through the close of the season.

13-9   Ball and Bull. Charles C. Foster. November 14, 1917. Newspaper.

A humorous paper published in honor of the meeting of the National Association of Professional Baseball Leagues in Louisville, Kentucky.

13-10   Baseball Laughs. A. Saroni. 1925. Paperbound.

13-11   Humorous Baseball Stories. J.G. Taylor Spink. The Sporting News. 1927. Paperbound.

Major and minor league anecdotes.

13-12   Giving 'em Fitz. Tommy Fitzgerald. Louisville Courier Journal. 1946. Booklet.

Humorous incidents of the 1945 season, reprinted from columns in the Louisville Courier-Journal.

13-13   Tall Baseball Stories. Julius (Jiggs) Amarant. Association Press. 1948. Clothbound.

As told by Wee Willie Little, ex-mascot of the Lightfoot Lillies.

13-14   Diamond Laughs. A. (Rowsy) Rowswell. Ft. Pitt Brewing Co. 1948. Booklet.

Humorous anecdotes.

13-15   A Treasury of Baseball Humor. Stan Lomax and David Dachs*, (* pseudonym Dave Stanley), eds. Lantern Press. 1950, 1963. Clothbound.

Humorous stories and anecdotes by various authors.

13-16   Butchered Baseball. Frederick S. Pearson. A.S. Barnes & Co. 1952. Clothbound.

Humorous definitions of baseball terms.

13-17   Laughs of a Lifetime. Jay Hanna (Dizzy) Dean. Colson & Co., Inc. 1952. Paperbound.

Humorous stories and cartoons.

13-18   Dizzy Baseball. Jay Hanna (Dizzy) Dean. Greenberg. 1952. Booklet.

A humorous glossary of baseball terms used by broadcasters.

13-19   Complete Baseball Joke Book. Johan J. Smertenko* (pseudonym Dan Morgan). Stravon Publishers. 1953. Cover title of paperback edition: Laffed on Base. Clothbound and Paperbound.

Humorous anecdotes.

13-20   Curve Ball Laughs. Herman Masin. Scholastic Book Services. 1955. Paperbound. Pyramid Books. 1958, reissue. Paperbound.

Humorous anecdotes of the major leagues.

13-20A   Baseball Laughs. Herman Masin. Scholastic Book Services. 1964. Paperbound.

Abridged edition of 13-20.

13-21   How to Watch a Baseball Game. Fred Schwed, Jr. Harper Brothers. 1957. Clothbound.

A light-hearted explanation of the game. Anecdotes.

13-22   Comedians and Pranksters of Baseball. Fred Lieb, ed. The Sporting News. 1958, 1959. Cover title: Comedians of Baseball Down Through the Years. Paperbound.

Anecdotes by Bob Burnes. Diamond slang by J.G. Taylor Spink. The lighter side by Les Biederman.

13-23   Out of My League. George Plimpton. Harper & Row. 1961. Clothbound. Pocket Books. 1967, reissue. Paperbound.

A humorous autobiographical account of a writer's pitching experience in a major league exhibition game.

13-24   The Zen of Base and Ball. Tom Ziegler and Hal Barnell. Simon & Schuster. 1964. Clothbound.

A satire employing zen philosophy to explain the game of baseball. Japanese sketches.

13-25   The Best of Baseball. R.A. Bender. 1964. Booklet.

An amusing explanation of the game.

13-26   Love Letters to the Mets. Bill Adler. Simon & Schuster. 1965. Clothbound.

A compilation of humorous letters sent to the New York Mets and to Casey Stengel.

13-27   Laughs from the Dugout. Milton J. Shapiro. Julian Messner, Inc. 1966. Clothbound.

Humorous anecdotes and incidents.

13-28   Letters from Lefty. Mickey Herskowitz. Houston Post Co. 1966. Paperbound.

A collection of columns from the Houston Post, comprising humorous letters from an anonymous Houston Astro pitcher to his girl friend. Homespun insights into the Houston Club.

13-29   The Diamond Pinheads. J.A. Walpole. Theo. Gaus' Sons Inc. 1966. Paperbound.

A tale about a baseball player extraordinary.

13-30   Ed Hamman's Indianapolis Clowns Baseball Laff Books. Ed Hamman. Baseball Associates. No date. Booklet.

A joke book.

This is called a dead ball.

14. Drama, Verse, Ballads

14-1   A Base Hit. Thomas W. King. 1888. Booklet.

A three-act play.

14-2   A Base Hit. H. Bown. 1889. Booklet.

A musical comedy version of 14-1.

14-3   Casey at the Bat. Ernest Thayer. New Amsterdam Book Co.
1901. Booklet.

The most famous of all sports ballads. Written by
Thayer in 1888 and first published in the San Francisco Examiner on June 3, 1888. First appearance in
book form.

14-3A   Casey at the Bat. Ernest Thayer. M. Witmark & Sons. 1904.
Booklet.

DeWolf Hopper's version. Hopper, a singer and
comedian, popularized the poem through recitations
around the country.

14-3B   Casey at the Bat. Ernest Thayer. Henry G. Pert. 1905. Booklet.

With a tribute to Henry Chadwick.

14-3C   Casey at the Bat. Ernest Thayer. R.A. Lyon. 1906. Booklet.

14-3D   Casey at the Bat. Ernest Thayer. McClurg & Co. 1912. Clothbound.

14-3E   Casey at the Bat. Ernest Thayer. Franklin Watts. 1964. Clothbound.

Introduction by Casey Stengel.

14-3F   Casey at the Bat. Ernest Thayer. Prentice-Hall. 1964. Clothbound.

14-4 The Annotated Casey at the Bat. Martin Gardner. Clarkson N. Potter, Inc. 1967. Clothbound.

Background notes on the writing of the ballad by Ernest Thayer and its popularization through William DeWolf Hopper's recitations. A compilations of subsequent ballads about Casey.

14-5 The Baseball Crank. Frank Dumont. 1902. Booklet.

A humorous monologue for stage delivery.

14-6 Ballads of Baseball. W.A. Phelon. Metropolitan Syndicate Press. 1906. Paperbound.

Humorous verses.

14-7 The Baseball Bug. T.P. Jackson. 1908. Booklet.

A one-act play.

14-8 Two Strikes. Thacher H. Guild. W.H. Baker & Co. 1910. Booklet.

A baseball comedy in two acts.

14-9 Baseball Ballads. Grantland Rice. Tennessean Co. 1910. Clothbound. Finch Press. 1972, reissue. Clothbound.

Verses encompassing a variety of baseball topics.

14-10 Baseball-itis. V.H. Smalley. 1910. Booklet.

A one-act comedy.

14-11 Baseball at Spruceville. R. Nesmith. 1911. Booklet.

A rural farce.

14-12 Right Off the Bat. William F. Kirk. G.W. Dillingham Co. 1911. Clothbound.

Baseball ballads.

14-13 Baseballogy. Edward V. Cooks. Forbes & Co. 1912. Clothbound.

Baseball ballads incorporating mention of prominent players.

14-14 The Girl and the Pennant. Rida J. Young. Samuel French. 1913. Paperbound.

A baseball comedy in three acts.

14-15 Wanted - A Pitcher. M.N. Beebe. W.H. Baker & Co. 1913. Booklet.

A one-act farce.

14-16 Chick Gandil's Great Hit. Gilbert M. Eiseman. Press of Judd and Detweiler. 1914. Paperbound.

A paraphrase of 14-3, describing Gandil's hit which enabled the Washington Senators to win a game from the Boston Red Sox.

14-17 Play Ball! P.J. Connor. The Print Shop. 1914. Paperbound.

Baseball in verse and song.

14-18 Baseball. G.H. Kashner. 1916. Booklet.

A vaudeville sketch.

14-19 Us Baseballers and Our Baseball Teams. Marshall Breeden. 1923. Clothbound.

Facts, fiction, and verse covering each major and high minor league team.

14-20 Baseball Fanthology. Edward Lyman, ed. Edward Branch Lyman. 1924. Paperbound.

Hits and skits of the game. Baseball poems by various authors.

14-21 One Hundred Baseball Limericks. Charles M. Best. 1925. Booklet.

14-22 Batter Up. Moe Jaffe. Mills Music Inc. 1938. Paperbound.

Major league team songs. Photos.

14-23 Play Ball. Stanley Kauffman* (*pseudonym Spranger Barry). Samuel French. 1940. Booklet.

A one-act comedy concerning a wealthy minor league rookie.

14-24 Mose's Baseball Poems. Al (Mose) Bland. 1940. Paperbound.

Humorous poems in dialect covering the 1940 Cincinnati Reds' championship season.

14-25 Baseball in Music and Song. Harry Dichter. 1954. Paperbound.

A facsimile series of nineteenth century sheet music.

14-26 Damn Yankees. Jerrold Rosenberg. Random House. 1956. Clothbound.

The libretto of the musical based on 12-102A. The music was written by Rosenberg under the pseudonym Jerry Ross.

14-27   Dozens O'Diamond Ditties. H. Casey. 1959, 1963. Paper-
        bound.

        Words and music to 30 baseball songs.

14-28   The Old Ball Game. Tristram Coffin. Herder and Herder. 1971.
        Clothbound.

        An examination of baseball's myths, legends, super-
        stititions, and personalities. The contribution of the
        sport to America's language, literature, and conscious-
        ness.

"Pulling down"
a high fly.

15. Pictorials

15-1   Baseball As Viewed By a Muffin. S. Van Campen. Taber Brothers. 1867. Paperbound.

Humorous lithographs and captions of baseball scenes.

15-2   Baseball A.B.C. McLoughlin Brothers. 1885. Clothbound.

An alphabet primer using baseball terms for each letter. Color illustrations of baseball action. "A stands for Arthur, a boy full of fun; When baseball he plays, none like him can run." "Z stands for Zero, this boy rather tall; Who thinks there's no fun like a game of baseball."

15-3   Goodwin's Album. Goodwin Tobacco Co. 1888. Paperbound.

A baseball-shaped publication containing color sketches, player and team records covering the 1887 season.

15-4   Pictorial Baseball Album. C.D. Harper and William P. Mussey. Mussey & Harper. 1888. Booklet.

Illustrations and sketches of leading players. 1887 World Series box scores, other facts.

15-5   Art Gallery of Prominent Baseball Players of America. National Copper Plate Co. 1898. Booklet.

15-6   The Garry -- A Book of Humorous Cartoons: Pickings from the Diamond. J.F. Collins. 1904. Clothbound.

Humorous cartoons of Garry Hermann, owner of the Cincinnati Reds. A review of the 1904 season.

15-7   Sporting Life's Portfolio. The Sporting Life. 1905. Paperbound.

Team pictures of all major league and pennant-winning minor league teams.

15-8   Character Sketches, Prominent Fans, Baseball Stars and Other Sports. E.A. Bushnell. Hubbell Printing Co. 1907. Clothbound.

Humorous cartoons.

15-9   Smitty at the Ball Game. Walter Berndt. Cupples and Leon. 1929. Clothbound.

      Reprints of daily "Smitty" comic strips with a baseball theme.

15-10   Baseball, 1944. Victory Publishing Co. 1944. Paperbound.

      Reviews, schedules, records, rosters. Color pin-up pictures.

15-11   Hall of Fame Cartoons of Major League Ball Parks. Gene Mack. Globe Newspaper Co. 1947. Booklet.

      Sketches of each park with notations of famous feats and events.

15-12   Gene Mack's Hall of Fame Cartoons. Gene Mack. Library Broadcasting System. 1950. Booklet.

      Updated edition of 15-11.

15-13   Official Sportstamp Baseball Album. Eureka Sportstamps. 1949. Booklet.

      American and National League editions. Color stamps of players with sketches of each.

15-14   Topps Baseball Stamp Album. Topps Chewing Gum Co. 1961, 1962. Booklet.

      Album for player stamps. Sketches, statistics.

15-15   All-Star Baseball "Pin-Up" Book. Rudolph Gutmann and Sam Nisenson. Garden City Publishing Co. 1950. Clothbound.

      Pictures, playing instructions.

15-16   How to Get to First Base. Marc Simont and Red Smith. H. Schuman. 1952. Paperbound.

      Humorous illustrations and captions. Player caricatures.

15-17   Baseball Picture Book. William Jacobellis. 1952. Paperbound.

      Photos of major leaguers.

15-17A Baseball Pictorial. William Jacobellis. 1954, 1956. Paperbound.

      Continuation of 15-17.

15-18   Li'l Leaguer. Al Liederman. Pocket Books. 1960. Paperbound. Cartoons.

15-19   Baseball Photo and Autograph Album.   JKW Sports Publications.
         1960-63. Magazine.

         Seven hundred pictures of major leaguers.

15-20   Old Timer's Baseball Photo Album.   JKW Sports Publications.
         1960, 1963, 1966, 1971. Magazine.

         Three hundred pictures with averages, facts.

15-21   Major League All-Star Baseball Player Stamp Album.   Wheaties.
         General Mills. 1963. Paperbound.

         The history of the All-Star game.   Color stamps of
         the players in the 1963 game.   Statistics, historical
         sketch of baseball, Hall of Fame.

15-22   Major League Baseball Fun Coloring Book.   W. Cook and B. Fan-
         ter. 1963. Paperbound.

         Humorous captions.

15-23   What They're Really Saying at White Sox Park.   Chicago White
         Sox. 1965. Booklet.

         Photos of game action with humorous captions.

15-24   Playball. Chicago White Sox. 1967. Booklet.

         Photos of game action with humorous captions.

15-25   The Art of Baseball.   Howie Roberts.   Chicago White Sox.
         1967. Booklet.

         Reproductions of paintings with humorous baseball
         captions.

15-26   Little Big Leaguers. Earl Hochman. Arrow Books. 1967. Pa-
         perbound.

         Caricatures and cartoons of Little League baseball.

15-27   On the Sidelines. Earl Hochman. Arrow Books. 1967. Paper-
         bound.

         Caricatures and cartoons of Little League baseball.

16. Schedule and Record Booklets

16-1   American Manual of Baseball. E.B. Patterson. Baseball Manual
        Publishing Co. 1879, 1880. Booklet.

        Rosters, umpires, schedules. The 1880 edition includ-
        ed averages.

16-2   Official Schedule and Score of the National League. Kenney
        Co. 1880. Booklet.

        List of clubs, averages, umpires.

16-3   Official Schedule of the National League of Professional Baseball
        Clubs. A.C. Stevens Co. 1881. Booklet.

        Blocks for scores and tabular results.

16-4   League Games. Aldine Printing Co. 1882. Booklet.

        With score blanks.

16-5   Official Schedule, Baseball Games Throughout the United States.
        W.A. Andrews. Billstein & Son. 1884. Booklet.

        Home and away schedule of each major and minor
        league team.

16-6   League Schedule and Game Book. Wright & Ditson. 1884. Book-
        let.

        Player and umpire rosters. Blanks for runs, hits,
        errors.

16-7   Champion Pocket League Schedule. Wright & Ditson. 1888.
        Booklet.

16-8   Eddleman's Pocket Baseball Schedule. Henry W. Eddleman. 1884.
        Booklet.

        Boxes for game scores.

16-9   Official Schedule of League Games. A.G. Spalding & Brothers.
        1889. Booklet.

16-10   Daily Schedule of League Games. Chicago & Northwestern Rail-
         way. Poole Brothers. 1889-93. Booklet.

16-11   Daily Schedule of the National League and Players' League Base-
         ball Games. Chicago Daily News. 1890.- Booklet.

16-12   Hughes' Official Baseball Schedule. Fred B. Hughes. 1891.
         Booklet.

              Schedule of the Western Association. Major league
              records.

16-13   Little Casino Schedule of the National League and American As-
         sociation. Charles A. Leimgruber. 1891-98. Booklet.

              Blanks for runs, hits, errors, pitchers. Records.

16-14   The Official Baseball Schedule for the Southern Association and
         National League. D. Oscar Groff. 1894. Booklet.

              Scorecards, recapitualtion sheets, and a sketch of
              Savannah, Georgia.

16-15   Brooklyn Daily Eagle Baseball Schedules. Brooklyn Daily Eagle.
         1895. Booklet.

16-16   Baseball Schedule of the National League and American Associa-
         tion. Emil Grossman. 1895. Booklet.

              Unusual facts.

16-17   Official Schedule of the National League and American Associa-
         tion. L. Laffan. 1896. Booklet.

16-18   Official American League Baseball Schedule and Record. Myers
         Co. 1900. Booklet.

              First publication covering the American League.

16-19   Official and Complete Schedule of the National League. Union
         Cigar Co. 1900. Booklet.

16-20   Sporting Life's Official Schedule and Record Book. The Sporting
         Life Publishing Co. 1904-07. Booklet.

              Separate American and National League editions.
              Schedules, averages, records, team pictures.

16-20A   Sporting Life's Official Playing Schedule. The Sporting Life Pub-
         lishing Co. 1908-14. Booklet.

              Continuation of 16-20.

16-21   Napolean Lajoie's Official Schedule and Records. American
         League Publishing Co. 1906-08. Booklet.

Separate American and National League editions. Schedules, averages, record, team pictures.

16-22   National League Schedule. Chicago Cubs. 1907. Booklet.

16-23   Baseball Schedule Book. Baseball Publishing Co. 1912. Booklet. American Association playing schedule.

16-24   Official Playing Schedule. M.J. O'Regan. 1916. Booklet. American, National, and Eastern Leagues.

16-25   Major and Minor Leagues Official Baseball Schedules. John L. Glaser. Herald-Nathan Press. 1931. Booklet.

Coverage of major and high minor leagues. Boxes for innings and runs, percentage tables.

16-26   Texaco Baseball Score Book. Hal Totten. Texaco, Inc. 1936, 1937. Booklet.

Schedules, records, facts. Chicago White Sox and Cubs photos and rosters.

16-27   Baseball Facts. J.M. Sheehan. C.H. Pearson. 1937-59. Booklet.

Records, statistics. Overprinted by various commercial firms for advertising purposes. Titles of overprinted editions vary.

16-27A   The Original Baseball Facts. M.J. Sheehan, ed. C.H. Pearson. 1960-to date. Booklet.

Continuation of 16-27.

16-28   Baseball Calendar. A. Goes. 1939-41. Booklet.

Overprinted for advertising purposes by various firms. Review, all-time records, biographies, facts, schedules.

16-29   Baseball Schedules. New York Times. 1939. Booklet.

American, National, and International League Schedules.

16-30   Square Deal Baseball Schedule and Record Book. Square Deal Racing Syndicate. 1939-42. Booklet.

16-31   Baseball Schedules and Statistics. Mascot Racing Syndicate. 1940. Booklet.

Club records, statistics, data.

16-32   Brown-Forman's Baseball Schedule. Brown-Forman Distillers.

1948-62. Booklet.

Major and minor league schedules and facts.

16-33 Professional Baseball Schedule and Information Handbook. Premo Sport Publications. 1951-52. Booklet.

Schedules, records, data. Overprinted by various firms for advertising purposes. Titles of overprinted editions vary.

16-33A Baseball Schedule. Premo Sport Publications. 1953-58. Booklet.

Continuation of 16-33.

16-33B Baseball Schedule and Information Handbook. Premo Sports Publications. 1959-to date. Booklet.

Continuation of 16-33A.

16-34 Baseball. Union Paste Co. 1951. Booklet.

Records, statistics, data.

16-35 Baseball Schedule and Record Book. Athletic Publications. 1952-61. Booklet.

Records, rosters, Hall of Fame, World Series. Overprinted by various firms for advertising purposes.

16-36 Baseball Major and Minor Leagues Schedules, Statistics, Information Guide. Woodrow Press. 1952-54. Booklet.

Schedules, facts, statistics, records. Overprinted by various firms for advertising purposes.

16-37 Kessler Baseball Fans' Guide. C.H. Pearson. 1953-to date. Booklet.

Rosters, records, statistics.

16-38 Baseball. C.H. Pearson. 1953-56. Booklet.

Records, World Series review, data.

16-39 Baseball Handbook. National Research Bureau of Chicago. 1953, 1954. Booklet.

Records, data. photos.

16-40 At a Glance Six-League Baseball Schedule. Novel Printing Co. 1954. Booklet.

Major and minor league schedules. Records.

16-41 "Whitey" White Owl Baseball Almanac. Gus Steiger. White

Owl Cigars. 1954. Booklet.

Records, rosters, data, facts.

16-42   Roster and Schedule, Dodgers, Giants, Yankees, Phillies. Curtis Paper Co. 1955. Booklet.

Rosters, records, schedules.

16-43   Baseball Handbook and Schedules. The Sporting News. 1955-64. Booklet.

Rosters, photos, records, data.

16-44   Official American and National League Schedules and Records. The Sporting News. 1965-to date. Booklet.

16-45   Baseball Schedule. Allied Photo-Litho Plate Service. 1955. Booklet.

Daily major and minor league schedules.

16-46   Baseball Handbook and Schedules. United Press International. 1956-to date. Booklet.

Overprinted by various commercial firms for advertising purposes.

16-47   Game-of-the-Week Baseball Guide. Masthead Corp. 1959. Booklet.

Rosters, schedules, statistics, records.

16-48   Baseball Schedules. Chicago Steel Service Co. 1959. Booklet.

Major and minor league schedules.

16-49   Gil Hodges' 1960 Baseball Schedule and Fact Book. J.M. Sheehan. C.H. Pearson. 1960. Booklet.

Previews, rosters, records, schedules.

16-50   Baseball's Incredible Year. Major League Baseball. The Benjamin Co. 1968. Booklet.

Team previews, rosters, schedules.

16-51   The Family TV Baseball Handbook. Zander Hollander. Associated Features. 1968. Booklet.

Rosters, reviews, schedules.

17. Calculators

17-1   Maxfield's Table of Baseball Percentages. C.E. Maxfield. Pioneer Press. 1889. Paperbound.

       Fold-out chart.

17-2   Chicago Daily News Baseball Percentage Tables. Victor F. Lawson. Chicago Daily News. 1891. Paperbound.

17-3   Kelley's System of Baseball Percentage. Thomas H. Kelley. 1891. Paperbound.

       Including forms for player and team records.

17-4   Percentage Book of Baseball. C. Tutty. 1900. Paperbound.

17-5   Baseball Percentage Book. John B. Foster. A.G. Spalding & Brothers. 1905. Booklet.

       Percentage tables to calculate club standings.

17-6   Ready Reckoner of Club Standings. John B. Foster. A.G. Spalding & Brothers. 1905, 1908, 1912, 1914, 1915, 1923, 1927, 1935. Booklet.

17-7   Ready Reckoner of Baseball Percentages. John B. Foster. A.G. Spalding & Brothers. 1908, 1912, 1914, 1915, 1923, 1927, 1935. Booklet.

17-8   Ready Reckoner of Club Standings. The Sporting News. 1946, 1948, reissue. Booklet.

       Percentage tables arranged according to games won.

17-8A   Ready Reckoner of Baseball Club Standings. The Sporting News. 1963. Booklet.

       Continuation of 17-8.

17-8B   Ready Reckoner of Team Standings. Rudolph Weber. The Sporting News. 1967. Booklet.

       Revised and amplified edition of 17-8.

17-9   Ready Reckoner of Baseball Percentages. The Sporting News. 1947. Booklet.

17-10   Batting Averages at a Glance. Paul Rickart. The Sporting News. 1952, 1960, reissue, 1962, 1965, reissue. Paperbound.

        At-bat and hit tables.

17-11   Batting and Pitching Averages at a Glance. The Sporting News. 1966, 1967. Paperbound.

        Tables for determining batting, pitching, and fielding averages.

17-12   Table of Baseball Percentages. William H. Floody. Brandow Printing Co. 1908. Clothbound.

17-13   Compilers' Baseball Batting Average Calculator. C.C. Kerr. Sentinel Printing Co. 1912. Paperbound.

        Tables arranged by times at bat.

17-14   Moreland's Percentage Tables of 220 Games. George Moreland. Moreland News Bureau. 1913. Paperbound.

17-15   The Baseball and Bowling Standard Calculator. Carl H. Baumgarten and Joseph Gorski. Drovers Journal Press. 1915. Clothbound.

        Team percentages, batting, fielding, and pitching averages, earned run averages, base stealing and run scoring figures.

17-16   Handy: A Compendium of Baseball Percentages. Morris Uri. 1924. Paperbound.

        Batting and pitching averages, team percentages.

17-17   Baseball's Pot of Gold and O.K. Guide. The Mirror-Review. 1933. Booklet.

        Betting systems, baseball glossary, team rosters.

17-18   Picking the Winners. Samuel Georgeson. 1947. Booklet.

17-19   Baseball Hi-Scores. Novel Printing Co. 1949. Booklet.

        An obscure numbers system.

17-20   Baseball Performance Index. Edwin Bartee. 1952. Paperbound.

        A new method for determining player efficiency.

17-21   Baseball Confidential. Mort Lowry. Baseball Confidential, Inc. 1960. Booklet.

        Player ratings according to a system which calculates

offensive percentage.

17-22   <u>What Are the Odds?</u> Baseball-For-Fans Publications. 1968-to
         date. Paperbound.

         Performance odds calculated for all major league
         players.

17-23   <u>Inside the Pitcher E.R.A.</u> Baseball-For-Fans Publications. 1968.
         Paperbound.

         An analysis and critique of pitcher earned run average
         calculations.

17-24   <u>The Baseball Rating Handbook.</u> Robert Kalich. A.S. Barnes &
         Co. 1969. Clothbound and Paperbound.

         A mathematical player rating system in which points
         are assigned to six categories. Ratings of current
         major leaguers and all-time stars. Profiles of great
         players, managers, and teams.

17-25   <u>How to Pick the Winner of a Baseball Game.</u> Stephen Chaplin.
         Lem Publishing Co. 1970. Paperbound.

         Pitcher and team factors, evaluating a game.

17-26   <u>Earned Run Averages at a Glance.</u> Negamco. 1970. Paper-
         bound.

18. Economic Matters

General

18-1   Millenium Plan of the Sporting Life. Francis Richter. The Sport-
        Life. 1888. Booklet.

        Reprinted from the December 7, 1887 issue of Sporting
        Life. A plan for strengthening organized baseball by
        reorganizing the National Agreement in order to halt
        major league exploitation of the minors.

18-2   How to Make Money in Baseball. Frederick G. Page. 1910.
        Title page: Baseball Secrets. Booklet.

        How to make $1,000-$5,000 a year in the baseball
        business by promoting and managing your own club.

18-3   Report by the Bureau of Franchises upon the Application of the
        Automatic Scoreboard Co., Inc. Board of Estimate and Apportion-
        ment, City of New York. M.B. Brown Printing & Binding Co.
        1917. Booklet.

        An application to construct, maintain, and operate
        electrical conductors in New York City for the pur-
        pose of operating automatic baseball scoreboards to
        be located on the premises of subscribers.

18-4   Final Report of the Clark C. Griffith Ball and Bat Fund. Charles
        Genslinger. 1919. Clothbound.

        The fund was started during World War I to provide
        balls and bats for troop recreation.

18-5   The Law of Baseball. J. Norman Lewis and James P. Durante.
        New York Law Journal. 1945. Booklet.

        An explanation of the baseball contract.

18-6   The Unionization of Baseball. Richard Armstrong. Princeton Uni-
        versity. 1947. Paperbound.

        A college thesis.

18-7   American Baseball Needs Four Major Leagues. H.D. Robins.
        Western Technical Press. 1947. Paperbound.

        Potential sites for new teams. A suggested program
        for expansion. Population and attendance figures. A
        plan for four Class AAA minor leagues.

18-8   The Business Side of Major League Baseball. Robert W. Smith.
        Princeton University. 1948. Paperbound.

        A college thesis.

18-9   Organized Baseball. Peter S. Craig. Oberlin College. 1950.
        Paperbound.

        A college thesis discussing the evolution of organized
        baseball, the player's status, baseball and the law,
        financial management of the game.

18-10   Monopsony in Manpower: Organized Baseball Meets the Antitrust
        Laws. Peter S. Craig. Yale Law Journal. 1953. Paperbound.

        An examination of the baseball contract.

18-11   So You Want to Run a Ball Club. Milt Woodard and J.G. Tay-
        lor Spink. The Sporting News. 1951. Booklet.

        Administrative facts from all viewpoints with a dis-
        cussion of each facet.

18-12   Baseball Is Their Business. Harold Rosenthal, ed. Random House.
        1952. Clothbound.

        Advice and information on business careers within or-
        ganized baseball by various officials. Scouting,
        broadcasting, managing, record keeping, etc.

18-13   Can You Buy a Baseball Star? Fred Lieb. Packard Motor Car
        Co. 1953. Booklet.

        Sketches of players obtained by purchase from other
        teams or by bonus payments.

18-14   Making Money in the Minors. Bill Leighty. Packard Motor Car
        Co. 1954. Booklet.

        An account of the successful return to minor league
        baseball by Peoria, Illinois.

18-15   The Onus of the Bonus. Harold Rosenthal. Packard Motor Car
        Co. 1955. Booklet.

        Sketches, records, photos of bonus players who failed
        and succeded in the major leagues.

18-16   The Baseball Player. Paul Gregory. Public Affairs Press. 1956.

Clothbound.
A discussion of the individual player's monetary value, player rewards, legal aspects of the game.

18-17   The Baseball Players' Labor Market. Simon Rottenberg. Journal of Political Economy. 1956. Booklet.
A criticism of the reserve clause.

18-18   Ball, Bat and Bar. Harold Seymour. Cleveland-Marshall Law Review. 1957. Booklet.
An evaluation of the reserve clause.

18-19   Baseball and Softball Gloves. U.S. Tariff Commission. 1961. Paperbound.
A report in response to President Kennedy's request for information on tariff prices.

18-20   Baseball: The Game, the Career, the Opportunity. Frank Slocum. Baseball Commissioner's Office. 1963. Booklet.
Published for prospective players. A discussion of opportunities, education, travel, security.

18-21   Major League Baseball Players Benefit Plan. Major League Baseball Pension Committee. 1963. Paperbound.
A detailed explanation of the plan.

18-22   A Financial Analysis of the Major League Baseball Players Benefit Plan. James Hannan. New York University Graduate School. 1965. Paperbound.
A thesis prepared by Hannan, a major league pitcher, as a requirement for his Master of Business Administration degree.

18-23   No Joy in Mudville. Dr. Ralph Andreano. Schenkman Publishing Co. 1965. Clothbound.
An economic study of baseball since 1950, with a pessimistic forecast of its future.

18-24   The Economic Impact of the Braves on Atlanta. William Schaffer, George Houser and Robert Weinberg. Industrial Management Center, Georgia Institute of Technology. 1967. Booklet.
An assessment of the economic benefits to Atlanta, Georgia, as the result of the obtaining of a major league baseball franchise.

18-25   The Development of Organized Baseball's Government. Jeffrey T. Mortimer. Bard College. 1967. Clothbound.

A college thesis.

18-26   A Proposal to Create a New Baseball League. James Maloney.
          1971. Paperbound.

          A privately-printed proposal to create publicly-held
          city teams.

Congressional Hearings

18-27   Monuments to Symbolize the National Game. Robert Luce. U.S.
          Congress. 1924. Paperbound.

          Hearings before the House of Representatives.

18-28   Organized Baseball. U.S. Congress. 1952. Paperbound.

          Report of the Monopoly Subcommittee.

18-29   Broadcasting and Televising Baseball Games. U.S. Congress.
          1953. Paperbound.

          Report of the Interstate and Foreign Commerce Com-
          mission concerning hearings on a bill to authorize
          rules.

18-30   Subjecting Professional Baseball Clubs to the Antitrust Laws. U.S.
          Congress. 1954. Paperbound.

          Hearings before a Subcommittee of the U.S. Senate
          Judiciary Committee.

18-31   Organized Professional Team Sports. U.S. Congress. 1958, 1960.
          Paperbound.

          Hearings to make the antitrust laws and FTC Act ap-
          plicable to baseball, and to limit the applicability of
          such laws so as to exempt certain aspects of baseball
          and football.

18-32   Statement of Organized Baseball on the Professional Sports Anti-
          trust Act of 1960. U.S. Congress. 1960. Booklet.

          A statement in defense of baseball by Ford Frick,
          Warren Giles, Joseph Cronin, and George Taitman.

18-33   Organized Baseball and the Congress. Paul A. Porter. Baseball
          Commissioner's Office. 1961. Booklet.

          A review and chronology from 1950-60.

18-34   Pro Athletes and Senate Bill 2391. Leslie O'Connor. Baseball
          Commissioner's Office. 1964. Paperbound.

A discussion of baseball's reserve clause.

Legal Proceedings

18-35   Robert L. Graham, et al vs. Charles D. Gaither. Court of Appeals of Maryland. 1921. Paperbound.

An appellee's brief concerning a petition to abolish Sunday baseball in Maryland. Petition was denied.

18-36   Federal Baseball Club of Baltimore, Inc. vs. National League of Professional Baseball Clubs and American League of Professional Baseball Clubs. U.S. Supreme Court. 1922. Two volumes. Clothbound.

When the Federal League was disbanded in 1915 the American and National Leagues compensated all the teams except Baltimore. The Baltimore Club sued and was awarded damages by a circuit court. The major leagues appealed and in 1922 the Supreme Court, in a landmark decision, ruled that organized baseball was not subject to anti-trust laws.

18-37   Milwaukee American Association and St. Louis American League Baseball Clubs vs. K.M. Landis and Fred Bennett. District Court of the United States. 1930.

A suit involving the reserve clause.

18-37A   Milwaukee American Association and St. Louis American League Baseball Clubs vs. K.M. Landis and Fred Bennett. U.S. Circuit Court of Appeals. 1930, 1931. Paperbound.

18-38   Fred Martin and Max Lanier against Albert B. Chandler and Organized Baseball. District Court of the United States for the Southern District of New York. 1948. Paperbound.

Memorandum in opposition to motion for preliminary injunction.

18-38A   Fred Martin and Max Lanier vs. St. Louis National League Baseball Club. U.S. Circuit Court of Appeals. 1948. Paperbound.

A suit filed in connection with Martin's and Lanier's suspension after jumping to the Mexican League.

18-38B   Fred Martin and Max Lanier vs. St. Louis National League Baseball Club. District Court of the United States for the Southern District of New York. 1949. Paperbound.

Answer of defendant St. Louis National Baseball Club.

18-38C   Fred Martin and Max Lanier against Albert B. Chandler and the National League except St. Louis National League Baseball Club. District Court of the United States for the Southern District of New York. 1949. Paperbound.

> Answer of defendants Ford C. Frick and members of the National League except St. Louis National League Baseball Club.

18-38D   Fred Martin and Max Lanier against Albert B. Chandler and Organized Baseball. District Court of the United States for the Southern District of New York. 1949. Paperbound.

> Several answers of president and members of the American League.

18-38E   Documents in the Case of Martin and Lanier vs. Chandler, et al. Pandick Press. 1950. Two volumes. Paperbound.

18-39   Daniel L. Gardella against Albert B. Chandler and Organized Baseball. U.S. Court of Appeals for the Second Circuit. 1949. Paperbound.

> A suit filed in connection with Gardella's suspension after jumping to the Mexican League.

18-40   The Gardella Case: Organized Baseball and the Anti-Trust Laws. Fred W. Trezise. Harvard Law School. 1949. Paperbound.

> A law school thesis which discusses the law suit brought by player Danny Gardella against baseball.

18-41   Presentation before Commissioner A.B. Chandler on Behalf of Dodier Realty and Investment Co. St. Louis Law Printing Co. 1949. Paperbound.

> A petition requesting that the St. Louis Cardinals vacate Sportsman's Park.

18-41A   Dodier Realty and Investment Co. vs. St. Louis National Baseball Club, Inc. and American League Baseball Co. of St. Louis. Supreme Court of Missouri. 1950. Paperbound.

18-42   Baseball - Sport or Commerce. John Eckler. University of Chicago Law Review. 1949. Booklet.

> A review of past litigation involving baseball.

18-43   Walter J. Kowalski vs. Albert B. Chandler, George Trautman, and Cincinnati Baseball Club. U.S. Court of Appeals for the Sixth District. 1951. Three volumes: 1. Appellee's Brief. 2. Replay Brief of Plaintiff-Appellant. 3. Brief of Plaintiff-Appellant. Paperbound.

> A suit involving the reserve clause.

18-43A   Walter J. Kowalski vs. Albert B. Chandler, et al. Supreme
          Court of the United States. Seven volumes: 1. Reply Brief of
          Petitioner. 1952. 2. Petition for Writ of Certiorari to the U.S.
          Court of Appeals for the Sixth District. 1952. 3. Brief for Res-
          pondents in Opposition to Petition for Certiorari. 1952. 4. Brief
          for Petition. 1953. 5. Petitioner's Reply Brief. 6. Brief for
          Respondents. 7. Transcript of Record. Paperbound.

18-44   Jack Corbett, et al vs. Albert B. Chandler. Supreme Court of
          the United States. Seven volumes: 1. Appellee's Brief. 1952.
          2. Reply Brief of Plaintiffs. 1952. 3. Reply Brief of Petitioners.
          1952. 4. Petition for Writ of Certiorari. 1952. 5. Brief of
          Respondents in Opposition to Petition for Certiorari. 1952. 6.
          On Writ of Certiorari to the U.S. Court of Appeals for the Sixth
          District. 1953. 7. Brief for Respondents. 1953. Paperbound.

          A suit brought by a minor league club owner in con-
          nection with the reserve clause.

18-45   State of Wisconsin vs. Milwaukee Braves, Inc., et al. Supreme
          Court of the United States. 1966. Paperbound.

          Petition for Writ of Certiorari to the Supreme Court
          of Wisconsin. A suit filed to prevent the Braves from
          moving to Atlanta.

18-46   George Earl Toolson vs. New York Yankees, Inc. U.S. Court of
          Appeals for the Ninth Circuit. No date. Paperbound.

          Appellee's reply brief. A suit filed in connection
          with the reserve clause.

19. Yearbooks

19-1   George Wright's Record Book of the Boston Club. George Wright. 1875. Booklet.

        Coverage of the 1875 season.

19-2   Who's Who in Boston Major League Baseball. Harold (Speed) Johnson. 1936. Paperbound.

        Photos, sketches, records of Boston Red Sox and Braves players.

19-3   How the Braves Won the Pennant in 1914. Kenneth M. Brett and W.J. Rosen. 1938. Paperbound.

        An account of the season, from spring training through the World Series, in which the Boston Braves rose from last place in July to win the pennant and World Series. Box scores of important games.

19-4   Milwaukee Braves, the Miracle Boys. William Sunners. National Library Publications. 1954. Paperbound.

        The story of the 1953 season, in which the Braves rose from seventh to second in their first season in Milwaukee. Sketches, statistics, records, box scores, photos.

19-5   Meet Your Braves. Milwaukee Journal. 1953. Booklet.

        Player sketches and photos of the Milwaukee Braves.

19-6   Atlanta Braves Photo Album. 1966. Magazine.

        Photos and autographs.

19-7   Ups and Downs of the Worcester Baseball Club. F.E. Pollard. 1880. Booklet.

        A review of the 1880 season.

19-8   St. Louis Browns Championship Baseball Club of the World. Merrell's Family Medicines. 1887. Booklet.

Pictures of players with endorsements of a liniment. Historical sketch of the game.

19-9   Meet the Browns. Kellogg Co. 1937. Booklet.

Photos of St. Louis Browns players.

19-10   The 1959 Baltimore Orioles Story. Phillies Cigars. 1959. Booklet.

Records, statistics, rosters, sketches, photos.

19-11   Birds on the Wing. Gordon Beard. Doubleday & Co. 1967. Clothbound. 1967, reissue. Paperbound.

The story of the 1966 World Champion Baltimore Orioles. Photos.

19-12   Putting it All Together. Brooks Robinson and Red Bauer. Hawthorn Books. 1971. Clothbound.

An account of the Baltimore Orioles 1971 championship season by their star third baseman. Autobiographical recollections.

19-13   Sketches of the New York Baseball Club. June Rankin. R.K. Fox. 1887. Title page: The New York Baseball Club. Booklet.

Sketch and illustration of each player. History of baseball.

19-14   Sketches of the New York and Brooklyn Baseball Clubs. June Rankin. R.K. Fox. 1888. Title page: The New York and Brooklyn Baseball Clubs. Booklet.

Sketch and illustration of each player. History of baseball.

19-15   The Giants of New York. Gary Schumacher. New York Giants. 1947-49. Magazine.

Articles, pictures, history. Sketches, photos, statistics of current players.

19-16   The Incredible Giants. Tom Meany. A.S. Barnes & Co. 1955. Clothbound.

The story of the 1954 World Champion New York Giants.

19-17   The Brooklyn Dodgers. Dispatch Press. 1940. Booklet.

Team and player records and statistics.

19-18   The Dodgers Today and Yesterday in Brooklyn Baseball. Clinton H. Hoard and Charles Dexter. W.H. Baseball Publishing Co.

1941. Magazine.

Sketches and records of present and past teams.

19-19 Baseball's Beloved Bums. Joe Hasel. Weiser Publishing Co. 1947. Paperbound.

Sketches, photos of the Brooklyn Dodgers. Historical background. Averages, World Series records.

19-20 Los Angeles Dodgers, San Francisco Giants Scouting Report. Sports Illustrated. 1958. Booklet.

Strong points, new faces, general outlook, rosters. Issued to acquaint fans with the newly-arrived Brooklyn Dodgers and New York Giants.

19-21 Line Drives at the Pittsburgh Pirates. Pittsburgh Press. 1910. Booklet.

Records, sketches, photos.

19-22 The 1959 Pittsburgh Pirates Story. Phillies Cigars. 1959. Booklet.

Records, rosters, statistics, sketches, photos.

19-23 The World Champion Pittsburgh Pirates. Bill Surface and Dick Groat. Coward-McCann. 1961. Clothbound.

The story of the 1960 World Series winners. All-time records and roster.

19-24 Pittsburgh Pirates Photo Album. Foodland. Century Printing. 1969. Magazine.

Color photos.

19-25 Word's Baseball Album and Sketchbook, Detroit Tigers. Andrew H. Word. Houghton-Jacobson. 1912. Booklet.

Sketches, photos.

19-26 Detroit Tigers in Picture. Free Press Photogravure Co. 1934. Booklet.

Player sketches and photos.

19-27 Following the Tigers. Al Nagler. 1935. Booklet.

Player sketches, records, and statistics of the Detroit Tigers. By the Detroit play-by-play announcer.

19-28 Tiger Facts. Fred T. Smith. 1951-53. Booklet.

Sketches, records of current Detroit Tiger players.

19-29   Year of the Tiger. Jerry Green. Coward-McCann. 1969.
Clothbound.

A daily account of the Detroit Tigers' 1968 pennant
and World Series winning season.

19-30   Sketchbook of the Chicago White Sox. 1915. Booklet.

19-31   Sketch Book and Complete Records of Our Sox and Cubs. A. Prusank. 1919. Booklet.

Sketches, records of Chicago White Sox and Cubs
players.

19-32   The Cubs of 1934. Murray Book Corp. 1934. Title page: Complete Roster of Chicago Cubs. Magazine.

Records, sketches, photos of the 1934 Chicago Cubs.

19-33   The Cubs of 1935. Harold (Speed) Johnson. 1935. Booklet.

Records, sketches, photos of the 1935 Chicago Cubs.

19-34   Who's Who in Chicago Major League Baseball. Harold (Speed)
Johnson. 1936-38. Paperbound.

Photos, sketches, records of Chicago White Sox and
Cubs players.

19-35   Chicago Cubs Autograph Book. Chicago National League Ball
Club. 1937. Booklet.

19-36   Player's Records, Chicago National League Ball Club. Neely
Printing Co. 1939. Booklet.

Player records and sketches.

19-36A   Chicago Cubs Players' History and Record Book. Neely Printing
Co. 1940, 1941. Booklet.

Continuation of 19-36.

19-36B   Chicago Cubs Player Roster and Record Book. Neely Printing Co.
1942. Booklet.

Continuation of 19-36A.

19-37   Picture Parade of the Chicago Cubs. 1946. Booklet.

19-38   The 1959 Chicago Cubs Story. Phillies Cigars. 1959. Booklet.

Records, rosters, statistics, sketches, photos.

19-39   Sketchbook of the Cleveland Indians. W.R. Blackwood. Davis
& Cannon Printers. 1918. Booklet.

Sketches, statistics, records.

19-40   Baseball Reference and Scoring Book. Jimmy Dudley.   Standard
          Brewing. 1948. Paperbound.

              Data on the Cleveland Indians.

19-41   Jimmy Dudley's Cleveland Indians Picture Scorebook. Jimmy Dud-
          ley. 1957. Paperbound.

              Player statistics, records, scoresheets.

19-42   Reds. Cino Publishing Co. 1930. Booklet.

              Cincinnati Reds' photos and sketches.

19-43   Pennant Race. Jim Brosnan. Harper & Row. 1962. Clothbound.
          Dell Publishing Co. 1963, reissue. Paperbound.

              The story of the 1961 pennant-winning Cincinnati Reds
              by their star relief pitcher. A candid view of the
              game and its players.

19-44   Cincinnati Riverfront Stadium Opening Souvenir Magazine. Tom
          Seeberg, ed. Cincinnati Reds. 1970. Magazine.

              A description of the new stadium.

19-45   New York Mirror Yankees Guide. Charles Segar. New York
          Mirror. 1937. Booklet.

19-46   New York Mirror Yanks, Giants, Dodgers Guide. New York
          Mirror. 1938. Booklet.

19-47   Ballplayers are Human, Too. Ralph Houk. G.P. Putnam's Sons.
          1962. Clothbound.

              The inside story of the 1961 season, by the manager
              of the New York Yankees. In the clubhouse, on the
              bench, team meetings, disciplinary problems. Yankee
              techniques, Houk's tactics, photos. Text transcribed
              from tape recordings.

19-48   Photo Book of the Washington Senators. Herbert Smart, Jr. 1947.
          Booklet.

19-49   Introducing the 1950 Washington Senators. 1950. Magazine.

              Picture album.

19-50   The Whiz Kids. Harry Paxton. David McKay Co. 1950. Cloth-
          bound.

              The story of the pennant-winning 1950 Philadelphia
              Phillies.

19-51   The 1959 Philadelphia Phillies Story. Phillies Cigars. 1959.
          Booklet.

Records, rosters, statistics, sketches, photos.

19-52   The Boston Red Sox of 1955. E.J. Chouinard. Meador Publishing Co. 1956. Clothbound.

Game scores, records, statistics.

19-53   The Impossible Dream. Bill McSweeny. Coward-McCann. 1968. Clothbound.

The story of the 1967 pennant-winning Boston Red Sox.

19-54   The Long Season. Jim Brosnan. Harper & Bros. 1960. Clothbound. Dell Publishing Co. 1961, reissue. Paperbound.

An inside account of the 1959 St. Louis Cardinals season by their star relief pitcher. A candid view of the game and its players.

19-55   Cardinals Caravan. Anheuser-Busch. 1969. Booklet.

St. Louis Cardinal team and player facts, statistics, records.

19-56   Original Minnesota Twins Cartoon Book. Promotions Diversified. 1961. Paperbound.

Player sketches and records.

19-57   The Minnesota Twins Coloring Book. Bob Blewett. Phelps Offset Printing. 1965. Booklet.

Captioned sketches.

19-58   Paul's Post. Paul Foss Printing & Litho. 1970. Booklet.

Minnesota Twins' player sketches and photos.

19-59   Highlights - Kansas City A's Baseball Season. Station WDAF. 1962-67. Booklet.

Review of the season by play-by-play announcers Monte Moore and George Bryson.

19-59A   Highlights - Exciting Days with the Oakland A's. Monte Moore. 1968-to date. Booklet.

Continuation of 19-59.

19-60   They're Our Mets. Joe King and Larry Fox. New York World Telegram. 1963. Booklet.

Reprinted from a series in the New York World Telegram. Player sketches and photos of the New York Mets.

19-61 Can't Anybody Here Play This Game. Jimmy Breslin. Viking Press. 1963. Clothbound. Avon Books. 1965, reissue. Paperbound.

 A humorous account of the 1962 New York Mets.

19-62 Shea Stadium Official Dedication Magazine. New York Mets. 1964. Magazine.

 Photos, roster of the New York Mets.

19-63 The New York Mets. Complete Sports. 1965. Magazine.

 Photos, feature stories.

19-64 Mets Coloring Book. Meredith Press. 1965. Paperbound.

 Captioned illustrations of the New York Met players.

19-65 The Year the Mets Lost Last Place. Paul Zimmerman and Dick Schaap. World Publishing Co. 1969. Clothbound. Signet. 1969. Paperbound.

 An account of the New York Mets' 1969 season from July 8-16, in which they battled toward an eventual pennant. Flashbacks to their previous ignominious seasons. The paperback edition contains a chapter covering the remainder of the season.

19-66 Amazing: The Miracle of The Mets. Joseph Durso. Houghton Mifflin Co. 1970. Clothbound.

 The story of the New York Mets 1969 championship season.

19-67 The Astros First Year in the Astrodome. Houston Sports Association, Inc. 1965. Booklet.

 Photos.

19-68 Team Roster Booklets. Booklet.

 Issued at start of season. Formats vary, but generally contain player sketches, records, data. Various titles.

19-68A Boston Braves. 1931-46.

19-68B Brooklyn Dodgers. 1928-40.

19-68C Chicago Cubs. 1922-41.

19-68D Cincinnati Reds. 1930-39.

19-68E New York Giants. 1927-39.

19-68F   Philadelphia Phillies. 1930-63.

19-68G   Pittsburgh Pirates. 1930-63.

19-68H   St. Louis Cardinals. 1930-47.

19-68I   Baltimore Orioles. 1954.

19-68J   Boston Red Sox. 1939-54.

19-68K   Chicago White Sox. 1933-46.

19-68L   Cleveland Indians. 1939-47.

19-68M   Detroit Tigers. 1932-47.

19-68N   New York Yankees. 1931-54.

19-68P   Philadelphia Athletics. 1930-51.

19-68Q   St. Louis Browns. 1923-51.

19-68R   Washington Senators. 1930-45.

19-69   Team Press Guides. Booklet and Paperbound.

        These evolved from the roster booklets. Issued to journalists at the beginning of the season. Rosters, records, sketches, reviews. Various titles.

19-69A   Atlanta Braves. 1966-to date.

19-69B   Boston Braves. 1947-52.

19-69C   Brooklyn Dodgers. 1941-57.

19-69D   Chicago Cubs. 1942-to date.

19-69E   Cincinnati Reds. 1940-to date.

19-69F   Houston Colts, Astros. 1962-to date.

19-69G   Los Angeles Dodgers. 1958-to date.

19-69H   Milwaukee Braves. 1960-65.

19-69I   Montreal Expos. 1969-to date.

19-69J   New York Giants. 1940-57.

19-69K   New York Mets. 1962-to date.

19-69L   Philadelphia Phillies. 1964-to date.

19-69M   Pittsburgh Pirates. 1964-to date.

19-69N   St. Louis Cardinals. 1948-to date.

19-69P   San Diego Padres. 1969-to date.

19-69Q   San Francisco Giants. 1958-to date.

19-69R   Baltimore Orioles. 1955-to date.

19-69S   Boston Red Sox. 1955-to date.

19-69T   California Angels. 1966-to date.

19-69U   Chicago White Sox. 1947-to date.

19-69V   Cleveland Indians. 1948-to date.

19-69W   Detroit Tigers. 1948-to date.

19-69X   Kansas City Athletics. 1955-67.

19-69Y   Kansas City Royals. 1969-to date.

19-69Z   Los Angeles Angels. 1961-65.

19-69AA   Milwaukee Brewers. 1970-to date.

19-69BB   Minnesota Twins. 1961-to date.

19-69CC   New York Yankees. 1955-to date.

19-69DD   Oakland Athletics. 1968-to date.

19-69EE   St. Louis Browns. 1952.

19-69FF   Seattle Pilots. 1969, 1970.

19-69GG   Texas Rangers. 1972.

19-69HH   Washington Senators. 1946-71.

19-70   Team Official Yearbooks, Modern Series. Magazine.
         History, player records, and sketches, team records,
         data, photos. Revised editions issued during season
         by many clubs. Various titles.

19-70A   Atlanta Braves. 1966-to date.

19-70B   Boston Braves. 1946-52.

19-70C   Brooklyn Dodgers. 1947-57.

19-70D   Chicago Cubs. 1948-57.

19-70E   Cincinnati Reds. 1947-to date.

19-70F   Houston Colts, Astros. 1962, 1964-66.

19-70G   Los Angeles Dodgers. 1958-to date.

19-70H   Milwaukee Braves. 1953-65.

19-70I   Montreal Expos. 1969-to date.

19-70J   New York Giants. 1947-57.

19-70K   New York Mets. 1962-to date.

19-70L   Philadelphia Phillies. 1949-to date.

19-70M   Pittsburgh Pirates. 1951-to date.

19-70N   St. Louis Cardinals. 1951-to date.

19-70P   San Diego Padres. 1969.

19-70Q   San Francisco Giants. 1958-to date.

19-70R   Baltimore Orioles. 1954-to date.

19-70S   Boston Red Sox. 1951-to date.

19-70T   California Angels. 1966, 1967.

19-70U   Chicago White Sox. 1948-70. 1948-63. Magazine. 1964-70. Paperbound.

19-70V   Cleveland Indians. 1948-to date.

19-70W   Detroit Tigers. 1955, 1957-to date.

19-70X   Kansas City Athletics. 1955-67.

19-70Y   Kansas City Royals. 1969-to date.

19-70Z   Los Angeles Angels. 1962-65.

19-70AA   Milwaukee Brewers. 1970, 1972.

19-70BB   Minnesota Twins. 1961-to date.

19-70CC	New York Yankees. 1950-to date.
19-70DD	Oakland Athletics. 1968-to date.
19-70EE	Philadelphia Athletics. 1949-54.
19-70FF	St. Louis Browns. 1950-52.
19-70GG	Seattle Pilots. 1969.
19-70HH	Washington Senators. 1950-68.
19-71	Jay Publishing Co. Yearbooks. Magazine.
19-71A	Kansas City Athletics. 1955, 1965.
19-71B	New York Yankees. 1955-65.

These were published in addition to the official team yearbooks. Jay also published the official yearbooks for various teams in various years.

19-72	Organization Sketch Books. William J. Weiss. Paperbound.

Yearly statistics for all players under contract to the major league club. Various titles. Dates are approximate.

19-72A	Atlanta Braves. 1969-to date.
19-72B	Chicago Cubs. 1969-to date.
19-72C	Cincinnati Reds. 1971-to date.
19-72D	Houston Astros. 1971-to date.
19-72E	Milwaukee Braves. 1955.
19-72F	Montreal Expos. 1970-to date.
19-72G	New York Mets. 1966-to date.
19-72H	Philadelphia Phillies. 1963-to date.
19-72I	San Francisco Giants. 1970-to date.
19-72J	St. Louis Cardinals. 1972.
19-72K	Boston Red Sox. 1971-to date.
19-72L	California Angels. 1966-to date.
19-72M	Chicago White Sox. 1967-to date.

19-72N   Cleveland Indians. 1967-to date.

19-72P   Detroit Tigers. 1969-to date.

19-72Q   Kansas City Royals. 1970-to date.

19-72R   Los Angeles Angels. 1965.

19-72S   New York Yankees. 1971-to date.

19-72T   Oakland Athletics. 1969-to date.

19-72U   Seattle Pilots. 1969.

19-72V   Texas Rangers. 1972.

19-72W   Washington Senators. 1963-71.

19-73   Major League All Stars. Greater Sports, Inc. 1950. Booklet.

              A guide to American and National League all-star
              teams making a post-season exhibition tour. Player
              sketches and records.

19-74   Golden Stamp Books. Golden Press. 1955. Magazine.

              Player sketches with color stamps.

19-74A   New York Giants.

19-74B   Brooklyn Dodgers.

19-74C   Milwaukee Braves.

19-74D   Cleveland Indians.

19-75   Royals Recipes. Lou Ann Carmean. Kansas City Royals. 1969.
              Paperbound.

              Favorite recipes of wives of the Kansas City Royals
              and Omaha Royals. Player sketches and photos.

19-76   Major League Baseball Players Association Yearbook Series. Major
              League Baseball Players Association. Sports Collectors, Inc. 1971.
              Today's (Team Name).

              Four sets covering all 24 teams. Statistics, schedules,
              color stamps of players.

19-77   Cactus League Yearbook. Ed Prell. Prell Press. 1971. Maga-
              zine.

              Issued to celebrate the 25th year of spring training in
              Arizona. Articles, records, photos covering the An-

gels, A's, Brewers, Cubs, Giants, Indians, and Padres.

No, this is not Macmonnies' Bacchante. It is the average pitcher showing the proper curves for a curved ball.

20. Minor League

General

20-1   <u>Spalding's Minor League Guide</u>. Henry Chadwick. A.G. Spalding & Brothers. 1889. Paperbound.

               Standings, individual and team statistics covering ten minor leagues. College records.

20-2   <u>Official Guide of the National Association of Professional Baseball Leagues</u>. Timothy H. Murnane. A.G. Spalding & Brothers. 1902-19. Booklet.

               Minor league history since 1883. Rules, major and minor league averages, records, facts.

20-3   <u>Minor League Digest</u>. Heilbroner Baseball Bureau. 1936-51. Baseball Blue Book, Inc. 1952-to date. Paperbound.

               Detailed statistical coverage of all minor league players. Administrative information.

20-4   <u>History of the National Association of Professional Baseball Leagues</u>. John B. Foster. National Association of Professional Baseball Leagues. 1926. Cover title: <u>National Association of Professional Baseball Leagues</u>. <u>Silver Jubilee</u>. Clothbound.

               Issued in honor of the 25th anniversary of the National Association. Organization, resumes of meetings, history of each league.

20-5   <u>The Story of Minor League Baseball</u>. Robert L. Finch, L.H. Addington and Ben M. Morgan. The National Association of Professional Baseball Leagues. 1953. Clothbound.

               History. Team, player, and league records.

20-6   <u>Humor among the Minors</u>. Edward Ashenback and Jack Ryder. M.A. Donohue & Co. 1911. Clothbound.

               Anecdotes, history, photos.

20-7   <u>Financial Controls for Minor League Baseball Operations</u>. Theodore

Herrick. Ohio State University. University Microfilms. 1959. Paperbound.

A college thesis.

20-8   A Minor League Directory. Raymond Nemec. 1971. Booklet.

A listing of minor leagues in operation from 1877–1901.

Administrative

20-9   National Association of Professional Baseball Leagues, Administrative Manuals. National Association of Professional Baseball Leagues. Paperbound.

20-9A   Minutes of Meeting. 1901–to date.

Report of the annual convention.

20-9B   Annual Report of the Secretary. 1902–to date.

Draft, reserve lists, National Board of Arbitration.

20-9C   Annual Convention. 1903–to date.

Minutes of meeting, registration list.

20-9D   Official Bulletin of the President-Treasurer. 1924–38.

Issued irregularly.

20-9E   President's Annual Report. 1933–to date.

20-9F   Private Telegraphic Code of the National Association of Professional Baseball Leagues. William G. Bramham. 1933. Clothbound.

A glossary of code words.

20-9G   Official Bulletin. 1933–46.

Issued monthly. Player trades and transfers.

20-9H   Bulletin. 1947–to date.

Continuation of 20-9G.

20-9I   Final Reserve List. 1934–to date.

Lists of players by teams and leagues.

20-9J   Administrative Rules and Regulations of Organized Baseball. 1937.

20-9K   Manual for Official Scorers and League Statisticians. 1940–49.

20-9L   Manual. 1946. Booklet.

        Explanations of rules, contracts, terms, etc.

20-9M   Instructions and Advice to Association Umpires. 1947-65.

20-9N   Manual for Umpires. 1966-to date.

        Continuation of 20-9M.

20-9P   Baseball Handbook for Club Executives. 1948.

        Digest of discussions and conclusions of the Baseball
        Executives Conference.

20-9Q   Highlights. 1948-to date.

        Records, standings, data covering each minor league.

20-9R   Qualification Register. 1949-to date.

        Lists of eligible players and the clubs to which they
        are under contract.

20-9S   Handbook. 1960-to date.

        Information for leagues and clubs. Golden Anniver-
        sary Edition in 1951 listed plans and program for 50th
        anniversary celebration.

20-10   Speeches Delivered at the Houston Promotional Clinic. National
Association of Professional Baseball Leagues. December 1954. Paperbound.

        Talks by minor league officials on various business
        topics.

20-11   National Association Baseball Almanac. National Association of
Professional Baseball Leagues. 1960. Magazine.

        Articles, features on minor league baseball.

20-12   Seventy Nights in a Ball Park. National Association of Professional Baseball Leagues. 1963. Paperbound.

        A guide for staging promotional "nights."

Biographical

20-13   The Real Baseball Story. Howard Palmer. Pageant Press. 1953.
Clothbound.

        An autobiographical account of a long minor league
        career.

20-14   Five Straight Errors on Ladies Day. Walter H. Nagle and Bryson Reinhardt. Caxton. 1965. Clothbound.

Autobiography, reminiscences, and observations of an old-time minor-league pitcher.

20-15   Low and Outside. Jerry Kettle. Coward-McCann. 1965. Clothbound.

An amusing autobiographical account of a five-year minor league career.

20-16   Up from the Minor Leagues. Donald Honig. Cowles Book Co. 1970. Clothbound.

Seven major leaguers relate their minor league experiences.

League Publications

20-17   Constitution and Playing Rules of the International Baseball Association. Heege and Kiffe. 1877, 1878. Booklet.

First minor league guide. Averages, convention proceedings.

20-18   Constitution and Playing Rules of the International Association of Professional Baseball Clubs. A.G. Spalding & Brothers. 1889. Booklet.

20-19   Constitution and Playing Rules of the National Baseball Association. Louis H. Mahn. 1879, 1880. Booklet.

The National Baseball Association succeeded the International Association.

20-20   Constitution and Playing Rules of the California Baseball League of Professional Ball Players. Liddle and Kaeding. 1880. Booklet.

20-21   Your California League. Robert Freitas. Globe Printing & Publishing Co. 1949. Booklet.

Player records, photos.

20-22   California League Record Book. William Weiss. 1949-to date. Booklet.

Team and player records.

20-23   California League Gold Book. William Weiss. California League. 1950-to date. Paperbound.

Player records.

20-24   Baseball Guide, Ohio State Association. A.J. Reach & Co.
            1884. Booklet.

            Constitution, rules, rosters.

20-25   Shibe's Official Eastern League Baseball Guide. J.D. Shibe &
            Co. 1884, 1885. Paperbound.

            Standings, rosters, schedules. Averages for the East-
            ern League, American Association, and National
            League. Playing rules, Eastern League constitution.

20-26   Spalding's Eastern League Guide. A.G. Spalding & Brothers.
            1886, 1892, 1894. Booklet.

            Averages, constitution, rules, review.

20-27   Eastern League Record Book. The Eastern League. 1947-to date.
            Booklet.

            Records, reviews.

20-28   Eastern Baseball League Pilot. Heilbroner Baseball Bureau. 1950-
            52. Booklet. Eastern Baseball League. 1953-57. Booklet.

            Records, sketches, photos.

20-28A   Eastern League Press, Radio, TV Information Book. Eastern Base-
            ball League. 1958-to date. Booklet.

            Continuation of 20-28.

20-29   Spalding's Official New England League Baseball Guide. A.G.
            Spalding & Brothers. 1886. Booklet.

            Rules, constitution, records, averages.

20-30   New England Official Baseball Guide. Timothy H. Murnane.
            1895. Booklet.

            Coverage of the New England League and New Eng-
            land Association. Review, rules, schedules, constitu-
            tion, averages.

20-31   Keith's Official Guide of the New England League of Professional
            Baseball Clubs. John Morse. Keith Co. 1896-98. Paperbound.

            Constitution, records, rules, statistics.

20-32   Reach's Official Southern Association Guide. A.J. Reach & Co.
            1889. Booklet.

20-33   Big League Prospects in the Southern Association. W.G. (Billy)
            Evans. 1943. Booklet.

            Sketches and records of promising players.

20-33A   Southern Association Prospects. W.G. (Billy) Evans. 1944-46. Paperbound.

Continuation of 20-33.

20-34   Southern Association Regulations. Southern Association. 1943. Booklet.

Instructions to managers, umpires, and players.

20-35   Southern Association Roundup. 1943-63. Booklet.

Edited by the various sports editors in the league cities. Rosters, sketches, facts.

20-36   Baseball Records, Southern Association. The Southern Association. 1944-63. Paperbound.

League, team, and player records.

20-37   Southern Association Scoring Rules. W.G. (Billy) Evans. 1944. Booklet.

Instructions to official scorers.

20-38   Who's Who in the Southern Association. W.G. (Billy) Evans. 1946. Paperbound.

Player records.

20-39   Southern Association Press Book. Southern Association. 1957-60. Booklet.

20-40   Southern Association Player Record. J.P. Friend. Friends News Service. 1960-to date. Paperbound.

Player sketches and records.

20-41   Official Western Association Records. F.B. Hughes. 1893. Booklet.

20-42   Through the Years with the Western League. Bill Bryson and Leighton Housh. Western Baseball League. 1951-53. Booklet.

History since 1885. Records, statistics, stories, photos.

20-43   Western Baseball League Managers' and Umpires' Careers. Western Baseball League. 1953. Booklet.

Sketches and records.

20-44   Western League Rosters. Western Baseball League. 1953. Booklet.

Team rosters.

20-45   The Western League Register. Western Baseball League. 1956-59.

Paperbound.

Player records and sketches.

20-46   Three I League Official Schedule. Rock Island Union. 1905.
Booklet.

Schedules, averages, photos.

20-47   Three I League Record Book. Three I League. 1949-60. Paperbound.

20-48   Three I League Dope, Data. Three I League. 1955, 1956.
Booklet. 1955 – two volumes. Subtitles: 1. Road Maps, Winning Streaks, All-Star Team, etc. 2. League Directory, Club
Directory, etc. 1956 – three volumes. Subtitles: 1. and 2. as
above. 3. Record Book.

20-49   The Three I League File. Harold Totten. Three I League. 1958.
Paperbound.

Player sketches and records.

20-50   Three I League of Professional Baseball Clubs All-Time Records.
Vern Hoschert. Three I League. 1961, 1962, 1963.

Player records.

20-51   Spalding's Official Pacific Coast League Baseball Book. G.V.
McKeever. A.G. Spalding & Brothers. 1910, 1911. Booklet.

20-52   Calpet Baseball Handbook of the Pacific Coast League. Leo
Moriarty. California Petroleum Co. 1926. Booklet.

League and player records and statistics. Highlights,
schedules.

20-53   Baseball Records of the Pacific Coast League. Leo Moriarty.
1928. Paperbound.

Records, history since 1903.

20-54   History of Baseball in California and Pacific Coast Leagues. Fred
Lange. 1938. Paperbound.

"Memories and musings of an old-time player." Season-by-season summaries, rosters, sketches of stars.

20-55   Pacific Coast League Baseball Record. W.R. Schroeder. Helms
Athletic Foundation. 1940. Paperbound.

All-time player and team records.

20-56   Pacific Coast Baseball League Records. Pacific Coast Baseball
League. 1940-to date. David G. Rowe. 1940-56. William

Weiss. 1962-to date. Booklet.

20-57   Pacific Coast League Team Record Books. Pacific Coast Baseball
League. 1946-48, 1950. Booklet.

A separate volume for each team. The 1946 series
included teams no longer in operation. Player and
team statistics.

20-58   Pacific Coast Baseball League. Pacific Coast Baseball League.
1946-50. Booklet. 1946 and 1950 - two volumes. Subtitles:
1. Club Records and Other Features. 2. No Hit Games, Extra
Inning Games, Individual Player Fielding Records, Miscellaneous
Records. 1947-49 - three volumes. Subtitles: 1. and 2. Same
as above. 3. Club Records.

20-59   Coast League Annual. John B. Old. Houlgate House. 1947,
1948. Booklet.

All-time records of the Pacific Coast League.

20-60   Pacific Coast League Baseball News. Los Angeles. 1947-51.
Newspaper.

Semi-monthly, April through October.

20-61   Pacific Coast League Blue Book. The Pacific Coast Baseball
League. Sports Publishing. 1947-to date. Booklet.

Records, statistics, data.

20-62   Pacific Coast League Record Book. Pacific Coast Baseball League.
1950. Booklet.

All-time team and player records.

20-63   Pacific Coast League Team Sketch Books. Pacific Coast Baseball
League. 1951. Booklet.

One volume for each team. Player sketches and
records.

20-64   Pacific Coast League Thumbnail Sketches. Pacific Coast Baseball
League. 1952. Paperbound.

Player sketches and records.

20-64A   Pacific Coast League Sketch Book. Pacific Coast Baseball League.
1953-59. Paperbound.

Continuation of 20-64.

20-64B   Pacific Coast Baseball League Press, Radio, TV Players Guide.
Pacific Coast Baseball League. 1960. Booklet.

Continuation of 20-64A.

20-64C   Pacific Coast League Player Guide. Pacific Coast Baseball League. 1961-to date.

          Continuation of 20-64B.

20-65   Sporting Life's Official Playing Schedule of Tri-State League Baseball Clubs. Sporting Life Publishing Co. 1911. Booklet.

          Statistics, schedules.

20-66   Official Playing Schedule, American Association. Baseball Publishing Co. 1912. Booklet.

20-67   American Association Record Book. American Association. 1926-58, 1962. Booklet.

          League, team, and player records.

20-68   The American Association on Parade. Fred Hutchinson. 1935, 1936. Booklet.

          Player records, photos.

20-68A   Who's Who in the American Association. Fred Hutchinson and Tom Briere. 1947-50. Booklet.

          Continuation of 20-68.

20-68B   Fifty Golden Years and Who's Who in the American Association. Robert French. 1951. Booklet.

          Golden anniversary issue of 20-68A.

20-69   The Record Makers of the American Association. American Association. 1936-54. L.S. McKenna. 1936-44. Halsey Hall. 1945-54. Booklet.

          Player records.

20-70   American Association Sketch Book. American Association. 1937-62, 1970-to date. Booklet.

          Records, rosters, other data. Spring and summer issues.

20-71   American Association Register. William Weiss. American Association. 1958-62. 1964-to date. Booklet.

          Player records.

20-72   All-Time Records and Highlights of the American Association. American Association. 1962, 1970-to date. Booklet.

20-73   Pocket Edition of Rules and Regulations Governing the Conduct of Umpires, Managers, and Players. P.B. Farrell. 1930. Booklet.

For the New York-Pennsylvania league.

20-74   New York-Pennsylvania Baseball League Manual. Frank Hyde.
New York-Pennsylvania League. 1963-to date. Booklet.

20-75   History of the Texas League. William Ruggles. Texas Baseball
League. 1932. 1951. Clothbound and Paperbound.

Season by season. Rosters, records, playoffs, player
index.

20-76   Texas League Record Book. William Ruggles. Texas Baseball
League. 1932, 1947-to date. Booklet.

Team and player records.

20-77   Texas League Schedule and Record Book. Ziggy Sears and Zeke
Handler. Texas Baseball League. 1948, 1949. Booklet.

20-78   Texas League Sketches. J.P. Friend. Friends News Service.
1961-to date. Paperbound.

Player sketches and records.

20-79   International League White Book. Herbert Simmons. 1937-to date.
Booklet.

Two editions in some years. Records, team reviews.

20-80   International League Players Index. The International League.
1952-to date. Paperbound.

Detailed lifetime player statistics.

20-81   Canadian-American League Orange Book. The Canadian-American
League. 1940-52. Booklet.

Team and player records.

20-82   Pioneer League Baseball Guide. 1940. Booklet.

An edition was published by each team. Schedules,
statistics.

20-83   Pioneer League Record Book. Ernie Hoff. 1949-to date. Booklet.

Records, statistics.

20-84   Pioneer League Index. William Weiss. 1952-to date. Paperbound.

Player records and sketches.

20-85   Visit the Appalachian League. Chris Tunnell. 1944. Magazine.
Team photos and facts.

20-86   Appalachian League Black Book. Karl Wingler. Appalachian
          League. 1949-to date. Booklet.

20-87   A Sketch History of the Middle Atlantic League. Russell Hocken-
          bury. 1947. Booklet.

          Yearly history, standings, records.

20-88   Middle Atlantic League Sketch Book. Middle Atlantic League.
          1948-52. Booklet.

          League, team, and player records.

20-89   Middle Atlantic League Silver Anniversary. Charles Kramer.
          Middle Atlantic League. 1949. Paperbound.

          History, records, photos.

20-90   Eastern Shore League Record Book. Ed Nichols. Salisbury Times.
          1947, 1948. Booklet.

          Team and player records since 1937.

20-91   The Official Coastal Plain League Record Book. J. Gaskill Mc-
          Daniel. Owen G. Dunn Co. 1947. Paperbound.

          Statistics, records from 1934-46.

20-92   The First Decade of Interstate League Baseball. Interstate League.
          1948. Booklet.

          History, player records.

20-93   South Atlantic League Dope Book. Cecil Darby. South Atlantic
          League. 1948-63. Booklet.

          Records, statistics.

20-93A   Southern League Record Book. J.P. Friend. Southern League.
          1964-to date.

          Continuation of 20-93.

20-94   South Atlantic League Player Index. J.P. Friend. Friend News
          Service. 1956-63. Booklet.

20-95   Record Makers of the South Atlantic League. J.P. Friend. Friend
          News Service. 1959-63. Booklet.

20-96   Carolina League Record Book. Jack Horner. Carolina League.
          1948-to date. Booklet.

20-97   All-Time Pony League Record Book. Pony League. Pierce Print-
          ing Co. 1949. Booklet.

          Season and game records since 1939.

20-98   Pony League Baseball Guide and Digest. Pony League. 1950-54.
          Booklet.

          Team and player records.

20-99   Georgia-Alabama League Highlights and Records. Walker Printing
          Co. 1949-51. Booklet.

          All-time league and team records.

20-100   Wisconsin State League Official Averages. Otto Kaufman. 1950.
          Booklet.

          Player records.

20-101   Wisconsin State League Record Book. Otto Kaufman. 1951-53.
          Booklet.

          Team and player records.

20-102   Florida International League Record Book. Florida International
          League. 1950-55. Booklet.

          League, team, and player statistics.

20-103   Florida State League All-Time Record Book. Florida State League.
          1965-to date. Booklet.

20-104   Northern League Record Book. Northern League. 1950. Booklet.

          Season and game records since 1933.

20-105   Western International League Record Book. Western International
          League. 1950. Booklet.

          Season and game records since 1937.

20-106   Cotton States League Golden Anniversary. J.P. Friend. Friend
          News Service. 1951. Magazine.

          History, records, statistics.

20-107   Cotton States League Record Book. Cotton States League. 1951-
          55. Booklet.

          History and records since 1902.

20-108   Longhorn League Official Averages. Buck Francis. 1951-55.
          Booklet.

          Player records.

20-109   Big State League and Gulf Coast League Baseball Record Book.
          Roy Edwards. Big State League and Gulf Coast League. 1952.
          Booklet.

          History, records, photos.

20-110   Sooner State Baseball League Record Book. Eddie Miller and Ed
          Williams. Waco Turner. 1954. Booklet.

          Team and player records.

20-111   West Texas-New Mexico League Records and Data Book. West
          Texas-New Mexico League. 1954. Paperbound.

          History, player and team records and statistics.

20-112   Northwest Roundup. William Weiss. Northwest League. 1955-
          69. Paperbound.

          Player records and sketches.

20-112A   Northwest League Record Book. William Weiss. Northwest League.
          1970-to date. Paperbound.

          Continuation of 20-112.

                              Team Publications

20-113   Souvenir, Richmond Baseball Club. F.W. Jennings. 1908. Book-
          let.

          Averages, sketches, photos covering the Richmond,
          Virginia, team of the Virginia State League.

20-114   Oshkosh in Baseball. Castle Pierce Press. 1913. Booklet.

          The history of baseball in Oshkosh, Wisconsin, from
          the amateur days of the 1860's to the minor leagues.
          Photos.

20-115   Sliding Home with Father Time. George Buchanan. 1929. Pa-
          perbound.

          History of baseball in Sheboygan, Wisconsin.

20-116   Introducing the 1934 Millers. Wheaties. 1934. Booklet.

          Photos of the Columbus, Ohio, team.

20-117   Milwaukee Brewers Pennant Winners. Howard Purser. Wisconsin
          News. 1936. Title page: Milwaukee American Association
          Champions. Booklet.

          Player sketches and records.

20-118   Milwaukee Brewers News. 1945, 1946. Newspaper.

          Monthly news of the Milwaukee, Wisconsin, team.

20-119   Milwaukee Brewers Sketch Book. Harold L. Esch. Sports Record

Bureau. 1947. Magazine.

20-120   Los Angeles Angels Baseball Autograph and Picture Book. 1937.
          Magazine.

20-121   The Los Angeles Angels Baseball Club and All-Time Record Book.
          George Goodale. 1951. Booklet.

          History of the Los Angeles, California, minor league
          team. Records, player sketches.

20-122   Angels Year Book. Los Angeles Angels. 1956, 1957. Magazine.

          Player sketches, statistics, records, photos.

20-123   Seventy-Five Years on Louisville Diamonds. A.H. Tarvin. Schuh-
          mann Publications. 1940. Paperbound.

          A narrative history of baseball in Louisville, Kentucky.

20-124   Springfield Browns and Three I League Record Book. 1940. Book-
          let.

          Records, photos.

20-125   Red Wing Annual. Easton Associates. 1940. Paperbound.

          Team and player records and statistics of the Roches-
          ter, New York, team.

20-126   Rochester Diamond Echoes. William E. McCarthy. Scheible Press.
          1949. Paperbound.

          A yearly review of baseball in Rochester, New York,
          since 1880. Records, statistics, facts.

20-127   The Red Wings - A Love Story. John L. Remington. 1969.
          Magazine.

          A pictorial history of baseball in Rochester, New York.

20-128   The Sioux Falls Canaries Cross Bats in League Play, 1933-40.
          Dwight K. Miller. Will A. Beach Printing Co. 1941. Booklet.

          History of the Sioux Falls, South Dakota, team.

20-129   Toledo Baseball Guide. Ralph Linweber. 1944. Booklet.

          History of baseball in Toledo, Ohio, since 1865. Re-
          cords, statistics.

20-130   Buffalo Bisons Pictorial Yearbook. 1945. Magazine.

          Photos of the Buffalo, New York, team.

20-131   Buffalo Bisons Sketch Book. Joseph Overfield. Kelly Letter Ser-
          vice. 1953. Paperbound.

Record of the Buffalo, New York, team since 1878.
Records, statistics of current players.

20-132 Buffalo Bisons Baseball Guide. The Sporting News. 1963. Booklet.

Team and player records, roster.

20-133 Know Your Chicks. John B. Sabbatini. 1947-52. Booklet and Magazine.

Autographed player photos of the Memphis, Tennessee, team.

20-134 Fifty Years with the Memphis Chicks. John Rogers and Henry Reynolds. Memphis Baseball Club. 1951, 1952. Booklet.

History of baseball in Memphis, Tennessee, since 1901.

20-135 The House of Barons. Zipp Newman and Frank McGowan. Cather Brothers Publishing Co. 1948. Magazine.

All-time records of the Birmingham Barons since 1900.

20-136 Your Houston Buffs. Morris Frank and Adie Marks. Houston Baseball Association. 1948. Booklet.

Player sketches of Houston, Texas, team.

20-137 Indianapolis Indians. Luke Walton. Indianapolis Star. 1949. Paperbound.

A review of the team's championship season.

20-138 Albany Senators Eastern League Champions. Argus Co. 1949. Magazine.

A pictorial review of the 1949 season of the Albany, New York, team.

20-139 Know Your Vols. John B. Sabbatini. 1949-51. Booklet.

Autographed player photos of the Nashville, Tennessee, team.

20-140 Vol Feats. Fred Russell and George Leonard. Nashville Banner. 1950. Booklet.

Fiftieth anniversary issue. All-time records of the Nashville, Tennessee, team.

20-141 San Francisco Seals Yearbook. San Francisco Baseball Club. 1949-57. Magazine and Paperbound.

20-142 Padre Parade. 1949-51. Booklet.

History of baseball in San Diego, California, and
the Pacific Coast League. Records and sketches of
the San Diego team.

20-143 Records of the San Diego Padres. San Diego Evening Tribune.
1966. Booklet.

All-time records of the San Diego, California, team.

20-144 Fifty Years of Professional Baseball in Alabama. Zip Newman
and Frank McGowan. Cather Brothers Publishing Co. 1950.
Magazine.

History of the various leagues in the state. Records,
statistics, photos.

20-145 The Triplets Baseball Book. Binghamton Press. 1950, 1951. Booklet.

History, records, photos of the Binghamton, New York,
team.

20-146 Tulsa Oilers All-Time Texas League Record Book. 1950. Booklet.

20-147 Tulsa Oilers All-Time History and Record Book. Grayle N. How-
lett. 1952. Paperbound.

History of the Tulsa, Oklahoma, team since 1905.
Records, photos, stories.

20-148 Seattle Rainiers Yearbook. Seattle Rainiers. 1951. Magazine.

20-149 Caricatures of Your Favorite Denver Bears. B. Bowie. 1951.
Booklet.

Player sketches.

20-150 Rollie Truitt's Scrapbook. Rollie Truitt. 1951-56. Paperbound.

History of the Portland, Oregon Beavers in the Pacific
Coast League. Yearly review, records, photos.

20-151 Erie Baseball Record Book. Jim Laughlin. 1954. Booklet.

Yearly supplements. History of baseball in Erie,
Pennsylvania, since 1890.

20-152 Your Lookouts Since 1885. Wirt Gammon. Chattanooga Publishing Co. 1955. Booklet.

History of baseball in Chattanooga, Tennessee.

20-153 Omaha Cardinals Booster Club. Omaha Booster Club. 1956-59.
Booklet.

A season review of the Omaha team and the American Association.

20-153A   Omaha Dodgers Boosters. Omaha Booster Club. 1961, 1962. Booklet.

Continuation of 20-153.

20-154   Seventy Years with the Pelicans. New Orleans Pelicans. 1958. Booklet.

History since 1887. Records, statistics, facts.

20-155   Fresno Giants Sketch Book. 1962. Booklet.

20-156   Batter Up: Fort Wayne's Baseball History. Bob Parker. Allen County-Fort Wayne Historical Society. 1967. Booklet.

A narrative historical sketch.

20-157   Spartanburg Phillies Yearbook. Spartanburg Baseball Club. 1968. Magazine.

Articles, photos.

20-158   Minor League Constitutions. Various titles. Southern League. 1892. Western League. 1897. American Association. 1903. Ohio State League. 1908. Ohio and Pennsylvania League. 1911. International League. 1912. Mississippi Valley League. 1920. Middle Atlantic League. 1927. West Dixie League. 1934. Pennsylvania State Association. 1935. South Atlantic League. 1936. Southern Association. 1939. Canadian-American League. 1939. North Atlantic League. 1950. Three-I League. 1953. Texas League. 1954. Booklets.

Dates represent first year issued and are approximate.

20-159   Minor League Team Roster Booklets. Various titles. Ardmore. 1955. Atlanta. 1954. Beaumont. 1954. Birmingham. 1945. Buffalo. 1945. Chatanooga. 1953. Columbus, Ohio. 1946. Dallas. 1952. Des Moines. 1954. Hollywood. 1946. Houston. 1953. Indianapolis. 1950. Jersey City. 1939. Kansas City, Missouri. 1946. Los Angeles. 1938. Louisville. 1946. Memphis. 1953. Miami. 1956. Milwaukee. 1947. Minneapolis. 1951. Montreal. 1947. Newark. 1946. Oakland. 1947. Omaha. 1958. Pueblo. 1954. Rochester. 1945. Sacramento. 1950. Saint Paul. 1944. San Antonio. 1951. San Diego. 1954. San Francisco. 1942. Seattle. 1945. Syracuse. 1949. Toronto. 1954. Tulsa. 1954. Vancouver. 1959. Waterloo. 1955. Booklets.

Issued at start of season. Player sketches, records, data. Dates listed represent the year first issued, and are approximate.

20-160   Minor League Team Press Guides. Buffalo. 1947. Columbus.
           1958. Dallas. 1953. Denver. 1952. Houston. 1953. In-
           dianapolis. 1948. Kansas City. 1953. New Orleans. 1953.
           Omaha. 1957. Seattle. 1947. Syracuse. 1968. Toronto.
           1950. Booklets and Paperbound.

           These evolved from the roster booklets. Issued to
           journalists at the beginning of the season. Rosters,
           records, sketches, reviews. Various titles. Dates
           listed represent the year first issued, and are approxi-
           mate.

21. Amateur and Semi-Pro

General

21-1   Ryan's American Amateur Association Baseball Guide. Michael
        J. Ryan. 1885. Paperbound.

> Reviews of various amateur associations, rules, re-
> cords. College statistics, major league coverage.

21-2   Spalding's Amateur Baseball Guide. A.G. Spalding & Brothers.
        1890. Booklet.

21-3   Baseball for Girls and Women. Gladys Palmer. A.S. Barnes &
        Co. 1929. Clothbound.

> How to play. Illustrations.

21-4   Global World Series of Baseball. George Marr, ed. Richard S.
        Falk. 1955-57. Magazine.

> The official souvenir book of the amateur open cham-
> pionship series played in Milwaukee, Wisconsin. Pho-
> tos, records.

Organizations

21-5   Constitution and By-Laws of the National Association of Junior
        Baseball Players. H.W. Karn. William D. Roe & Co. 1866.
        Booklet.

21-6   Baseball Manual of the National Association of Junior Baseball
        Players. W.H. Kelley. National Association of Junior Baseball
        Players. 1871. Booklet.

> Rules, constitution, and by-laws, minutes of the con-
> vention, history. Color illustrations.

21-7   Constitution and Rules of the National Association of Amateur
        Baseball Players. National Amateur Association. 1871-76. Pa-

perbound.

> The splintering of the National Association of Base-
> ball Players in 1870 resulted in the formation of two
> groups: The National Association of Professional Base-
> ball Players, which formed the first major league, and
> the National Association of Amateur Baseball Players.

21-8   Spalding's Indoor Baseball Rules. A.G. Spalding & Brothers. 1893-
1924. Booklet.

> Rules and constitution of the Indoor Baseball Associa-
> tion.

21-8A   Spalding's Indoor Baseball Rules. A.G. Spalding & Brothers. 1925-
26. Booklet.

> Also rules for playground baseball. Continuation of
> 21-8.

21-8B   Spalding's Indoor Baseball. A.G. Spalding & Brothers. 1927-30.
Booklet.

> Continuation of 21-8A.

21-9   Spalding's National Amateur Playground Association Handbook. A.
G. Spalding & Brothers. 1908-11. Booklet.

21-10   Spalding's Official Rules of Playground Baseball. A.G. Spalding
& Brothers. 1929-34. Booklet.

21-11   Outdoor Baseball for Girls and Women. A.G. Spalding & Brothers.
1929-37. Booklet.

> Official publication of the National Section on Wo-
> men's Athletics of the American Physical Education
> Association.

21-12   The American Legion Junior Baseball Handbook. The American
Legion. 1931, 1932. Booklet.

> Rules, advice, review, photos.

21-13   Junior Baseball, the American Legion. 1949-60. Booklet.

> Rules, review, information, photos.

21-13A   American Legion Baseball. The American Legion. 1961-to date.
Booklet.

> Continuation of 21-13.

21-14   Babe Ruth Boys' Club News. Esso, Inc. January 3, 1934. Newspaper.

21-15   Official Handbook of the American Baseball Congress. American
         Baseball Congress. 1935-60. Paperbound.

         Directory, rules, other information.

21-15A   Official Handbook of the American Amateur Baseball Congress.
         American Amateur Baseball Congress. 1961-to date. Paperbound.

         Continuation of 21-15. Published in two editions
         from 1966-69.

21-16   The Financing of Amateur Baseball. American Baseball Congress.
         1942. Paperbound.

         Two volumes.

21-17   ABC News. American Baseball Congress and Babe Ruth League.
         1944-60. Newspaper. Monthly. January - September.

21-17A   Amateur Baseball News. American Baseball Congress and Babe
         Ruth League. 1961-to date. Newspaper. Monthly, February -
         September.

         Continuation of 21-17. The Babe Ruth League became
         a separate organization in 1964.

21-18   Tournament Management and Operation. American (Amateur) Base-
         ball Congress. 1954-to date.

         Organization, planning, promotion, management.

21-19   The Executive's Handbook. American (Amateur) Baseball Congress.
         1954-to date. Paperbound.

         An operating manual.

21-20   The Umpire's Handbook. Amaerican (Amateur) Baseball Congress.
         1954-to date. Paperbound.

         Mechanics, rule interpretations, plays.

21-21   The Scorer's Handbook. American (Amateur) Baseball Congress.
         1954-to date. Booklet.

         A complete course in scoring.

21-22   How to Organize a Baseball League. American (Amateur) Baseball
         Congress. 1954-62. Booklet.

         Administration, operation, financing.

21-23   Baseball Schools and Clinics. American (Amateur) Baseball Con-
         gress. 1954-62. Paperbound.

         An outline for players and managers.

21-24   Managers Handbook. American (Amateur) Baseball Congress. 1955-

68. Paperbound.

An operating manual.

21-25 Babe Ruth League Rules and Regulations. American (Amateur) Baseball Congress and Babe Ruth League. 1954-63. Booklet.

Official handbook.

21-25A Rules and Regulations, Babe Ruth League. Babe Ruth Baseball, Inc. 1964-to date. Booklet.

Continuation of 21-25.

21-26 Official Babe Ruth League Magazine. Teen Sports Publishing Corporation. 1965. Magazine.

Biographical sketch of Ruth, yearly history of the league. Photos.

21-27 United States Amateur Baseball Association Constitution. Office of National Director. c1930. Booklet.

The purpose of this association was to create a permanent organization to represent amateur baseball.

21-28 Constitution and By-Laws, U.S.A. Baseball Congress. Office of the Secretary. 1932. Booklet.

An amateur organization organized in 1932.

21-29 Baseball Around the World. International Amateur Baseball Federation. 1939. Booklet.

History of the Federation, photos.

21-30 Little League Baseball Official Rules. Little League Baseball, Inc. 1951-71. Booklet.

Rules and regulations.

21-30A This Is Little League Baseball. Little League Baseball, Inc. 1972. Booklet.

Continuation of 21-30.

21-31 At Bat with the Little League. Carl E. Stotz and M.W. Baldwin. Macrae-Smith. 1952. Clothbound.

The history of Little League baseball. Stotz is the founder of the Little League.

21-32 Little Leaguer. Little League Baseball, Inc. May 1953-to date. Magazine.

Monthly during season; six per year. Articles, photos.

21-33   Official Encyclopedia of Little League Baseball. Hy Turkin. A.
         S. Barnes & Co. 1954. Clothbound.

         History, rules, playing instructions, organizations,
         policies.

21-34   How You Can Play Little League Baseball. Whitney Martin and
         John McCallum. Prentice-Hall. 1954. Clothbound.

         Fundamentals, conditioning, care of equipment. Stories
         of major leaguers.

21-35   Inside Baseball for Little Leaguers. Mickey McConnell. Wonder
         Books. 1955-57. Paperbound.

         Step-by-step pictorial instructions by J. Robinson,
         Roberts, Musial, Williams, Mathews, others.

21-36   Baseball Lessons for Little Leaguers. Chicago Tribune. 1957.
         Booklet.

         Instructions by present and past major league players.
         Photos.

21-37   How to Play Little League Baseball. Mickey McConnell. Ronald
         Press. 1960. Clothbound.

         Official Little League instruction book.

21-38   This Is the Little League. Little League Baseball, Inc. 1960.
         Booklet.

         Twentieth anniversary edition.

21-39   Seven Years in Little League Baseball. Robert Starling. Reel &
         Starling. 1963. Clothbound.

         Reminiscences of a Greenville, North Carolina, Little
         League coach. Playing tips.

21-40   Little League Baseball Training Handbook. Little League Baseball,
         Inc. 1966. Paperbound.

         Official publication. Detailed playing instructions.

21-41   How to Coach, Manage and Play Little League Baseball. Charles
         Einstein. Simon & Schuster. 1968. Clothbound. 1970, reissue.
         Paperbound.

         A general instructional manual.

21-42   Successful Little League Baseball for the Boy, the Parents and the
         Manager. Dick Bard. Nash Publishing Co. 1971. Clothbound.

         Advice on organizing and training a Little League
         team. Playing strategy, batting, pitching, catching.

21-43   Warm Up for Little League Baseball. Dean Morris A. Shirts. Athletic Institute. Sterling Publishing Co. 1971. Clothbound.

Illustrated playing instructions.

21-44   Jackie Robinson's Little League Baseball Book. Jackie Robinson. Prentice-Hall. 1972. Clothbound.

A primer and instructional by a Hall of Famer. Attitude, teamwork, sportsmanship, the role of parents.

21-45   Laughing and Crying with Little League. Catherine and Loren Broadus. Harper & Row. 1972. Clothbound.

A humorous explanation of Little League baseball.

21-46   Senior League Rules and Regulations. Little League Baseball, Inc. 1972. Booklet.

Rules for play in the ages 13-15 division of Little League baseball.

21-47   Pony League Baseball Official Rules. Poney League Baseball, Inc. 1951-69. Booklet.

Playing rules of organized leagues for boys 13-16 years old.

21-47A   Rules and Regulations for Pony League. Boys Baseball, Inc. 1970-to date.

Continuation of 21-47.

21-48   Pony League Yearbook. Pony League Baseball, Inc. 1955. Magazine.

Rules, records, review.

21-48A   Pony League Record Book. Pony League Baseball, Inc. 1956. Magazine.

Continuation of 21-48.

21-49   This You Should Know. Pony League Baseball, Inc. 1959. Magazine.

Organization, administration, and history of the Pony Leagues.

21-50   Teen-Age League Baseball. Teen-Age League. 1954. Magazine.

A program of organized baseball for junior teen leaguers, age 13-14, and senior teen leaguers, age 15-16.

21-51   Baseball Rules. National Federation of State High School Athletic Associations. National Baseball Congress of America. 1945-to date. Paperbound.

Codified rules with interpretations and play situations.

21-52   Baseball Case Book. National Federation of State High School
Athletic Associations. 1953-to date. Booklet.

Official rule interpretations.

Regional

21-53   Pacific Baseball Guide. A. Roman & Co. 1867. Booklet.

A history of Pacific Coast baseball since 1860. Rules
and regulations of the Pacific Baseball Convention of
California.

21-54   Baseball Directory. Jason Wentworth. F.A. Searle. 1867. Booklet.

A directory of clubs in and proceedings of the New
England Baseball Association. Meetings, rules.

21-55   Manual of the New York State Association of Baseball Players.
New York State Association of Baseball Players. 1868. Booklet.

Constitution, playing rules.

21-56   Central New York State Amateur Baseball Handbook. Sherlock
& Smith. 1876. Booklet.

Constitution, by-laws, rules.

21-57   Bryce's Canadian Baseball Guide. William Bryce. 1876. Booklet.

21-58   Spalding's Official Canadian Baseball Guide. A.G. Spalding &
Brothers. 1910-25. Booklet.

21-59   The Life and Baseball Career of "Frog Eye." Howard L. Hastings.
J.F. Williams. 1895. Booklet.

A biography of Claude T. Meredyth, a player on the
Shelbyville, Kentucky, team. Sketches of his team-
mates. The first baseball biography.

21-60   A Brief History of Lee Baseball Teams. Kinnie Ostewig. 1897.
Paperbound.

An account of baseball in Lee, Illinois. Box scores
of outstanding games, statistics, player sketches.

21-61   The Early History of Amateur Baseball in the State of Maryland.
William R. Griffith. John Cox. 1897. Paperbound.

History from 1858-1871. Game lineups, newspaper reports, player lists. Coverage of the Pastime, Maryland, Excelsior, and Waverly Clubs.

21-62   Fun and Frolic with an Indian Ball Team. Guy W. Green. 1900, 1902, 1903, 1904, 1907. Cover title: On the Diamond, the Nebraska Indians. 1903. Paperbound.

Experiences and anecdotes of the Nebraska Indians, a traveling amateur team. Accounts of tours, yearly records since 1897.

21-63   Spalding's Municipal Amateur Guides. A.G. Spalding & Brothers. Paperbound and Booklet.

21-63A   Chicago Amateur Baseball Annual and Inter-City Baseball Association Yearbook. 1904-05.

21-63B   Spalding's Official Chicago Baseball Guide. H.G. Fisher. 1910-13.

21-63C   Constitution of the Chicago Inter-City Baseball Association. 1911. Booklet.

21-63D   Spalding's Official St. Louis Amateur Baseball Yearbook. J.W. McConaughy. 1905.

21-63E   Spalding's Official St. Louis Baseball Book. 1909-10.

21-63F   Spalding's Washington Amateur Baseball Yearbook. J.F. Luitich. 1905.

21-63G   Constitution, Rules, and By-Laws of the Amateur Baseball Commission of the District of Columbia. 1911-12.

21-63H   Spalding's Official Metropolitan Baseball Book and Official Inter-City Baseball Association Guide. J.R. Price. 1905-13.

Coverage of New York City.

21-63I   Spalding's Minneapolis Amateur Baseball Yearbook. 1905.

21-63J   Spalding's Official Denver Baseball Book. 1905-14.

21-63K   Spalding's Buffalo Amateur Baseball Yearbook. Walter Mason. 1905.

21-63L   Official Handbook of the City Baseball League of Cleveland. 1908.

21-63M   Spalding's Official Cleveland Baseball Book. 1910-11.

21-63N   Official Guide of the Cleveland Amateur Baseball Association. C.C. Townes. 1913.

21-63P   Spalding's Official Boston Baseball Book. 1910-11.

21-63Q   Spalding's Official Philadelphia Baseball Book. 1910-11.

21-63R   Spalding's Official Pittsburgh Baseball Book. 1910-11.

21-63S   Constitution, Rules, and By-Laws of the Amateur Baseball Commission of Richmond, Virginia. 1912.

21-64   Hudson Dispatch Record Book. Dispatch Printing Co. 1917. Booklet.

            Baseball in Hudson County, New York.

21-65   Fifty Years of the Baseball War between Franklin and Oil City. New Herald Printing Co. 1918. Booklet.

            An account of the rivalry between two Pennsylvania towns.

21-66   Siskiyou Pioneer. Spring, 1954. Magazine.

            Issue devoted to baseball in the Siskiyou Valley, California.

21-67   Diamond Dust. George Hungerford. Advocate Publishing Co. 1941. Paperbound.

            An account of amateur baseball in Kansas in the early 1900's. Major league facts.

21-68   Take Me Out to the Ball Game. Frederick D. Suydam. Wayne County Historical Society. 1947. Paperbound.

            The history of baseball in Honesdale, Pennsylvania, since 1897.

21-69   Textile Baseball Yearbook. 1947. Booklet.

            Records and photos of players in the semi-pro leagues of Georgia, North and South Carolina.

21-70   Old Timers Hot Stove League of St. Paul. Frank Salvus. 1948. Title page: St. Paul Baseball with the Amateurs and Semi-Pros. Paperbound.

            A history of baseball in St. Paul, Minnesota, from 1860-1919, with emphasis on amateur and semi-pro leagues.

21-71   Annual Report. Brooklyn Amateur Baseball Federation. 1949. Paperbound.

Review of the season, program for 1950, photos.

21-72   Sandlot Baseball in Milwaukee's South Side. George Reimann.
         Robert W. Wiesian & Associates. 1968. Booklet.

         Historical facts, photos.

Semi-Pro

21-73   National Semi-Pro Baseball Congress Official Guide. National
         Semi-Pro Baseball Congress. 1938. Paperbound.

         Rules, directory, tournament results.

21-73A   Official Guide, National Semi-Pro Baseball. National Semi-Pro
         Baseball Congress. 1939-45. Paperbound.

         Continuation of 21-73.

21-73B   Baseball Annual. National Baseball Congress of America. 1946-
         47. Paperbound.

         Continuation of 2I-73A.

21-73C   Official Baseball Annual. National Baseball Congress of America.
         1948-to date. Paperbound.

         Continuation of 21-73B.

·21-74   Baseball Rules. National Baseball Congress of America. 1952-to
         date. Booklet.

         Playing and scoring rules, with amendments for semi-
         pro baseball.

21-75   The Official Umpire's Guide. National Baseball Congress. 1968-
         to date. Paperbound.

         Rules, instructions, knotty problems.

Collegiate - Guides

21-76   American Collegiate Baseball Association Guide. Wright & Ditson.
         1884, 1885. Paperbound.

21-77   Spalding's Official American Collegiate Guide. A.G. Spalding &
         Brothers. 1886. Paperbound.

21-78   Spalding's Official Collegiate Baseball Annual. E.B. Moss. A.
         G. Spalding & Brothers. 1911-14. Paperbound.

21-79   National Collegiate Athletic Association College Baseball Guide.
         A.G. Spalding & Brothers. 1930, 1931. Paperbound.

21-80   Official National Collegiate Athletic Association Baseball Guide.
         National Collegiate Athletic Association. 1958-to date. Paper-
         bound.

Collegiate - General

21-81   Baseball. Walter Camp. A.G. Spalding & Brothers. 1893. Pa-
         perbound.

         Specially adapted for colleges and prep schools. The
         history of college baseball since 1886. The play of
         each position, batting, and baserunning. A chapter
         for parents discussing the benefits of athletics. Re-
         view of the 1890 season.

21-82   Harvard University Baseball Club. Harvard University. 1903.
         Paperbound.

         The history of baseball at Harvard since 1865. Box
         scores, records, rosters, photos.

21-83   Collegiate Press Guides. c1947-to date. Booklet.

         Issued to journalists at the beginning of each season.
         History, records, sketches, preview.

21-84   Collegiate Baseball Digest. (Name later changed to Collegiate
         Baseball.) American Association of Collegiate Baseball Coaches.
         January 1958 - to date. Monthly, 1958, 1959, semi-monthly,
         January - June 1960 - to date. Paperbound and Newspaper.

         Articles on a variety of topics.

21-85   The Best from Collegiate Baseball. American Association of Col-
         legiate Baseball Coaches. 1972. Booklet.

         Reprints of articles.

21-86   Fast Balls and College Halls. Charles Keith. Vantage Press.
         1959. Clothbound.

         The autobiography of an amateur player and college
         professor.

21-87   The Big Ten. Kenneth L. Wilson and Jerry Brondfield. Prentice-
         Hall. 1967. Clothbound.

         A yearly summary of games in all sports. Player
         sketches, photos, records, chronology.

Collegiate - Athletic Histories

General athletic histories of individual colleges, with baseball coverage.

21-88   A History of Yale Athletics. Richard M. Hurd. 1888, 1892. Cover title: Yale Athletics. Clothbound.

The 1892 edition bears an 1888 copyright date. It is identical to the first volume except for an appendix covering the years 1888-92.

21-89   Yale, Her Campus, Classrooms and Athletics. Walter Camp and L.S. Welch. L.C. Page & Co. 1899. Clothbound.

21-90   Dartmouth Athletics. John H. Bartlett and John P. Gifford. Dartmouth College. 1893. Clothbound.

21-91   Athletics at Dartmouth. Horace G. Pender and Raymond M. McPartlin. Dartmouth College Athletics Council. 1923. Clothbound.

21-92   A History of Athletics at Pennsylvania. George W. Orton. Athletic Association, University of Pennsylvania. 1896. Clothbound.

21-93   The History of Athletics at the University of Pennsylvania. Edward R. Bushnell. Athletic Association, University of Pennsylvania. 1909. Clothbound.

21-94   Harvard Teams. W.B. Wheelwright and A.M. Goodridge. 1899. Clothbound.

21-95   Ten Years Athletics at Harvard. W.S. Cooledge. 1901. Booklet.

21-96   The H Book of Harvard Athletics. John A. Blanchard. Harvard Varsity Club. 1923. Clothbound.

21-97   The Second H Book of Harvard Athletics. Geoffrey H. Movius. Harvard Varsity Club. 1964. Clothbound.

21-98   The Games of California and Stanford. Jack F. Sheehan and Louis Honig. Commercial Publishing Co. 1900. Clothbound.

21-99   Fifty Years on the Quad. Norris E. James. Stanford Alumni Association. 1938. Clothbound.

21-100   Great Moments in Stanford Sports. Peter Grothe. Pacific Books. 1952. Paperbound.

21-101   Athletics at Princeton. Frank Presbry and James H. Moffat. Frank Presbry Co. 1901. Clothbound.

21-102   Cornell University, a History. Waterman T. Hewett. University
          Publishing Society. 1905. Vol. Three. Clothbound.

21-103   Athletics at Lafayette College. Francis A. March, Jr. Lafayette
          College. 1926. Clothbound.

21-104   Athletics in the University of North Carolina. Centra Alumni
          Office. 1927. Paperbound.

21-105   The M Book of Athletics, Mississippi A & M College. John W.
          Bailey. Curtiss Printing Co. 1930. Clothbound.

21-106   The M Book of Athletics, Mississippi State College. John W.
          Bailey. Williams Printing Co. 1947. Clothbound.

21-107   A Glance at Amherst Athletics. W.L. Tower. 1935. Paperbound.

21-108   One Hundred Years of Athletics, the University of Michigan.
          Phil Pack. Michigan M Club. 1937. Paperbound.

21-109   Michigan's All-Time Athletic Record. University of Michigan.
          1953. Title page: Athletic Record of the University of Michigan.
          Booklet.

21-110   Memorable Moments in Michigan Sports. Sigma Delta Chi. Kays
          Press. 1953. Paperbound.

21-111   Michigan All-Time Athletic Record Book. University of Michigan.
          1968. Paperbound.

21-112   Athletics at Wesleyan. Frank W. Nicolson. Wesleyan University
          Alumni Council. 1938. Clothbound and Paperbound.

21-113   Who's Who in Minnesota Athletics. Richard C. Fisher and Peter
          W. DeGrote. Who's Who in Minnesota Athletics. 1941. Cloth-
          bound.

21-114   A Sports History of the University of the South. Sewanee Alumni
          News. Alumni Association of The University of the South. 1949.
          Paperbound.

21-115   University of Southern California Athletics. Greater Alumni As-
          sociation. 1950. Paperbound.

21-116   The Tale of the Wildcats. Walter Paulison. Northwestern Uni-
          versity Alumni Association. 1951. Clothbound.

21-117   Ohio State Athletics. James E. Pollard. Ohio State University
          Athletic Department. 1959. Clothbound and Paperbound.

21-118   The Iowa Conference Story. J.E. Turnbull. State Historical
          Society of Iowa. 1961. Paperbound.

21-119   History of Athletics at Maryville College. Ken D. Kribbs. Man-
          grum Printers. 1969. Clothbound.

21-120   Varsity Athletic Record Book, University of Maine. Stuart P.
          Haskell, Jr., ed. University of Maine. 1970. Paperbound.

21-121   Spartan Saga. Lyman L. Frimodig and Fred W. Stabley. Michi-
          gan State University. 1971. Paperbound.

21-122   The Gladiators. John McCallum. Pacific Lutheran University
          Press. 1972. Clothbound.

          Collegiate - Major Conference Official Record Book

          Scores, rosters, records, all-time data, other facts. Published by
          the individual conferences. (* indicates other sports covered)

21-123   *Official Western Conference Records Book of Big Nine Sports.
          1946, 1948, 1949. Title page: The Western Conference Records
          Book. Paperbound.

21-123A   *Big Ten Records Book. 1950-to date. Title page: The Western
          Conference Records Book. 1950-61. Paperbound.

21-124   *Pacific Coast Conference Spring Sports. 1947-59. Paperbound.

21-124A   Big Five AAWU Spring Sports Information. 1960, 1961. Booklet.

21-124B   *AAWU Spring Sports Information. 1962, 1963. Booklet.

21-124C   *Athletic Association of Western Universities Spring Sports Infor-
          mation. 1964-66. Booklet.

21-124D   *Pacific Eight Spring Sports Information. 1967-to date. Booklet.

21-125   *Pacific Coast Conference Records Book. 1949-59. Booklet.

21-126   *Southern Conference Spring Brochure. 1952-63. Cover title:
          Southern Conference Spring Sports Press Data. Booklet.

21-126A   *Southern Conference Spring Press Data. 1964-to date. Paper-
          bound.

21-127   *Atlantic Coast Conference Spring Sports. 1954-to date. Paper-
          bound.

21-128   *Missouri Valley Conference All Sports Handbook. 1957-64. Pa-
          perbound.

21-128A   *Missouri Valley Conference Records Book. 1965-to date. Paperbound.

21-129   *Western Athletic Conference Yearbook. 1963-to date. Paperbound.

21-130   Official Southeastern Conference Baseball Record Book. 1967-to date. Cover title: Southeastern Conference Baseball Data Book. Paperbound.

           The following Conferences include baseball coverage in their spring sports or miscellaneous sports brochures. Dates are approximate.

                   Southeastern Conference. 1949-66. Missouri Valley Intercollegiate Athletic Association. 1949-to date. Southwest Athletic Conference. 1950-to date. Eastern College Athletic Conference. 1952-to date. Ivy League. 1954-to date. Border Conference. 1958-62. Mountain States Athletic Conference (Skyline). 1958-62. Mid-American Conference. 1963-to date.

21-131   Big Eight Conference Track, Baseball, Tennis, Golf Yearbook. 1968-to date. Paperbound.

22. Rule Books

22-1   Draper and Maynard Official Baseball Rules. Draper-Maynard Co.
        1909-28. Paperbound.

        Early editions included averages. Later editions added
        rules of other sports.

22-2   Diamond Dope. P. Goldsmith Sons. 1910-20. Paperbound.

        Later editions were entitled Diamond Dope and Rules.
        Rules, facts.

22-2A   Official Baseball Rules. P. Goldsmith Sons; MacGregor Sporting
        Goods Co. 1937-52. Booklet.

        Continuation of 22-2.

22-3   Heilbroner's Official Book of Rules. Heilbroner Baseball Bureau.
        1914-15. Paperbound.

22-4   Regles de Baseball. Y.M.C.A. Les Foyers Du Soldat et Du Mar-
        in. 1918. Paperbound.

        Official professional baseball playing rules printed in
        French and English and published in Paris.

22-5   Official Rule Books.

        From 1920-42 these were printed in the Spalding,
        Reach, Spalding-Reach, and Sporting News Official
        Guides in detachable booklet form.

22-5A   Official Baseball Rules. A.G. Spalding & Brothers. 1920-39.
        Booklet.

        Explanatory notes by John B. Foster. Knotty problems.

22-5B   Official Baseball Rules. A.J. Reach & Co. 1922-39. Booklet.

22-5C   Official Baseball Rules. Spalding-Reach. 1940, 1941. Booklet.

22-5D   Official Baseball Rules. Sporting News. 1942, 1950-to date.
        Booklet.

22-6   Knotty Problems in Baseball. John B. Foster. A.G. Spalding & Brothers. 1920-35. Paperbound.

          Rule interpretations covering unusual and difficult situations.

22-6A   Knotty Problems of Baseball. A.G. Spalding & Brothers. 1936-39. The Sporting News. 1950, 1954, 1956, 1958-to date. John B. Foster. 1936-39. Paperbound.

          Continuation of 22-6.

22-7   What's What in Baseball. W.G. (Billy) Evans. 1921, 1947-49. Booklet.

          Rule explanations, records, facts. By a major league umpire.

22-8   Umpire Billy Evans' Simplified Baseball Rule Book. W.G. (Billy) Evans. 1922, 1923. Booklet.

          Questions, answers, rule interpretations, plays that puzzle.

22-9   Fisher's Baseball Decisions. H.G. Fisher. 1925. Paperbound.

          Safe or out? Scoring instructions.

22-10   Official Baseball Rules. Stall and Dean. 1925. Booklet.

          As adopted by the American and National Leagues and the National Association of Professional Baseball Leagues.

22-11   Digest of Baseball Rules and Regulations. The National League. 1930-33. Booklet.

          Methods of procedure, constructions and practical applications.

22-12   Baseball As You Should Know It. John H. Hobbs. 1936. Paperbound.

          Rule interpretations.

22-13   Official Rules of Baseball. Thomas E. Wilson & Co. 1939. Booklet.

22-14   Baseball and Softball Rules. Hubert G. Johnson. Sport Tips and Teaching Aids. 1941. Paperbound.

          Interpretive comparisons of baseball and softball rules.

22-15   Baseball Rules and Decisions Book. Martin Rothan. Baseball Decisions Co. 1947, 1949. Paperbound.

Rules explained through game action. Interpretations, terms.

22-16   Bauer and Black's Official Baseball Rules and 1947 Major Records. Bauer and Black. 1948. Paperbound.

Statistics.

22-17   Listen, Ump. Thomas F. Pyle. 1948. Paperbound.

Five hundred knotty problems.

22-18   Baseball Rules in Pictures. G. Jacobs and J.R. McCrory. Grosset & Dunlap. 1957, 1966. Paperbound.

For boys.

22-19   Baseball Rule Book. Hillerich and Bradsby. 1961. Booklet.

Rules, schedules.

23. Umpiring

23-1   DeWitt's Baseball Umpires' Guide. Henry Chadwick. R.M. De-
Witt. 1875, 1875, revised. Paperbound.

Rules with an explanatory appendix. Duties of the
umpire.

23-2   The Toughest Decision I Ever Made. W.G. (Billy) Evans, ed.
1912. Booklet.

Interesting plays recounted by leading major and minor
league umpires. A reprint of magazine articles.

23-3   Billy Evans Course in Umpiring. W.G. (Billy) Evans. 1926. Paperbound.

The proper angle, single and double umpire systems,
things to remember. Puzzling situations, a review of
the rules. By a major league umpire.

23-4   Umpiring from the Inside. W.G. (Billy) Evans. 1947. Clothbound.

A discussion of rules, do's and don't's. Bill Klem's
words of wisdom.

23-5   Brick Owen's Instructions for Umpires. Clarence (Brick) Owens.
Booklet. E. Callahan. 1940. Paperbound.

A ten-lesson course of instruction for beginners, amateurs, and semi-pros by a former umpire.

23-6   National League Instructions to Umpires. The National League.
1943. Booklet.

Rule interpretations, duties.

23-7   Don't Kill the Umpire. Hy Gittlitz. Grosby Press. 1957. Clothbound.

A discussion of umpires and umpiring. Famous incidents, statistics.

23-8   Guides to Baseball Umpiring. Gilbert P. Augustine. 1960. Pa-

perbound.

Principles, techniques, philosophy, knotty problems.

23-9   Call 'em Right. C.G. Mittelbuscher. 1970. Booklet.

A textbook on umpiring.

23-10   Standing the Gaff. Harry (Steamboat) Johnson. Parthenon Press. 1935. Clothbound.

Recollections of a twenty-five-year minor league umpiring career.

23-11   The Umpire Story. James Kahn. G.P. Putnam's Sons. 1953. Clothbound.

The history of umpiring. Sketches and anecdotes of individual umpires. Chronology, all-time roster.

23-12   Mr. Ump. Babe Pinelli and Joe King. Westminster Press. 1953. Clothbound.

The autobiography of a former major league umpire. Anecdotes, umpiring tips.

23-13   Kill the Ump! Dusty Boggess and Ernie Helm. Lone Star Brewing Co. 1966. Paperbound.

The autobiography of a former major league umpire. Views on various aspects of the game.

23-14   Jocko. Jocko Conlan and Robert Creamer. J.B. Lippincott, Inc. 1967. Clothbound.

The autobiography of a colorful former major league umpire. An account of a twenty-year career. Revealing insights, outspoken views on umpiring, baseball and baseball players, past and present. Anecdotes and recollections.

See also 9-4V, 9-4W, 9-4X.

A slide to first.

24. World Series and All-Star Games

World Series - General Histories and Record Books

24-1   Charlie White's Red Book of Baseball. Charlie White. A.G.
        Spalding & Brothers. 1934. Booklet.

        A vest pocket edition of 4-104, containing World
        Series records.

24-2   World Series Wonders. Pfeiffer's Brewing Co. 1940. Booklet.

        Unusual World Series facts and records.

24-3   Baseball's Greatest Drama. Joseph J. Krueger. Classic Publish-
        ing Co. 1942, 1943, 1946. Clothbound.

        A history of the World Series. Game-by-game ac-
        counts.

24-4   The Story of the World Series. Fred Lieb. G.P. Putnam's Sons.
        1949, 1950, 1965. Clothbound.

        An informal history since 1882.

24-5   The World Series and Highlights of Baseball. Lamont Buchanan.
        E.P. Dutton & Co. 1951. Clothbound.

        A combined history of baseball, its stars, and the
        World Series. Records, illustrations, photos.

24-6   Happy Felton's Official Radio and TV World Series Score Book.
        Associated Oil. 1952. Paperbound.

        History, records, scoring instructions.

24-7   World Series Record Book. The Sporting News. 1953-to date.
        Booklet.

        The box score and account of every game. All-time
        player and team records.

24-7A   Gillette World Series Record Book. Hy Turkin, ed. The Sporting

News. 1953, 1954. Booklet.

Condensation of 24-7.

24-8   World Series Encyclopedia. Don Schiffer. Thomas Nelson & Sons. 1961. Clothbound and Paperbound.

Detailed player records. Line scores.

24-9   World Series Thrills. Joseph Bell. Julian Messner, Inc. 1962. Clothbound.

The ten most exciting incidents. Capsule biographies, records, box scores.

24-10   Highlights of the World Series. John Durant. Hastings House. 1963, 1971. Clothbound.

Cobb vs. Wagner, the Miracle Braves, the Black Sox. The rise of the Yankees. The A's and the Gashouse Gang, Casey Stengel. Records, yearly results.

24-11   Heroes of the World Series. Al Silverman. G.P. Putnam's Sons. 1964. Clothbound.

Mathewson, Baker, Gowdy, Alexander, Ruth, Pepper Martin, Dean, Newsom, Casey, Billy Martin, Rhodes, Larsen, Burdette, Koufax. A chapter on "goats."

24-12   Stars of the Series. Joseph Gies and Robert Shoemaker. Thomas Y. Crowell Co. 1964. Clothbound.

A narrative yearly history of the World Series. Records.

24-13   Greatest World Series Thrillers. Ray Robinson. Random House Little League Library. 1965. Reissued as Major League Library. Clothbound.

Exciting games that made baseball history.

24-14   World Series Annual. Lou Sahadi. Complete Sports. 1966. Paperbound.

Feature stories on games and players. Photos.

24-15   Joe Garagiola's World Series Fun 'n Facts Scorebook. Joe Garagiola. Chrysler-Plymouth. 1966. Booklet.

Score sheets, scoring instructions. World Series facts, amusing incidents, records.

24-16   World Series. Robert Smith. Doubleday & Co. 1967. Clothbound.

The games and the players. Highlights, scores, records, photos.

24-17   **The World Series: The Statistical Record.** Harold Paretchan. A. S. Barnes & Co. 1968. Clothbound.

        Player and team records and statistics. Game-winning hits.

24-18   **The World Series.** Lee Allen. G.P. Putnam's Sons. 1969. Clothbound.

        A narrative history. All-time player index.

24-19   **World Series Highlights: Four Famous Contests.** Guernsey Van Riper. Garrard Publishing Co. 1970. Clothbound.

        A brief history of baseball and the World Series. Highlights of the 1905, 1928, 1948, and 1968 World Series.

24-20   **World Series, Yesterday and Today.** Don Smith and Art Poretz. Stadia Sports Publishing. 1971. Booklet.

        Narrative review, outstanding feats, records.

24-21   **Showdown! The World Series.** Don Smith. Stadia Sports Publishing Co. 1972. Booklet.

        Continuation of 24-20.

24-22   **The World Series: a Pictorial History.** John Devaney and Burt Goldblatt. Rand, McNally & Co. 1972. Clothbound.

        Photos, illustrations, summaries, box scores covering each series.

World Series - Souvenir Booklets

Issued to commemorate league and/or World Championships. Sketches, photos, records, reviews.

24-23   **The Detroit Tribune's Epitome of Baseball.** Detroit Tribune. 1887.

24-24   **Complimentary Testimonial to the Champions.** Digby Bill, De-Wolff, and J. Barton Key. M.J. Rooney & Co. 1889. Booklet.

        Issued in connection with a testimonial and presentation to the New York Baseball Club championship team of 1889. Program league averages, player photos, chart of league race.

24-25   **Pennant Souvenir of Baltimore.** D.D. Guy. G.A. Meekins. 1894.

24-26   **Our Champions.** Standard Engraving Co. 1902. Booklet.
        Photos and sketches of the Philadelphia Athletics.

24-27   The Champion Athletics. Charles Dryden. 1905.

Sketches of the Philadelphia Athletics.

24-28   Sporting Life's Photographic and Biographic Album of Baseball Players of the New York Club of the National League. The Sporting
Life Publishing Co. 1906. Booklet.

A brief history of the New York club, player sketches.
Forerunner of 24-29.

24-29   Sporting Life's World Series Library. Francis Richter. The Sporting Life Publishing Co. 1907-10. Booklet.

Coverage of previous year's World Series winner.
Player sketches, box scores, game accounts. Reprints
of articles from Sporting Life. Various titles.

24-30   Portraits of Chicago Cubs and Philadelphia Athletics, the Champions of the National and American Baseball Leagues. Chicago
Daily News. 1910. Booklet.

24-31   Pennant-Winning Plays and Players. Philadelphia Evening Bulletin.
1911.

24-32   Philadelphia and New York. Philadelphia Bulletin. 1911.

24-33   The Red Sox Album. Brown and Leahy. Remington-Urguhart Press.
1912. Booklet.

Sketches and photos of the 1912 champion Boston Red
Sox.

24-34   Official Players Souvenir: The Reds of 1919. Cincinnati Reds.
1919.

24-35   Souvenir Record Book, World Championship Series, Chicago vs.
Cincinnati. A. Prusank. 1919.

24-36   Connie Mack's Philadelphia Athletics, American League Champions.
1929. Booklet.

24-37   Dodger Victory Book. Brooklyn Dodgers. 1942.

24-38   New York Yankees World Champions Album. Major Leaguers.
1943.

24-39   Champions, American League, 1944. St. Louis Browns. 1945.

24-40   Boston Red Sox, American League Champions. Boston Globe.
1946.

24-41   The 1957 World Series As Told by the Milwaukee Journal. Milwaukee Journal. 1957.

24-42   Tailor-Made Clothing Co.'s Official Score and Baseball Book.
        John J. Evers, ed. W.D. Cox & Co. 1912. Booklet.

        1911 World Series box scores and records. Other re-
        cords, score sheets.

24-43   The World Series for 1937. Dell Publishing Co. August 19, 1937.
        Magazine.

        Articles by different writers on the possible pennant
        winners: Yankees, Cubs, Giants, Cardinals, and Pi-
        rates. Photos.

24-44   The 1924 World Series. Dan Daniel. Packard Motor Car Co.
        1951. Booklet.

        Box scores, reviews, photos of the New York Giants-
        Washington Senators series.

24-45   A Day in the Bleachers. Arnold Hano. Thomas Y. Crowell Co.
        1955. Clothbound.

        A book-length account of the World Series game of
        September 29, 1954, as viewed from a bleacher seat.
        Detailed observations on the game and the spectators.

24-46   World Series. Complete Sports. 1961-65. Magazine.

        Articles, reviews of the past series, previews of the
        coming one. Records, photos.

24-47   The Book on the   (date)   World Series. Baseball-For-Fans
        Publications. 1966-to date. Paperbound.

        A description of each pitch and every play. Statis-
        tics. The 1971 edition includes the 1970 All-Star
        game.

24-48   Great Moments in Pitching. Baseball-For-Fans Publications. 1968.
        Paperbound.

        Pitch-by-pitch analysis of Bob Gibson's performance in
        the first game of the 1968 World Series.

All-Star Games

24-49   All Star Guide. Jack Koch. 1950. Booklet.

        All-time All-Star game rosters, scores, statistics, re-
        cords.

24-50   Baseball All-Star Game Thrills. Hal Butler. Julian Messner, Inc. 1968. Clothbound.

Accounts of 12 games.

Rooting for
the home team.

25. Tours

25-1   Baseball. Harry C. Palmer. A.G. Spalding & Brothers. 1888. Paperbound.

> Rules, theory of the game. Sketches of American players visiting in Australia.

25-2   Athletic Sports in America, England, and Australia. Harry C. Palmer, J.A. Fynes, Frank Richter, and W.I. Harris. W.A. Houghton. 1889. Clothbound.

> The origin and history of the game. A detailed account of the 1888-89 world tour by the Chicago and All-American teams. Color photos.

25-3   Sights around the World with the Baseball Boys. Harry C. Palmer. Edgewood Publishing Co. 1892. Clothbound.

> An account of famous sights seen while on a baseball tour around the world.

25-4   World Tour, National and American League Baseball Teams. Willsden & Co. 1914. Paperbound.

> A diary and photographic account of the October 1913 - March 1914 tour by the Chicago White Sox and New York Giants.

25-5   The Home Coming. Ring Lardner and E.G. Heeman. Blakeley Printing Co. 1914. Paperbound.

> Issued in honor of the March 6, 1914, homecoming of Charles A. Comiskey, owner of the Chicago White Sox, from the world tour. Pictures, cartoons, articles, verses, songs.

25-6   History of the World's Tour. Ted Sullivan. M.A. Donohue & Co. 1914. Paperbound.

> An account of the tour around the world by the Chicago White Sox and New York Giants in the winter of 1913-14. Photos, observations on various countries and people.

26. Dictionaries and Spectators' Guides

26-1 **Technical Terms of Baseball.** Henry Chadwick. A.G. Spalding & Brothers. 1897. Booklet.

Definitions of pitching, batting, fielding, and base-running terms.

26-2 **Historical Dictionary of Baseball Terminology.** Edward J. Nichols. Pennsylvania State College; University Microfilms. 1939. Paperbound.

Written as a doctoral thesis.

26-3 **The Dizzy Dean Dictionary.** Jay Hanna (Dizzy) Dean. Falstaff Brewing Co. 1943, 1949. Booklet.

Amusing definitions of baseball teams.

26-4 **Baseball Nicknames.** Gates-Vincent Publishers. 1946. Booklet.

An alphabetical listing with explanations of origins. General and specific nicknames.

26-5 **Dictionary of Baseball.** Parke Cummings. A.S. Barnes & Co. 1950. Clothbound.

Definitions of terms and phrases. Official rules.

26-6 **Baseball Lingo.** Zander Hollander. Phillies Cigars. 1959. Booklet.

A detailed glossary.

26-7 **Baseball Lingo.** Zander Hollander. W.W. Norton & Co. 1967. Clothbound.

An expanded edition of 26-6.

26-8 **Baseball Glossary.** Danny Litwhiler. 1961. Paperbound.

Terms in English, Dutch, Italian, and Spanish.

26-9 **The Baseball Dictionary.** Ron Rice and Chuck Moore. Ron Rice. 1968. Paperbound.

A glossary accompanied by humorous illustrations.

26-10 Baseball Talk for Beginners. Joe Archibald. Julian Messner, Inc. 1969. Clothbound.

A dictionary of terms and expressions.

26-11 Let's Talk Baseball. O'Keefe Brewery. 1969. Booklet.

A French-English explanation of the game to introduce Canadian fans to the new Montreal franchise.

26-12 Illustrated Baseball Dictionary for Young People. Henry Walker. Harvey House. 1970. Clothbound.

Official terminology and popular jargon.

26-13 The Long and Short of Baseball. Baseball Unlimited, Inc. 1953. Booklet.

An explanation and discussion of various aspects of the game.

26-14 Baseball Made Plain. Wilson Lloyd. Baseball Commissioner's Office. 1957. Booklet.

An illustrated explanation of the game.

26-15 How to Watch and Enjoy a Ball Game. Wilson Lloyd. Baseball Associates. 1970. Paperbound.

Explanations, humorous illustrations.

26-16 Baseball - Montreal. Bertrand B. Leblanc. Editions du jour. 1970. Paperbound.

A general explanation of the game written in French for Canadian fans in conjunction with the new major league franchise in Montreal.

26-17 Ladies' Day. Milwaukee Junior Chamber of Commerce. 1955. Booklet.

An explanation of the game for feminine fans. Illustrated by action photos of the Milwaukee Braves.

26-18 A Housewife's Guide to Baseball. Station KMPC. Golden West Broadcasters. 1958. Booklet.

Historical background, general explanation, glossary.

26-19 Milady's Guide to Baseball. Herb Heft. Minnesota Twins. 1963. Booklet.

An illustrated guide for feminine fans.

26-20   <u>Milady's Guide to Inside Baseball</u>. Sports Books. 1964. Booklet.
          Continuation of 26-19.

26-21   <u>A Wife's Guide to Baseball</u>. Charline Gibson and Michael Rich.
          Viking Press. 1970. Clothbound.

          An explanation of the game by the wife of pitching
          star Bob Gibson, with notes by Gibson.

27. Anecdotes and Recollections

27-1   Play Ball. Mike Kelly. Press of Emery and Hughes. 1888. Pa-
        perbound.

        Stories of the diamond field. An autobiography of
        Kelly, stories of other stars.

27-2   Stories of the Baseball Field. Harry C. Palmer. Rand, McNally.
        1890. Paperbound.

        A collection of dressing room yarns and humorous in-
        cidents in the lives of major league stars.

27-3   Touching Second. John J. Evers and Hugh S. Fullerton. Reilly
        & Britten. 1910. Clothbound.

        The history, development, and science of baseball.
        Anecdotes and observations by a star infielder.

27-3A   Baseball in the Big Leagues. John J. Evers and Hugh S. Fuller-
        ton. Reilly & Britten. 1913. Clothbound.

        Reissue of 27-3.

27-4   Pitching in a Pinch. Christy Mathewson. G.P. Putnam's Sons.
        1912. Clothbound. Grosset & Dunlap. 1912, reissue, 1923,
        reissue. Clothbound. Finch Press. 1972, reissue. Clothbound.

        Observations and anecdotes by an all-time great pitch-
        er.

27-5   Busting 'em. Ty Cobb. E.J. Clode. 1914. Clothbound.

        Anecdotes, recollections, and observations on the
        game by an immortal.

27-6   My Thirty Years in Baseball. John J. McGraw. Boni and Live-
        right. 1923. Clothbound. Finch Press. 1972, reissue. Cloth-
        bound.

        Anecdotes, recollections, and observations on the
        game by an all-time great player and manager.

27-7   Babe Ruth's Own Book of Baseball. George Herman Ruth. A.L. Burt Co. 1928. Clothbound. G.P. Putnam's Sons. 1928, re-issue. Clothbound. Gale Reprint Co. 1971, reissue. Cloth-bound.

> Autobiographical notes. Playing instructions, obser-vations, anecdotes, humorous accounts.

27-8   Magic Names of Baseball. Larry Woltz and Bill Cartan. Metro-politan Publishing Co. 1932. Paperbound.

> Anecdotes about Waddell, Lajoie, Cobb, Wagner, Mathewson, Speaker, Evers, Jackson, Schalk, Ruth.

27-9   Baseball Grins. John (Honus) Wagner. Laurel House. 1933. Booklet.

> Humorous anecdotes, reminiscences, poems. By an all-time great.

27-10   The Baseball Scrap Book. Harwell E. West. Diamond Publishing Co. 1938. Paperbound.

> A collection of unusual feats and odd incidents.

27-11   One Hundred Years of Baseball. Frank Salvus. Tolson Publishing Co. 1938. Paperbound.

> A yearly collection of events, outstanding performan-ces, records, and personal items.

27-11A Supplement. 1938. Booklet.

> Completes the 1938 season.

27-12   A Century of Baseball. A.H. Tarvin. Standard Printing Co. 1939. Paperbound.

> Anecdotes, unusual feats, and occurrences, historical facts.

27-13   Baseball Banter. Stan Carlson. 1940. Paperbound.

> A humorous collection of baseball anecdotes.

27-14   Aunt Minnie's Scrap Book. A. (Rowsy) Rowswell. Ft. Pitt Brew-ing Co. 1949. Booklet.

> Unusual anecdotes collected by a Pittsburgh sports writer.

27-15   Tales of the Diamond. A. (Rowsy) Rowswell. Ft. Pitt Brewing Co. 1950. Booklet.

> Similar to 27-14.

27-16   Bill Stern's Favorite Baseball Stories. Bill Stern. Blue Ribbon

Books. 1949. Clothbound. Pocket Books. 1949, reissue. Paperbound.

Anecdotes, accounts of unusual events.

27-17   Low and Inside. Ira Smith and H. Allen Smith. Doubleday & Co. 1949. Clothbound.

Pre-1918 anecdotes, oddities, and curiosities. Stories with a humorous twist.

27-18   Three Men on Third. Ira Smith and H. Allen Smith. Doubleday & Co. 1951. Clothbound.

Sequel to 27-17. Emphasis on the post-World War I era.

27-19   My 66 Years in the Big Leagues. Connie Mack. Holt, Rinehart, & Winston. 1950. Clothbound and Paperbound.

Anecdotes, autobiographical notes, and recollections, acounts of historical events. By an all-time great manager. An abridged prospectus was issued prior to publication.

27-20   Baseball Complete. Russ Hodges. Rudolph Field. 1952. Clothbound. Grosset & Dunlap. 1963, reissue. Clothbound.

Anecdotes, inside stories of players and events.

27-21   Lore and Legends of Baseball. Mac Davis. Lantern Press. 1953. Clothbound.

Stories, fables, unusual incidents.

27-21A   Teen-Age Baseball Jokes and Legends. Mac Davis. Grosset & Dunlap. 1959. Paperbound.

Reissue of 27-21.

27-22   Baseball's Unforgettables. Mac Davis. Bantam Books. 1966. Paperbound.

Little-known anecdotes and thrilling moments in the lives of the baseball greats.

27-23   Mighty Men of Baseball. Charles Verral. Aladdin Books. 1955. Clothbound.

Sketches of all-time stars at each position in the form of fictionalized reminiscences.

27-24   The Hot Stove League. Lee Allen. A.S. Barnes & Co. 1955. Clothbound.

Anecdotes, legends, and facts. The origin and make-up of the professional baseball player.

27-25   My Baseball Diary. James Farrell. A.S. Barnes & Co. 1957.
          Clothbound.

          Reminiscences of baseball in Chicago during the au-
          thor's boyhood. Observations on the game today.

27-26   Baseball Is a Funny Game. Joe Garagiola. J.B. Lippincott, Inc.
          1960. Clothbound. Bantam Books. 1962, reissue. Paperbound.

          Recollections by a former player, now a broadcaster.
          Humorous incidents, philosophy of the game.

27-27   My War with Baseball. Rogers Hornsby and Bill Surface. Cow-
          ard-McCann. 1962. Clothbound.

          The inside story of the struggles among the players,
          managers, and front offices. Facts behind selling
          and trading players and firing managers. Personal
          reminiscences. By an all-time great.

27-28   The Roar of the Crowd. William R. Burnett. Clarkson N. Pot-
          ter, Inc. 1964. Clothbound.

          Conversations between the author and an anonymous
          ex-major leaguer, who delivers opinions and reminisces
          on a variety of baseball topics.

27-29   You Can't Beat the Hours. Mel Allen and Ed Fitzgerald. Harper
          & Row. 1964. Clothbound.

          Anecdotes of past and present stars. Recollections
          by the longtime New York Yankee broadcaster.

27-30   The Glory of Their Times. Lawrence Ritter. Macmillan Co.
          1966. Clothbound and Paperbound.

          Reminiscences of 22 old-time players. Photos.

27-31   The Hustler's Handbook. Bill Veeck and Ed Linn. G.P. Putnam's
          Sons. 1965. Clothbound. Berkley Books. 1967, reissue.
          Paperbound.

          Sharp criticisms of today's administration of baseball
          by a former club owner.

27-32   Strange but True Baseball Stories. Furman Bisher. Random House
          Little League Library. 1966. Clothbound. Windward Books.
          1972, reissue. Paperbound. Reissued as Major League Library.

          Amusing, amazing, and offbeat incidents. Index,
          photos.

27-33   More Strange but True Baseball Stories. Howard Liss. Random
          House. 1972. Clothbound. Major League Library.

          Accounts of 34 unusual events.

27-34   Cuttin' the Corners. Tex Millard. A.S. Barnes & Co. 1966.
          Clothbound.

          Humorous anecdotes of major league baseball. By a
          major league scout.

27-35   Forty Years a Fan. Ed Doyle. Dorrance & Co. 1972. Cloth-
          bound.

          The best players at each position, covering the period
          from 1928-68. Lifetime statistics.

27-36   The Summer Game. Roger Angell. Viking Press. 1972. Cloth-
          bound.

          Observations on the game, its players and teams
          covering the years 1962-71.

28. Conditioning

28-1   Pedestrianism, Baseball Playing, Running, etc. Andrew Peck &
        Co. 1868. Booklet.

   Training instructions.

28-2   Hygiene for Baseball Players. A.H.P. Leuf, M.D. A.J. Reach
        & Co. 1888. Paperbound.

   The body as a mechanism, the art and science of
   curve pitching, causes and treatment of disabilities,
   hints to managers.

28-3   Baseball Exercises. C. Brown. 1962. Paperbound.

   Special emphasis on catchers. Illustrated.

28-4   Isometrics the Major League Way. Milt Bolling. 1966. Booklet.

   Twenty-eight exercises as developed by a major league
   scout and former player.

28-5   Conditioning for Baseball. Robert R. Spackman, Jr. Charles C.
        Thomas. 1966. Clothbound.

   Pre-season, regular season, and off-season drills and
   exercises.

29. Quizzes

29-1   Do You Know Your Baseball? Bill Brandt. Grosby Press. 1947.
        Clothbound.

       Questions and answers. Records, facts, box scores of
       unusual games.

29-2   Happy Felton's Flip Quiz Baseball Book. Larry McDonald. As-
        sociated Oil. 1950. Booklet.

       Facts, data.

29-3   Baseball Quizzle Book. Si Frankel. Samuel Gabriel Sons & Co.
        1953. Magazine.

       Cartoon quizzes for young readers.

29-4   Diamond Dilemmas. Everett Roundy. 1954. Booklet.

       Baseball word puzzles.

29-5   Do You Know Your Baseball? Hy Gittlitz. Grosby Press. 1955.
        Clothbound.

       Five hundred questions and answers covering every as-
       pect of the game.

29-6   Baseball Quiz Booklet. Les Keiter, ed. Adams Hat Co. 1955.
        Booklet.

       One hundred and twenty-five questions and answers.

29-7   So You Think You Know Baseball. Harry Simmons. Fawcett Pub-
        lishing Co. 1960. Paperbound.

       Reprinted from a series in the Saturday Evening Post.
       Knotty problems and their solutions.

29-8   Baseball Crossword and Almanac. Elgin Press. 1967. Paperbound.

       A baseball puzzle book.

29-9   Baseball Sportsword and Almanac. Elgin Press, Inc. 1968. Pa-
        perbound.

       Puzzles, quizzes, playing records.

30. Administrative Works

30-1   The National Agreement of Professional Baseball Associations and Agreements and Regulations Supplementary Thereto. National Agreement Arbitration Committee. 1882-84. Booklet.

> The National Agreement was the forerunner of the National Association of Professional Baseball Leagues, but differed in that the major leagues were members. Terms of the agreement, supplements, register of clubs and officers, regulations.

30-1A   The National Agreement of Professional Baseball Associations. National Agreement Board of Arbitration. 1885-1901. Booklet.

> Continuation of 30-1.

30-2   National Agreement of the National Association of Professional Baseball Leagues. National Association of Professional Baseball Leagues. 1901-32. Booklet.

> In 1901 the National League resigned from the National Agreement, and the minor leagues reorganized into the National Association. Terms of the agreement, minutes of meeting, rules and regulations.

30-2A   The National Association Agreement of Professional Baseball Leagues. National Association of Professional Baseball Leagues. 1933-47. Booklet.

> Continuation of 30-2.

30-2B   Agreement. National Association of Professional Baseball Leagues. 1948-to date. Paperbound.

> Continuation of 30-2A.

30-3   Major-Minor League Agreement and the Major-Minor League Rules. National Association of Professional Baseball Leagues. 1947. Booklet.

> In 1947 the Major-Minor League Agreement and Rules were revised. Terms, rules, regulations.

30-4   Proceedings of the Joint Playing Rules Committee of the American League, National Association of Professional Baseball Leagues and Spalding Faction of the National League. Knapp, Peck and Thomson. 1902. Booklet.

These proceedings formed the basis for the revised National Agreement and the World Series.

30-5   The National Commission. Armstrong News & Stationary Co. 1903. Paperbound.

The terms of the National Agreement for the government of professional baseball. The compact between the National, American, and minor leagues for the governing of organized baseball. Signed in Cincinnati, Ohio, in 1904.

30-6   Annual Report of the National Commission. National Commission. 1905-20. Paperbound.

Rules and regulations, proceedings, the National Agreement administrative reports. The 1905 edition contained the Cincinnati peace compact.

30-7   Board of Arbitration of the National League and American Association. Eagle Printing Co. 1888, 1889. Paperbound.

The peace agreement drawn up by the two leagues.

30-8   Leagues and Cities of Professional Baseball. Heilbroner Baseball Bureau. 1910-41. Paperbound.

The divisional makeup of organized baseball.

30-9   Heilbroner's Official Baseball Blue Book. Heilbroner Baseball Bureau. 1910-51. Paperbound.

The official adminstrative manual of organized baseball. Directory of all leagues and clubs in the National Agreement. Rules of the National Commission. Contracts, schedules. Supplements issued during the season. In later years, date of first publication was erroneously given as 1909.

30-9A   Baseball Blue Book. Baseball Blue Book, Inc. 1952-to date. Paperbound.

Continuation of 30-9.

30-10   Interclub Organization. 1936-66. Paperbound. Heilbroner Baseball Bureau. 1936-51. Baseball Blue Book, Inc. 1952-66.

Lists of the minor league teams which are owned by or have working agreements with each major league team. After 1966, this material was incorporated

into the Baseball Year and Note Book - Minor
League Digest.

30-11   Dimensions of Baseball Parks.   Heilbroner Baseball Bureau.   1940.
Paperbound.

Dimensions of all parks in organized baseball.

30-12   Professional Baseball in America.   Leslie O'Connor.   Baseball
Commissioner's Office.   1921, 1924, 1926, 1928, 1934, 1936.
Booklet.

Agreements and rules pertaining to relationships between leagues, clubs, and players.   Contracts, regulations.

30-13   Baseball.   Stephen Fitzgerald & Co.   1955.   Paperbound.

A two-volume study of results of a questionnaire on
baseball distributed to the public on behalf of the
Baseball Commissioner.

30-14   Facts.   Major League Baseball.   1965.   Supplements issued in
1966 and 1967.   Clothbound.

History, economic data, other information on a variety
of baseball topics.   Compiled for promotional use by
the team public relations directors.

30-15   Professional Baseball Rule 4.   Major League Baseball.   Baseball
Blue Book, Inc.   1965-67.   Booklet.

An explanation of the Free Agent negotiation rule.

30-16   Professional Baseball Rules.   Baseball Commissioner's Office.   1967-
to date.   Booklet.

Rules for free agent selection, high school, American
Legion, and college players and professional draft of
new players.

30-17   Constitution of the American League of Professional Baseball Clubs.
The American League.   1901-to date.   Paperbound.

30-18   Birthdays and Birthplaces of American League Players, Managers,
Coaches and Umpires, League and Club Officials.   Henry R. Edwards.   The American League.   1930-32.   Paperbound.

30-19   American League Official Scoring Rules and Instructions.   The
American League.   1930-40.   Booklet.

Adopted from the report of a special committee of the
Baseball Writers' Association of America.

30-20   American League Regulations.   The American League.   1932-to date. Booklet.

General rules for the conduct of games.

30-21 The American League and You. The American League. 1964, 1965. Booklet.

A discussion of the advantages of a baseball career as a player on an American League team.

30-22 American League Supplemental Regulations. The American League. 1966. Booklet.

Interpretations of the constitution.

30-23 A Working Manual for World Series, League Championship, All-Star Game. The American League. 1971. Booklet.

Instructions for team public relations directors.

30-24 Excerpts from National League Constitution and Rules and Agreements between Clubs and Player Representatives. The National League. 1965. Booklet.

Explanations for player representatives.

30-25 Yearbook of Baseball Players' Fraternity. Baseball Players' Fraternity. 1912. Booklet.

Officers, board, list of members, by-laws.

30-26 Constitution and By-Laws of the Association of Professional Ball Players. Association of Professional Ball Players. 1926. Booklet.

The Association was organized in 1924 as a charitable group for the purpose of aiding sick and indigent players.

30-27 Conduct of Judge Kenesaw Mountain Landis. U.S. Senate. 1921. Paperbound.

Hearings before the Judiciary Committee concerning the Standard Oil Co. antitrust trial. These were held after Landis became Baseball Commissioner.

30-28 Play Ball, America. National Baseball Centennial Commission. 1939. Booklet.

Instructions on organizing municipal observances of the Baseball Centennial. Messages from President Roosevelt, Judge Landis, others.

30-29 Baseball Writers' Association of America. Baseball Writers' Association of America. 1954. Booklet.

History, aims, rules, activities, procedures, reports.

30-30   Constitution. Baseball Writers' Association of America. 1967.
          Booklet.

30-31   Briggs Stadium: Baseball's Finest Playfield. Detroit Baseball Co.
          1948. Booklet.

          A description and photos of the stadium. Photos and
          sketches of Detroit Tiger officials.

30-32   Baltimore Baseball Club Survey. Baltimore Orioles. 1954. Book-
          let.

          Summaries of answers to questionnaires distributed to
          fans in 1954 concerning administrative procedures.

Promotional Booklets

Issued to prospective players to provide background information.
Dates are approximate.

30-33   Play Ball with the Yankees. New York Yankees. 1948-64.

30-34   Your Career in Baseball. New York Yankees. 1965-to date.

30-35   A Future with the Dodgers. Brooklyn Dodgers. 1949-54.

30-36   The Dodgers Want You. Brooklyn Dodgers. 1955-57.

30-37   Welcome to the Cardinals. St. Louis Cardinals. 1954-to date.

30-38   Getting Ahead Fast. Chicago Cubs. 1959-to date.

          See Also 9-4V, 9-4W, 9-4Y, 9-4Z, 9-4AA.

31. Hall of Fame

31-1   National Baseball Museum. National Baseball Hall of Fame and Museum. 1938. Booklet.

        History of the hall, sketch of Abner Doubleday, photos.

31-1A   National Baseball Museum and Hall of Fame. National Baseball Hall of Fame and Museum. 1939. Booklet.

        Continuation of 31-1.

31-1B   National Baseball Museum, Inc.: Hall of Fame. National Baseball Hall of Fame and Museum. 1942. Booklet.

        Story of Cooperstown and the museum. History of baseball, photos and sketches of Hall of Famers. Continuation of 31-1A.

31-1C   Hall of Fame: National Museum of Baseball. National Baseball Hall of Fame and Museum. 1945. Booklet.

        Continuation of 31-1B.

31-1D   National Baseball Hall of Fame and Museum. National Baseball Hall of Fame and Museum, Inc. 1946-to date. Paperbound.

        Continuation of 31-1C.

31-2   Baseball's Hall of Fame. Ken Smith. A.S. Barnes & Co. 1947, 1952. Clothbound. Grosset & Dunlap. 1958, 1962, 1970. Clothbound. Tempo Books. 1970, reissue. Paperbound.

        History of Cooperstown, development and dedication of the baseball shrine, description of the shrine and museum, sketches and records of members.

31-3   Doubleday Field. Rowan D. Spraker. Freeman's Journal Co. 1965. Booklet.

        An account of the development of the baseball field at Cooperstown, New York, the site of the Baseball Hall of Fame.

31-4   Baseball's Shrine: The National Baseball Hall of Fame and Museum.
        C. Paul Jackson. Hastings House. 1969. Clothbound.

        The development, and a description of the Hall of
        Fame.

31-5   Baseball Immortals. Lloyd Farmer. Educational Research Bureau.
        1942, 1947, reissue. Booklet.

        Biographies and records of Hall of Famers.

31-6   Baseball's Hall of Fame. B.E. Callahan. 1950-52. Booklet.

        Records, pictures, career highlights of Hall of Famers.
        Over-printed by various commercial firms for advertis-
        ing purposes.

31-7   Baseball Stars of Yesterday. A. (Rowsy) Rowswell. Fort Pitt
        Brewing Co. 1951. Booklet.

        Sketches of Hall of Famers.

31-8   National Baseball Hall of Fame Records and Pictures. 1952.
        Booklet.

31-9   A Treasure Chest of the Hall of Fame. Jerry Barton. Wilson-
        Hill. 1952. Paperbound.

        For younger readers. Sketches and records of all
        Hall of Fame members. Historical background, re-
        cords, other data.

31-10   Baseball Heroes. Charles Dexter. Fawcett Publishing Co. 1952.
        Booklet.

        Sketches in comic book form of Hall of Fame members.

31-11   Baseball's Immortals Series. Home Plate Press. Booklet.

        Biographies, playing records.

31-11A Babe Ruth. 1953.

31-11B Lou Gehrig. 1953.

31-11C Ty Cobb. 1953.

31-11D Joe DiMaggio. 1961.

31-11E Dizzy Dean. 1961.

31-11F Honus Wagner. 1961.

31-11G Christy Mathewson. 1961.

31-12   New York Giants Hall of Fame Story. Zander Hollander. As-
         sociated Features. 1957. Booklet.

         Sketches of New York Giant players in Hall of Fame.

31-13   The Hall of Fame Story Book. Associated Features. 1957. Book-
         let.

         Sketches and photos of players in the Hall of Fame.

31-14   Baseball's Hall of Fame. Robert Smith. Bantam Books. 1965.
         Paperbound.

         Divided by eras. Sketches, photos.

31-15   Kings of the Diamond. Lee Allen and Tom Meany. G.P. Put-
         nam's Sons. 1965. Clothbound.

         Biographical sketches of the members of the Hall of
         Fame.

31-16   Baseball: Hall of Fame - Stories of Champions. Samuel and
         Beryl Epstein. Garrard Publishing Co. 1965, 1966. Clothbound.
         Scholastic Book Services. 1968, reissue. Paperbound.

         Stories of Walter Johnson, Christy Mathewson, Ty
         Cobb, Babe Ruth, and Honus Wagner.

31-17   Hall of Famers. Pete Knowlton. 1969. Paperbound.

         Career statistics and highlights of DiMaggio, Hornsby,
         Musial, and Williams.

31-18   The Tocsin: Cooperstown Baseball Series. Ken Smith. The Vil-
         lage Printer. 1971. Booklet.

         Sketches, photos, and records of nine Hall of Famers.

32. Scoring

32-1   The National Baseball Score Book. Milton Bradley & Co. 1867.
        Clothbound and Paperbound.

32-2   Peck and Snyder's Amateur Score Book. Henry Chadwick. Peck
        and Snyder. 1883. Booklet.

        With full instructions for scoring a game.

32-3   Cosgrave's Symbol Scorebook for Baseball. John Paul Cosgrave.
        Stockton Mail Publishing House. 1887. Paperbound.

        A system of shorthand score keeping.

32-4   The Official Score Book. A.J. Reach & Co. Wright & Ditson.
        1890. Paperbound.

        Scoring instructions using the Harry Wright system.

32-5   National League Official Score. King. 1891. Booklet.

        The official scorebook issued for use in all games.
        Photos and sketches of stars.

32-6   Scott's Improved Individual Baseball Record. Charles H. Scott.
        1895. Booklet.

        Rules, schedules, rosters. Blanks for individual game
        records in each category.

32-7   Howe Baseball Scoring Record. Irwin Howe and Albert Barron.
        1910. Booklet.

32-8   How to Score. H.G. Fisher. 1925. Paperbound.

32-9   Radio Baseball Scorebook. John Trojack. 1936-46. Booklet.

        Scoring instructions, blanks.

32-10   How to Score. Fred Lieb. The Sporting News. 1939, 1946.
        Paperbound.

        A detailed method developed and used by the Sporting
        News.

32-11 Baseball Score Magazine. Baseball Statistical Service. 1947. Magazine.

> Score sheets, information on scoring, computing averages.

32-12 Bob Wolff's Official Box Score Book. Bob Wolff. 1948. Paperbound.

> Facts, scoring instructions by a major league broadcaster.

32-13 Byrum Saam's Official Baseball Score Book. Green Mountain Publishers. 1949. Paperbound.

> Scoring instructions, pictures of Philadelphia players, score sheets.

32-14 Food Fair Official Baseball Record and Score Book. Kirsh Publishing Co. 1954. Booklet.

> Scoring instructions, Baltimore Orioles schedule and roster, records, score sheets.

32-15 Statiscore. Gene Elston. 1959. Booklet.

> A scorebook developed by a major league broadcaster.

32-16 Baseball Scoring Instructions: Official Baseball Scoring Rules. Scoremaster Co. 1969. Title page: Basic Scoring Instructions. Booklet.

> Instructions and rules for scoring a baseball game.

See also 9-4Y, 9-4Z, 9-4AA, 9-4BB.

33. Miscellaneous

33-1   The Orr-Edwards Code for Reporting Baseball. Orr and Edwards.
        1890. Paperbound.

> A system for uniform reporting by telegraph. Symbols
> and code words for weather, attendance, game high-
> lights, line score, statistics.

33-2   Baseball Code Simplified. William T. Call. 1913. Paperbound.

> A method of transmitting games by telegraph.

33-3   The Spalding Baseball Collection. New York Public Library.
        1922. Paperbound.

> Titles in the collection of books, pamphlets, pictures,
> and other material on baseball and other sports, given
> to the library by Mrs. Albert G. Spalding. The col-
> lection was formerly owned by her late husband.

33-4   Collectors' Guide to Baseball Publications. Ernest Krotz. Base-
        ball Bureau. 1943. Booklet.

> Descriptions of well-known baseball publications.

33-5   Play Ball. Play Ball, Inc. 1941. Booklet.

> Signatures of four hundred and forty major leaguers.

33-6   Baseball Players' Home Addresses. Richard Burns. 1967. Paper-
        bound.

> Compiled as an aid to the autograph collector. Al-
> phabetical listing. Tips on autograph collecting.

33-7   The Metafysics and Psychology of Baseball. Emil Scharf. R.A.
        White Publishing Co. 1908. Booklet.

> Appendix by J.E. Grillo. An investigation and anal-
> ysis of the causes that produce the various phenomena
> of the game. Unusual spellings employed.

33-8   An Analysis of the Aerodynamics of Pitched Baseballs. Carl W.

Selin. University Microfilms. 1957. Paperbound.

A thesis written at the State University of Iowa.

33-9 Baseball-istics. Robert Froman. G.P. Putnam's Sons. 1967. Clothbound.

The basic physics of baseball explained for younger readers.

33-10 Scientific Study of Baseball. Arthur MacDonald. 1914. Booklet.

Reprinted from the American Physical Education Review. Authored by a criminologist, with statistical tables used as an anthropological study of the typical ballplayer.

33-11 Ballplayers Don't Hustle Anymore. Harry LeDue. Packard Motor Car Co. 1954. Booklet.

A comparison of present and past players.

33-12 Japan Is Big League in Thrills. John Holway. Tokyo News Service. 1955. Paperbound.

History of baseball in Japan since 1934. Data, photos of American stars. Published in Tokyo.

33-13 Slide, Sagittarius, Slide. Gwen Stiefbold. Voice of Astrology Publishing Co. 1964. Paperbound.

How the science of astrology can change the game of baseball.

33-14 Percentage Baseball. Earnshaw Cook and Wendell R. Garner. Williams and Wilkins. 1964. Clothbound. M.I.T. Press. 1966. Paperbound.

Charts, tables, formulae, and graphs expounding the authors' theories that much of modern strategy is faulty.

33-15 Percentage Baseball and the Computer. Earnshaw Cook and Donald L. Fink. Waverly Press. 1971. Clothbound.

A computer-developed simulation of major league game situations in order to analyze accepted principles of strategy.

33-16 A Comparative Analysis of the Major League Baseball Broadcasters. Mark Frankfurt. 1967. Booklet.

A privately-printed summary of answers to questionnaires submitted by the author.

Index

Index

H

J

P

From a photograph by J. W. Black, circa 1874

M'Vey (Right Field).   Al. Spaulding (Pitcher).
James O'Rourke (First Base).   Andrew Leonard (Left Field).   George Wright (Short Stop).